LIFE À LA
HENRI

HENRI CHARPENTIER
AND BOYDEN SPARKES

LIFE À LA
HENRI

Being the Memories of Henri Charpentier

RUTH REICHL
SERIES EDITOR

Introduction by Alice Waters

THE MODERN LIBRARY
NEW YORK

LIBRARY OF CONGRESS CATALOGING-IN-PUBLICATION DATA
Charpentier, Henri, 1880–1961.
Life à la Henri: being the memories of Henri Charpentier / Henri Charpentier
and Boyden Sparkes; introduction by Alice Waters.
p. cm.—(Modern Library food)
ISBN 0-375-75692-2
1. Charpentier, Henri, 1880–1961. 2. Cooks—France—Biography.
3. Cookery, French.
I. Sparkes, Boyden, 1890–1954. II. Title. III. Series.
TX649.C45   A3 2001
641.5'092—dc21   00-060956
[B]

Modern Library website address: www.modernlibrary.com

Introduction to the Modern Library Food Series

Ruth Reichl

My parents thought food was boring. This may explain why I began collecting cookbooks when I was very young. But although rebellion initially inspired my collection, economics and my mother's passion fueled it.

My mother was one of those people who found bargains irresistible. This meant she came screeching to a halt whenever she saw a tag sale, flea market, or secondhand store. While she scoured the tables, ever optimistic about finding a Steuben vase with only a small scratch, an overlooked piece of sterling, or even a lost Vermeer, I went off to inspect the cookbooks. In those days nobody was much interested in old cookbooks and you could get just about anything for a dime.

I bought piles of them and brought them home to pore over wonderful old pictures and read elaborate descriptions of dishes I could only imagine. I spent hours with my cookbooks, liking the taste of the words in my mouth as I lovingly repeated the names of exotic sauces: soubise, Mornay, dugléré. These things were never seen around our house.

As my collection grew, my parents became increasingly baffled. "Half of those cookbooks you find so compelling," my mother complained, "are absolutely useless. The recipes are so old you couldn't possibly use them."

How could I make her understand? I was not just reading recipes.

To me, the books were filled with ghosts. History books left me cold, but I had only to open an old cookbook to find myself standing in some other place or time. "Listen to this," I said, opening an old tome with suggestions for dinner on a hot summer evening. I read the first recipe, an appetizer made of lemon gelatin poured into a banana skin filled with little banana balls. "When opened, the banana looks like a mammoth yellow pea pod," I concluded triumphantly. "Can you imagine a world in which that sounds like a good idea?" I could. I could put myself in the dining room with its fussy papered walls and hot air. I could see the maid carrying in this masterpiece, hear the exclamations of pleasure from the tightly corseted woman of the house.

But the magic didn't work for Mom; to her this particular doorway to history was closed. So I tried again, choosing something more exotic. "Listen to this," I said, and began reading. " 'Wild strawberries were at their peak in the adjacent forests at this particular moment, and we bought baskets of them promiscuously from the picturesque old denizens of the woods who picked them in the early dawn and hawked them from door to door. . . . The pastry was hot and crisp and the whole thing was permeated with a mysterious perfume. . . . Accompanied by a cool Vouvray, . . . these wild strawberry tarts brought an indescribable sense of well-being. . . .' "

"Anything?" I asked. She shook her head.

Once I tried reading a passage from my very favorite old cookbook, a memoir by a famous chef who was raised in a small village in the south of France. In this story he recalls being sent to the butcher when he was a small boy. As I read I was transported to Provence at the end of the nineteenth century. I could see the village with its small stone houses and muddy streets. I could count the loaves of bread lined up at the *boulangerie* and watch the old men hunched over glasses of red wine at the café. I was right there in the kitchen as the boy handed the carefully wrapped morsel of meat to his mother, and I watched her put it into the pot hanging in the big fireplace. It sizzled; it was so real to me that I could actually smell the daube. My mother could not.

But then she was equally baffled by my passion for markets. I could stand for hours in the grocery store watching what people piled into their carts. "I can look through the food," I'd try to explain. "Just by paying attention to what people buy you can tell an awful lot about them." I would stand there, pointing out who was having hard times, who was religious, who lived alone. None of this interested my mother very much, but I found it fascinating.

In time, I came to understand that for people who really love it, food is a lens through which to view the world. For us, the way that people cook and eat, how they set their tables, and the utensils that they use all tell a story. If you choose to pay attention, cooking is an important cultural artifact, an expression of time, place, and personality.

I know hundreds of great cookbooks that deserve to be rescued from oblivion, but the ones I have chosen for the Modern Library Food Series are all very special, for they each offer more than recipes. You can certainly cook from these books, but you can also read through the recipes to the lives behind them. These are books for cooks and armchair cooks, for historians, for people who believe that what people eat—and why—is important.

Two are books I once read to my mother. *Clémentine in the Kitchen* introduces one of the most lovable and entertaining characters who ever picked up a whisk. She is the ultimate *bonne femme* and a nostalgic reminder of a long-gone life when people were truly connected to the land.

Life à la Henri, the memoir of the man who invented crêpes suzette, is more than a memoir and more than a cookbook; in the nearly one hundred years that he was alive, Henri Charpentier watched the world and its food change on two continents. He fed both Queen Victoria and Marilyn Monroe, he made and lost fortunes, and he never lost his sense of humor. I have been in love with Henri for most of my life, and I think it is time the rest of the world got to meet him.

Although Edouard de Pomiane must have breathed the same air as Henri Charpentier, they seem to belong to different ages. Henri's world is long gone, but Edouard de Pomiane seems thoroughly modern. If he turned up tomorrow in a time machine, he would be right at home. His first book, *Cooking with Pomiane,* was published in Paris in the thirties. It became Elizabeth David's favorite cookbook, and I find it hard to understand why it is not on every cook's shelf. If you forced me to depend on a single cookbook for the rest of my life, it would probably be this one, if only because having made the acquaintance of M. de Pomiane I am reluctant to lose his companionship. His book is filled with common sense, good humor, great writing, and wonderful recipes. It says a great deal, I think, that another book by this forgotten writer, *Cooking in Ten Minutes* (published in 1930), is probably the most widely imitated cookbook of our time.

There are, of course, people who are appalled by the notion of getting dinner on the table in ten minutes. You'll meet a number of them in *Perfection Salad,* which opens with this question from 1923: "Are Vegetables ever served at a buffet luncheon?"

The answer? As provided by a magazine called *American Cookery,* was yes, with a caveat that they "appear in a form that will not look messy on the plate." The magazine proceeded to offer a few suggestions, including "the plebian baked bean . . . or toasted marshmallows stuffed with raisins."

Did we ever live in a world in which women spent their time stuffing marshmallows with raisins? Apparently. One hundred years ago, in a frantic effort to control food and keep it in its place, American women were busily transforming the act of cooking into "domestic science." Laura Shapiro went back to recipes in old magazines and cookbooks to find out what those women were up to. It is a tragic tale that has had enormous repercussions for all of us. Still, the first time I read *Perfection Salad* I had only one thought: I wish my mom could read this.

I imagine myself handing this book over to my mother. "Okay," I would say, "I'll admit it. Food is sometimes boring." But then I'd tell her about those raisin-stuffed marshmallows and add, "But cookbooks never are."

Introduction

Alice Waters

Some of us, like the author of this book, are born with joie de vivre. But some of us need a revelation to show us how glorious life can be when all our senses are wide awake.

For me, that revelation came during my college year abroad in France. I was a typical product of a nineteen-fifties upbringing in suburban New Jersey, but somehow I made friends in Paris who—to my wonder—took great pains over what they ate. What's more, they took great pride in taking such pains. Today, over thirty years later, when I close my eyes I can still see the mussels we hauled in at Honfleur, scrubbed shiny and black, and steamed in a caldron. They were the first mussels I ever ate, and the best, tasting succulent and orange and reminding me of the smell of the high tide at midnight. I can still feel the cobblestones underfoot as my friends and I stood in line at the neighborhood bakery, inhaling the mesmerizing aroma of fresh baguettes. After we bought the loaves, we could never wait, and greedily broke them apart, still warm, to taste on the way home, where we spread homemade apricot jam on whatever was left. And I still see the tiny restaurant in Pont-Aven where we were treated as if we were long-lost family and feasted, as I had never been fed before, on food foraged, grown, and harvested by the same people who cooked and served it—food so exquisite and alive that I knew I had to make food like that a permanent part of my life.

The memoirs of Henri Charpentier have that same power to reveal the joys of living, and eating, with all your senses. Here is someone who never lost his almost infantile delight in life and whose alert senses never dulled. Henri was a proud and happy sensualist whose memoirs span the turn of the twentieth century, from the Belle Époque on the Riviera to the Depression at the brand-new Rockefeller Center. His seventy-year-long career began at a grand hotel as a ten-year-old page boy to kings and queens and ended at his own tiny California restaurant as a chef to Hollywood royalty, almost thirty years after this book was first published. In between he survived a series of picaresque reversals of fortune, at one time or another finding himself starving and homeless in Victorian London, the companion of a fabulously wealthy Russian prince in Morocco, and an outlaw restaurateur raided by revenuers during Prohibition on Long Island. Through it all, he never lost his discriminating appetite nor his unflappable charm.

Although his memoirs end on a note of triumph, with Henri basking in acclaim as the patron of Henri's at the Maison Française, his good fortune did not last. As the Depression worsened, he refused to compromise his standards, the restaurant failed to make enough money, and in 1935 he was evicted for nonpayment of back rent. A few years later, his Long Island property was confiscated to pay back taxes. Eternally resilient, he left the East Coast and landed in Los Angeles, where, again to enormous acclaim, he opened a new Henri's on Sunset Strip, only to fail once more. Until his death in 1961, Henri ran a restaurant in Redondo Beach that served only sixteen guests a night and was so popular that it was reserved four years in advance. To the end of his life, he insisted stubbornly on quality over quantity.

Reading Henri's book today, I am reminded a little of a cartoon French chef in white tunic and billowing toque making that familiar gesture in which the hand, held as if taking a big pinch of salt, points toward the mouth, gently touches pursed lips, and flies open as the fingertips are kissed with an appreciative smack. But he resembles even more a beaming, benevolent, and sometimes blustering grandpapa, white mustache dancing as he acts out for the little ones the extravagant story of his life. Does he exaggerate? Perhaps. But he does so for the sake of a good story, and with such ebullient innocence and pride that we can easily forgive him his flamboyance.

Henri had much to be proud of. He invented crêpes suzette for the prince who became Edward VII; poured rare Burgundies for Sarah Bernhardt; and hosted presidents, financiers, judges, and generals at his restaurants in New York. But the heart of his memoir is not so deeply concerned with the *haut monde* or even with *haute cuisine*. His most profound emotional attachment was to his foster parents and the tiny village in Provence where he spent his first ten years. It was there that he always returned, in triumph after his successes and in search of inspiration after his failures; and it was there that his appetite was first attuned to appreciate the bounty of creation and good simple things, lovingly prepared. In later life, even in the grandest settings, his culinary instincts always favored the unadorned.

In his love for simplicity and dislike for fancy garnishes he was ahead of his time—and our time, too. Even today, a hundred years after Escoffier banished much of the show from grand cuisine, many chefs still cannot resist the allure of multiple squeeze bottles, the vertical dessert, and the oversize plate. When culinary schools are still teaching their students how to make tomato roses, it is refreshing to hear Henri remind us that "there is beauty in a natural tomato, but something obscene in any effort to disguise its shape." In this, he was the disciple of his foster brother Jean Camous, who also left his home village and became a chef and who taught Henri the art of going to market.

Henri was an apprentice to his foster brother Camous at the Grand Hotel Frascati in Le Havre, where the clientele included the likes of Baron Rothschild, Bernhardt, and Félix Faure, the president of France. In Le Havre, Henri and Camous went to the marketplace together at dawn, and his descriptions of those morning buying excursions exemplify all that is best about this book. The market basket, he observes, is nothing less than a treasure chest, "an object of the utmost significance," and he suggests that it deserves to be superimposed on the tricolor as the emblem of France, whose greatness it has nourished. It is thanks to the market basket, he writes, that every French family happily looks forward to gathering at the dinner table.

So off to the marketplace Henri and Camous went, befriending the vendors, inspecting their wares, and striking bargains, always in search of the most beautiful products. He makes the scene come marvelously alive. "Vegetables cannot be good unless they are fresh," he says flatly, and he proceeds to pass along a great deal of advice on judging freshness and quality—poignant advice when we realize that freshness measured in hours, and not days or weeks, is a luxury even more out of reach of most Americans now than it was in the nineteen thirties. I think Henri would be happy to know that today there are more and more farmers and gardeners fighting to restore regional and local farmers' markets to something like the important place they held in France a hundred years ago. (The lucky patrons of such markets will profit by consulting the delightful appendix on page 241, "Advice for a Lady with a Market Basket.")

A brilliant restaurateur like Henri has another priceless asset besides a firm grip on his market basket: the heart of a great waiter. From his very first days at the Hotel Cap Martin, Henri displayed both a natural instinct for anticipating the needs of the guests and an ingenious aptitude for gratifying them. He had an unshakeable belief in the inherent dignity of service and an intuitive understanding that every little thing counts, from kind words to polished shoes. To spend a lifetime performing the grueling emotional labor of treating strangers as though they were your most cherished friends is difficult for most of us to imagine; Henri never seems to give it a second thought.

His career left Henri no room for a private life in the modern sense—he had no serious interests outside his restaurants—but he tells us that he and his wife and family enjoyed a harmonious and healthy partnership in which life and work were one. He is so lovable, we believe him. How can we help loving a man who bursts into tears of joy and gratitude in almost every chapter of his memoirs? We even believe him when he tells us that he was only fourteen years old when he invented my favorite dessert, crêpes suzette.

I do not remember exactly where I first tasted this archetypal dessert—probably at La Bourgogne, an old-fashioned French restaurant in San Francisco, in the nineteen sixties—but I immediately loved everything about it: the heat, the blue flame hovering over the oval copper pan, the bittersweet flavors, the texture of the paper-thin pancakes, the solemn theater of their presentation. Although I can't persuade my pastry chef to put them on the menu every day, we serve them often at my restaurant, Chez Panisse, slightly altered from Henri's recipe (buckwheat flour in the crêpe batter for a hint of rustic tanginess, some candied tangerine peel to augment the Grand Marnier). They are one of the immortal classics of French cooking.

Serving them connects us to an unbroken tradition that links the farm-house, the marketplace, and the grand hotel to our modest restaurant in California.

In France, it is only recently that these connections have begun to unravel. When I first visited there, I was able to have the same kinds of experiences that Henri had seventy-five years before, and to learn firsthand that neither his high standards nor his infectious joie de vivre were unique. Like Henri Charpentier, people took immense pride in their work and cared passionately about where their food came from. I am proud to have become part of this tradition, and humble, too, for there is really no great mystery to it. As Henri says, "the high art of the restaurateur is no more than a development of the thing which in the kitchen of the home is recognized for what it is, the love of the mother for her family."

———

ALICE WATERS is the founder and proprietor of Chez Panisse, a restaurant in Berkeley, California. She is the author of many cookbooks, including *Chez Panisse Café Cookbook*, *Chez Panisse Vegetables*, and *Fanny at Chez Panisse*.

CONTENTS

LIFE À LA
HENRI

CHAPTER I

LIFE IN CONTES

Should you hear me say that when I was a boy of ten a proud English duchess was my friend, that queens spoke tenderly to me, that kings acknowledged my salutations, that I shared the private chapel benedictions of an empress, that another empress, my favorite, in her boudoir traded bonbons for my point of view, what would you think? Especially if I told you that in half a year after I was ten I had made a fortune in gold coins, what then? Certainly you would think that such a boasting fellow must be a Gascon, which I am not at all; I am of Nice and we Niçois do not boast. The simple explanation is that in 1890 while I was still a tiny Frenchman I became a page boy in the Hotel Cap Martin, an establishment of the Riviera which I now suspect was truly more agreeable to European royalty than their various palaces.

I was born in Nice in 1880 but I was reared in Contes, a village some leagues distant. If I am moved to begin my memoirs with the earliest souvenirs of my existence it is because ten thousand times in my career it has been revealed to me that when ladies or gentlemen want to know how a particular dish is created they want details of the beginning. Consequently when they ask me to disclose the secrets of Lobster Henri, Special, I tell everything which has significance. What I am going to do now, I who invented Crêpes Suzette for the prince who became Edward VII, is to give the recipe for myself, for Henri Charpentier.

When I first became aware of myself I was not concerned because I bore one name and the other children of the family to which I was attached bore another. Most of the time I was simply Henri; today I remain Henri. Nevertheless I was a Charpentier and the others were called Camous. I will explain this now without regard to the chronology of my own discoveries among these facts. My mother was young when I was born; nineteen, a tender creature and herself excellently born. A marquise and a countess had contributed to her inheritance of the exquisite qualities of France. My father was a lawyer and no longer young. Their marriage had taken place despite the protestations of my mother's people, especially of her father. Consequently when, a few days after my birth, my father was killed by a fall from a horse, she was alone, entirely, and utterly grief-stricken.

In that time ladies in France were somewhat reluctant to nurse their children; that was vanity; but in the case of my mother the reluctance became common sense. Had she nursed me then certainly I would have grown up, if at all, to be a melancholy fellow, one nourished on tears. So, when I was only a few days old I was placed in the arms of one who had milk for me. She was the coachman's wife, that tender being, my *maman nourrice* who to me became and remains the most precious of all living creatures.

What a theme awaits the poet who shall sing of restaurateurs! I believe that; but always I shall think that no matter to what heights the art of preparing food shall be elevated by the chefs of extreme talent and inspiration, nothing they may create in food equals in sublimity those original meals offered by the mother to the infant. By that simple transfer of milk to my small sack of a stomach I really became the son of her who reared me. But suppose at that premier breakfast you had been permitted to regard, as did Papa Camous, the fuzzy, bobbing head of myself. Suppose you had witnessed the avidity of toothless, infant gums. Then, you too would have said: "This devouring person is a morsel of cannibal. He would eat his *maman nourrice.*"

Probably it was the small pension which my mother for a little while managed to provide which helped to make possible the retreat of the family Camous to their natal village of Contes. Even today I can sympathize with their hunger for it, in that valley where ten months in the year the Paillon is not a stream but only a path of gravel. My foster-father Rousson Camous was a good peasant soul who could do no evil to any living thing except flies, of which, as the friend of horses, he was the sworn enemy. From one end of the year to the other he saw hardly twenty francs. Through the week as he tended his few orange trees his whiskers sprouted thickly and stiffly until on Sunday morning he would be too bushy for an appropriate appearance in church. Then, if I had been good, I was allowed to wrap my small fingers about one of his great ones and run beside him as he slowly clumped through the narrow street that led to the shop of the village barber, Antoine Massiera.

There were never many customers, for a shave cost three sous and in that village a sou was of enormous circumference. Instead of a towel a basin was held beneath the chin of anyone who sat in the barber's chair. Deep in my mind I can hear right now the scrape, scrape, scrape of the razor through the heavy stubble of beard. I can hear the grumbles of Papa Camous as he told off three sous into the barber's hand and scolded the man for giving him a smarting face in place of a comfortable one. They had both been to the war in 1870; and Diedrick Toirant, the pharmacist and village notable, had actually been a captain.

Celestin and Cesarina Camous were my brother and sister; but then, all Contes was inhabited by people who seemed as one great family without secrets. In the whole of the closely massed buildings of white masonry not one drop of bitterness was distilled to tincture the disposition of the orphan boy. In that place I can remember nothing of cruelty; only kindness and love.

Indeed, it is mature reflection and not the actual memory which fixes a mood of sadness upon the final visit of my mother. I did not understand the circumstances which brought her. She came on one of those festival days when candles thicker than a little boy and taller than a man burned before the church. Some of their light ever since has seemed to flare in my mind to illuminate the memory of her face. I was midway between five and six when she expended some of her vanishing strength on this pilgrimage of farewell to her child. She spoke French and I a patois. Yet I know with what words she shaped the sacred injunction then laid upon my guardian.

"Godmother," she said, "take good care of my child. Already he has become a piece of your heart. See to it that when he grows up he will be good. I am dying. I feel it within me. I shall not be able to return what is due you except as I now give you my thanks." After so long a time the words can be repeated for the reason that simple people like Mama Camous who do not read and write are much more faithful than most to charge their memories with what they hear.

One day that was perhaps a season later as I came from the school conducted by M. Draghui who taught with fervor all that he knew of honor, politeness, respect and love, but with less emphasis what he knew of arithmetic, grammar and geography, I found my foster-mother in tears. She drew me tightly to her bosom as if I had been a loaf of bread that she would slice. "Your mother, Henri," she said, "has gone to heaven." Pushing myself free I asked, "But how? How could she go without Badou?"

The key to all mysteries of arrival and departure were centered for me then in Badou. Even the journeys into the great empty spaces over us and from which we foolishly shelter ourselves with hats, even those vastnesses, I thought, could be explored only as extensions of the daily migration of Badou who drove the diligence back and forth between Contes and Nice. None, it then seemed to me, ever went from our village or returned to it except in the vehicle of that old man. Badou was one of the first of my friends. He represented opportunity. Sometimes he brought a package too insignificant to be delivered from his vehicle to the door where it was expected. A small boy by carrying it could earn a sou.

The return of Badou from Nice each evening was our local excitement. When his rumbling, shabby black vehicle of stage coach proportions was still a mile away we could hear the pistol shot crackings of his long whip. The whip was long because Badou was tender-hearted. All the work of hauling through those hills of our province of Alps-Maritime was accomplished by his two horses. They were ancient beasts who were among equines even more patriarchal than Badou among men. They were never punished. The whip lash played upon the backs and burned the ears of four young, strong unreal horses that Badou kept taut in the traces of his fancy. That heavy diligence should have had more actual animals. The age of Badou himself would have been betrayed to anyone who observed, after his arrival in the public square, how with creakings he descended from the high box. True, a jaunty youthful beret covered his hair but his bulging moustache, except where it was stained a rusty brown by the tobacco of which he was almost always in want, was snowy white. No dull cravat such as protected the necks of ordinary men would do for Badou. A red handkerchief was tied about his throat in a manner reminiscent of adventures he must have had when he really drove six horses. Ah, but it was the voice of Badou that sang in my heart! It seemed to come from a larynx corded with the bass strings of a guitar and when he addressed me: "Henri, petit," I quivered.

We had little money in the Camous family, but we had big appetites. However, my foster-mother, my Mama Camous, when she had nothing she could still make something. At Christmas time her bread would acquire a smoother texture, was softer to the touch and had an exciting flavor. How was it done? Two spoons of olive oil, two of sugar and four of butter worked into the ordinary bread dough. But even Papa Camous would have been disappointed if she had stopped there. The bread must have appropriate shapes for the holidays. For my little foster-sister, Cesarina, she would make a *piate,* which is Niçois for *poupée,* by which I mean to say doll baby. One big loaf would be fashioned into the shape of a little bread girl with a bread dress to her bread ankles. Prunes pressed into the top of the head became the coiffure, the ears were thin pieces of orange skin, the eyes were raisins, the mouth was contrived out of cherries. There were cherry buttons on the dress and embroidery across the front fashioned out of apricots, prunes, raisins, figs and nuts. Celestin and Henri each had a loaf of this holiday bread in the shape of a chanticleer. For each rooster Mama Camous would cut a V of apricot to become the beak. One cherry became the eye and seven or eight cherries were the rooster's comb. The tail was a marvelously fruity thing with feathers richly colored with apricots, prunes and figs. The breast was iridescent with a glaze of jelly made of currants or peaches. Sometimes she painted a coating of sugar on these sweet effigies.

Christmas, of course, was best but on every saint's day we small ones could expect to be shoo'd out of doors as if we had been chickens strayed into her domain on a hunt for crumbs. She liked to work her kitchen sorcery in private. "It's to be a surprise," she would say and then command us sternly, "Go now!" At Easter she would make dyes for hard-boiled eggs. To transform beets into coloring matter they should be baked in ashes or sand. Peel them, mash them, with a little fat, in hot water. What you will get will be a ruby coloring, sufficient to paint a house, or anyway, a couple of dozen Easter eggs. Gold was found in the brown skins of onions. Green was acquired by mashing raw spinach and then bringing it to a boil with a little water to which fat was added. It was not so good a paint as the ruby and gold of the beets and onion skins, but it was indubitably green. All our food came to us by processes that to city people would seem extraordinary. How many, many days I saw the solitary nanny-goat of our household set forth in the morning with a withered, empty bag! She would mount to the top of that hill slope on which the small town of Contes is rooted. Up there was the rendezvous of all the goats of our village. All day she would browse but at sundown she would, with the other goats, return to the village coming to our door as faithfully as if she had been a dog. Always her bag was filled with excellent milk which she would have defended with her horns from any unauthorized person; but to me, Henri, who was her friend, she would surrender it to the last drop. So you see, I grew up in a family which had milk but no milk bill.

In Contes we had few ice-boxes, almost none, I think; but every family had a *garde à manger*. Often in the spring and summer months it would contain food for a picnic. I remember that at least twice a year the children would be dismissed from school and the men and women would leave their work for a great picnic in which the entire village joined. The first of these celebrations in the Spring had some ancient significance linked with the fruitfulness of the soil.

For that one my Mama Camous would prepare by fixing a number of pies of a kind which we called *tarte de blé*. She prepared flour dough as if to make bread and then spread it thin as pie crust in a baking pan heavily greased with butter or olive oil; never with ordinary fat since this was to be eaten cold. Next she would chop a Swiss chive into small pieces and after mixing it with butter, oil and salt, sauté it until much of the plant moisture had vanished as steam. Then two or three onions which she had thoroughly browned would be added to the mixture of chives along with bread crumbs, cheese crumbs and a couple of eggs. All this was mixed into a paste which was spread on the dough. Mama Camous always poured the paste into the middle of the dough and then with her fingers raked it smooth, being careful to leave about a three-inch margin of dough free of the paste. Next she would encircle the greenish paste with an inch-wide border of tomato purée that had been cooked with garlic and onions. Then over the vegetable surface she would crisscross fillets of anchovy and in each square place an olive. This structure was baked for twenty minutes and it came from the oven beautifully brown on top and with the outer margin of dough puffed high like the wall of a reservoir. In almost every kitchen in Contes such tarts were made for the picnic.

On the morning of the picnic all the people, except the village girls, would go to church to mass. Why the girls did not go I do not now remember; but I know that after the benediction the ladies would return home and the men and boys would march down to the picnic ground which was in a grove of chestnut trees on the banks of the brook in the valley below the village.

A great supply of food was always there in readiness. It was piled on a table that was used for this purpose, year after year. It was a very old table that had been fashioned of thick oak planks and its patina was a history of French wines. Half a dozen hams, numerous roasted rabbits, great discs and loaves of bread, sausages of many varieties and other good things would be piled on and under that magnificent table.

The village butcher was the carver and took pride in slicing the ham in transparent sheets, the *mortadella* of pigs' head and gelatine even thinner; and the salami was, literally, like paper. Then there was cheese, mountain cheese of a kind not to be had from stores. It had a dark skin as thick as the bark of trees to preserve the rich flavor and delicate aroma of the crumbly interior. Hah, between the French people and the German the difference is well expressed by their respective cheeses. The Germans have Limburger, for example; but in all of France you could not discover a cheese which was not a temptation. If you succumb to that temptation then you are compelled by the enchantment to eat some more. All through the day the men would eat and drink wine and talk and laugh; the boys would play and go swimming in the brook. But at four in the afternoon we would know the ladies were on their way. Right now it seems to me I can hear again the music to which they kept time as they marched from the village.

The ladies and girls would bring baskets of *beignets,* apple fritters that had been cooked with currant jelly and which were the especial and necessary dessert of our June picnics. The memory of those occasions that I enjoy most is of the musicians. There was Ganzi, a very tall fellow who held his violin upright on his shoulder so that one hand manipulated the frets high above his head while the other was sawing the bow back and forth in front of his ear. Ciroulin Zaveri who played the cornet did not have lungs enough and his notes sometimes came into the world misshapen and sour. François Baza, who played the bass fiddle had no teeth at all and his loose lips were constantly forming words to make merriment among the little boys who surrounded him. "Farandela, farandela," he would sing, and we would shout with delight. Dodouo had the trombone, but the one I admired most was my friend the leader, old Pepi Straforello who played the flute, a complete task for his lips and fingers so that he had left only his eyes with which to command his orchestra. And how his eyes would roll!

Badou would be there, too. On this day he would arrive in a brake, which had a top and curtains but no glass in its sides like the impressive, heavy-wheeled diligence. Dadou would bring strangers from Nice. Since it was a picnic even his thin old horses would have a treat, a meal of bran and a dried tree seed-pod which we called *couroulées*. They had a form like flat bananas, were very sweet and we boys would steal them from under the noses of the poor horses. Then night would come and Badou's passengers would discover they could not get back to Nice, but would have to sleep in the auberge. Something would have happened to the legs and voice of Badou. He would acknowledge that everything was not as it should be but he would deny with tears that he was drunk. Still he was the only one in our village who ever got tipsy at the picnics. He did, however, for even M. Draghui, our schoolmaster, would permit it to be said that Badou was drunk when the old man could no longer say to his horses, "Hie," which means go forward, or "Heue," which means stop. For some the picnic would last until there was no longer oil in the lamps or candles within the clear glass cylinders on the table, but for me the picnic was over when Papa Camous would volunteer to stable Badou's horses and put the old man himself to bed. When that happened I would be ready to pull myself to the top of that bed which was taller than little Henri, there to lie and dream that the future would be all picnics and eating out of doors.

CHAPTER II

HOUSEBROKEN

One morning as the diligence rumbled on its metal tires over the stones of the public square at the beginning of the journey to Nice, I was the passenger who sat beside Badou in his coupé, high above the bony backs of his nags. That morning the whip cracked in a way to make the villagers think the day was the 14th of July. In the interior of the vehicle cherishing a vast basket rode my foster-mother. We were on our way to see her oldest son, Jean Camous, a man who was taught to cook by the incomparable Escoffier. In that year, 1887, Jean was chef in the kitchen of the Grand Hotel in Monte Carlo.

When we had arrived there and my nose had twitched like a little dog's with all the fascinating odors to be encountered in the hidden passages of a big hotel we came at last into Jean's kitchen. Presently I sat at a fabulously long board table scrubbed until its planks were the yellow of cream and as soft. Jean stood there looking down upon me, glorious in white and with a cap that was like a white linen crown tilted stiffly to one side of his head. He was very blonde. His eyes were blue and his golden moustache and goatee were things to thrill creatures other than the small boy who rolled his eyes upward passionately after every suck at something delicious spooned from a saucer. It was coffee ice cream.

"Jean," I pleaded, "bring me here with you."

"Fellow," he protested, "first I should have to stretch your head farther from your feet. No one will give you a situation until you grow. Eat plenty of soup. Dream about meat and when you can eat a piece do so. You must grow bigger. Then we shall get you a situation."

I took that advice and in three years, when I was ten, once more Badou carried me away from Contes. This time I went by train from Nice to Mentone and then to Cap Martin and the Hotel Cap Martin. I had embarked on a great career. You think not? What made Caruso sing? His food, positively.

Jean Camous had become the chef of the Hotel Cap Martin and it was through his intercession that an arrangement had been made to attach me to the staff of the hotel, as you might add to the bottom of a dizzy column of figures one small digit. I arrived with an old trunk that had belonged to Jean, a trunk big enough to contain the wardrobe of a family, or even, if neatly fitted, the carcasses of ten boys the size of Henri Charpentier. In that cavern were stowed three pairs of stockings, two shirts, an old pair of shoes, a few handkerchiefs; practically nothing amid its emptiness. It was carried into the hotel by a porter who eyed me with curiosity as he weighed its lightness upon his back. Then Jean took me by the hand and delivered me into the office of the manager, the *patron,* as we called him in France; and before him I stood with my feet very close together to obtain the ultimate centimeter of height. I got the job and if you think it queer that one should begin the career of restaurateur while yet so young I would remind you that the admirals of the English began as young and did not have so much to learn.

In no time I was dressed as a page in a suit of blue cut in English schoolboy style with a wide collar of white linen. On my yellow hair was a cap of blue with a pert and glossy visor and on the top a big gold button as if to mark my presence and save me from being stepped on by the tall ones who thronged the lobby of that fashionable place. I remember so well how I looked because, I think, never until that day had I seen all of myself as one piece. In the mirror at home there would be reflected an ear and then at the cost of movement, a nose or one blue eye; never a complete countenance. But in the Hotel Cap Martin as I trod on Oriental carpets I was surrounded by mirrors and nothing they reflected could give me quite so much excitement as the sight of myself costumed for work.

Impressions came swiftly to overwhelm my small knowledge of the world. I was standing near the door admiring myself with puffed-out chest when I became aware of feet of astonishing length and then high above me a gruff voice spoke, "Boy." I thought I was being insulted. In my village we used the English word to designate a young rascal. My eyes began to move as I thought how quickly information about me had reached the hotel. I put my head back as I would today to see the face of a giant. The Englishman spoke again; two more English words. Then I said, in French, that I did not understand, whereupon with one French word he revealed to me his problem.

"Come, m'sieu," I said. I led him through a corridor and beyond a door where only employees were supposed to go. We descended a flight of narrow, twisting wooden stairs, traversed a long passage until we came to a cluster of idle porters, dishwashers and others. How should I have known this was not the place for customers? I think the man must have been amused by my midget proportions and my giant error. He gave me five francs, which made me feel like Monte Cristo; and then he told on me.

Mr. Ulrick, one of the two English proprietors, came to the desk of the German concierge to ask who had taken a gentleman below stairs. Proudly I claimed this distinction only to hear myself denounced as a farmer. "Excuse me," I said, "is there a difference in people?" Then Mr. Ulrick turned his anger on the concierge who was from that blue minute my enemy. When Mr. Ulrick vanished the German turned to another, bigger page and indicating me he said: "Take him to the toilet. Submerge his head in it. Next time he will know."

That page, Jean Baptiste Devisse, today is the concierge of the Riviera Palais in Nice and my warm friend. When he took me into a wonderful salon of porcelain, I looked upon that white magnificence of plumbing and refused to believe it. With an elbow and the back of my hand I menaced Jean to persuade him I was not taken in by his jest; but it was so. In America where everyone takes for granted the utmost in convenience and accommodations, it is difficult to appreciate how much in earnest I was when I declared that in Contes such a place would be made the kitchen. So I became housebroken.

Luncheon time for the hotel crew was my next mental earthquake. A big, fat cook, friend and subordinate of Jean Camous, beckoned to me and pointed to a plate which I took in my hands. Onto it he forked a piece of roast veal from which arose an incense with an intoxicating fragrance. The portion was nearly as big as my head. Innocently I asked him: "For how many is this piece?"

"You."

I think now that cook was having fun with me; but then I was solemn. I carried that beautiful piece of roast veal to a table protected by spotless white oil cloth. I had a glass of wine and my own napkin. There was more meat on my plate than would be eaten in a week by Papa and Mama, by Celestin and Cesarina, by Badou and even some others. Suddenly I was wretched with longing and sorrow; I began to cry and I never did eat that piece of veal. That was forty-four years ago, but today when I think of the poverty of Contes and the richness with which I was in contact, I can cry afresh from the original emotion.

CHAPTER III

The Queens and Duchesses in My Life

But I had an enemy! That concierge hated my small self for the humiliation my error had brought upon him. Every time guests were departing he would send me off with a dispatch to the tower telegraph station perched on the cliff edge so its semaphore signals could be seen by mariners' eyes on ships far out on that sapphire sea. It was such a place as any boy would delight to loiter in except when that boy knew he was missing his chance to receive pay for unrequited errands. Three times I came back to the Hotel Cap Martin to be hailed as stupid by the jeering concierge while other boys were bragging of their tips. Then suddenly I knew I was smarter. I took his next dispatch obediently but when I was beyond his sight I ran back and climbed through a first floor window. As the departing guests came down the curving steps, there hidden from the concierge by heavy draperies I saluted, I bowed and I made flattering remarks. To me none who departed was of less rank than baron; a few I made counts, occasionally in a burst of enthusiasm I said farewell to "mon prince." Some were flattered, but some, I think found my smallness wistful and pathetic. Where other boys would have received three francs, I received ten. I had a gold coin, a ten franc piece, in my pocket at the very moment that day when the concierge said again: "Stupid, you do not run fast enough. More guests have departed." I grinned behind my hand.

In all the hotel the one who impressed me the most was the general manager, the tall, dignified Mr. Charles Ulrick. No fleck of dust, no faintly unpleasant odor ever escaped detection by that pack of bloodhounds, his fierce eyes and alert nostrils. Naturally, even such small ones as my feet were caught in the gaze of his inspection.

"Change those shoes."

"Yes, sir." For the first time I compared my rough, stiff leather country shoes with his, soft as a lady's gloves and polished until they mirrored the blue pattern of the deep vase of Chinese porcelain beside which he was standing. Soon afterward I was cajoling Michel, the porter, to tell me where Mr. Ulrick bought his shoes. The place was in Mentone and I went there. In a tone which suggested that the matter was ended the shoemaker told me shoes such as Mr. Ulrick wore cost twenty francs. "Twenty-two francs if I have them by tomorrow night," I said and drew more than that sum out of my pocket. When I returned for those shoes the shoemaker threatened his big son with the back of his hand. "Take an example from this boy," he said. "He has worked but a few days and already he steps from these [he held up my old ones] into these [and now he held up Mr. Ulrick's shoes in miniature] which I make for him for eighteen francs, wishing I was rich enough to make them for nothing." A four-franc present, that one!

In the room in the employees' section of the hotel which I shared with my friend Jean and Antoni, a Swiss elevator boy, I woke twice that night to touch my shoes. In the morning wearing them I brought myself under the gaze of Mr. Ulrick before seven. But he paid no attention to me. Three times I said, "Bonjour, M'sieu Ulrick," before at last he exclaimed over them. Then when he realized what I had done he handed me twenty francs.

"I am giving you the price of your shoes," he said.

"But Verrane, the shoemaker, charged me only eighteen."

"Keep those two extra ones anyway for being so honest."

I worried less about the concierge from that moment; and even less when the Duchess of Rutland became my friend. I stood close by her chair as she read a newspaper before the dinner hour. Her hair was white and there were blue pencilings on the backs of her hands but each fingernail had been cared for as if it were a jewel. I followed the direction of her gaze and though I could not then read English I had marked her place as she rose. A gong had signaled the beginning of dinner. All degrees of greatness were thronging into the dining room, including daughters of the duchess, each of whom when the occasion demanded I must call "milady" and a son who was to be addressed as "milord."

When the duchess emerged two hours later I could have told her better than a clairvoyant why she beamed and filled with tightness those stiff corsets of 1890. I had actually seen her smile compounded. A boy of my size? I was all over the hotel, exploring like a mongoose and as long as I kept from under foot I was tolerated anywhere. So I had watched when the word came back to the kitchen that Madame la Duchesse desired to eat Chicken Beaulieu. I can and do make it today. Jean Camous himself supervised the whole operation and from a dozen limp, yellow candidates selected the plucked and drawn three-months-old baby chicken that two days before had been throttled.

When a lump of sweet butter with salt and freshly ground pepper had begun to bubble, the chicken was placed in the casserole and covered. Cooking separately were white onions only a little larger than the biggest pearls in the necklace of the duchess and potatoes of a similar size. Today I start the race of the vegetables and the chicken as carefully as at Belmont Park the two-year-olds are started in the Futurity. These are tender creatures and the heat of the fire is something to be measured carefully or the magic is spoiled. Remember: first the butter, and when it is hot enough to conquer, then the onions, then the potatoes, a few hazel nuts, the heart of an artichoke. If you use an entire clove of garlic be sure, before serving, to recover it if it is to be served to a duchess. Then add half a dozen ripe olives with the stones left in to help them resist the ordeal of cooking. Next put in a peeled tomato of a size no bigger than could be crowded into your mouth. Finally cook some slices of truffle in a glass of sherry. When this is done forty minutes will have gone from your life, but your chicken will be ready for his nest of vegetables, and like jeweled decorations he can wear upon his breast the truffles.

Did I say the duchess beamed after eating that? But listen: I placed her chair, I knelt to bring into position a footstool and then I handed her the newspaper and with my finger indicated the place where she had stopped reading.

"How did you know the very line?" She spoke with amazement in her voice.

"I followed Madame's eye. I hope I was not impertinent."

For an answer she put her hand to my face and patted it. My nostrils were filled with the delicate odor of her perfume of violets, and I heard her say, "What is your name, petit?"

"Henri," I said and with big eyes watched her withdraw from a little pocket in her skirt a purse of gold fabric, saw her open it and select a gold coin. Then it was in my hand, a louis, twenty francs. With sympathetic questions she learned my story and when I explained that I worked so that I could help Mama Camous, she exclaimed, "lovely."

Thereafter if we had not seen each other for twenty-four hours she would pretend to be worried and say, "Let me see, petit: Have you grown up?" Every Sunday she gave me a gold piece and from time to time she would commend me to the general manager. I knew that glowering concierge had lost his least power over me the first time she said: "Ulrick, I like this boy. He is polite and nice." She was patting my cheek again and I was inhaling the violet perfume. One day she showed me a big box of chocolates, ten pounds at least. She was sending it to Contes, to Mama Camous. Did I not say that a duchess was my friend?

Sometimes I would hold the door open for Queen Victoria's son, the Prince of Wales and for his tall friend, Leopold, King of the Belgians. One hand of Leopold was always occupied with a cane and a hat. The hat was gray of an old-fashioned, half hard form with a top like a melon. I have had, in my hands, that hat of his many times. Leopold was lame but there was a fine economy in his affliction because when he walked each step was a bow to the people who were so constantly saluting him that it was easier to carry his hat than to lift it. He never abandoned a table until he had sent a compliment to the chef. Usually he uttered it as he was preening his spade beard and his fine moustache that was grayer than his hat. After Cap Martin I saw him through many years at Aix les Bains, in Monte Carlo, in Paris, Ostend. His eyes alone could tell you that he knew every prerogative of his office of king; and yet, the thing that seemed to give him more pleasure than his luncheon was to say at the slightest excuse, *"Merci,"* "I thank you," *"Merci."* A real king that one.

At Cap Martin I knew the view from our terrace was lovely. You could drench your eyes with the blue of the sea and then turn them and your imagination upon Monte Carlo on the right and the Cap Antibes; and on the left Mentone and the spires of San Remo. The air was sweet with the odors of rare flowers, of thyme, rosemary bushes and eucalyptus trees. Nature seemed to have planned that place to be the resort of kings. But inside the hotel men had improved on nature.

Four tall, but shallow fireplaces were in the lobby. Each sent every least atom of smoke into its big stone chimney; but gave its heat and its feeling of cheer to the people in that splendid chamber, without regard to the individual's place in the world. I know I was as happy there as any king; yes, happier. The walls were cream, the marble stairs had been shaped to the curve dreamed by some fine architect. There were tapestries to soften voices, and thick carpets and rugs to cushion the feet of the finest people of Europe. As you entered, the concierge stood behind his desk on the left; the manager was in his bureau on the right. In the vestibule were tables on which were files of the great newspapers from Paris, London, St. Petersburg, Madrid, New York, Berlin, Buenos Aires. It was my duty to deduct each day one paper from the wooden splint in which it was held with its successors as I added the newest one. The old ones belonged to me. That was how I was kept alive to the duty and in the course of the season I made 250 francs—fifty dollars—from the sale of them to a dealer who resold them to readers more patient than those who patronized the Hotel Cap Martin. If what I used to fancy were true, those papers continued to be passed on at a smaller and smaller fee until even now somewhere there would be a humble citizen waiting his turn to read what was no longer news, but history.

History indeed! There came a time when a band of dark blue velvet was sewn to the right sleeve of my coat between the wrist and the forearm. It had an edging of gold lace and, also in gold lace, a device which was the two-headed eagle of Austria-Hungary. The Empress Elizabeth had come to stay at the Hotel Cap Martin. The significance of that decoration on my arm was that I had been assigned as the special page boy of her majesty. When she was arriving or departing a red carpet was unrolled in the porte-cochère. The small hackneys drawing her victoria would trot smartly to the door and then lean forward from their hind legs to guarantee a firm stand until she was safely out or else seated in the vehicle. My part was to stand stiffly with my arm extended so that she might use me as a living balustrade. She needed no support but invariably her fingers brushed the velvet on my arm. It was I who carried telegrams, packages and letters to the apartment of her majesty where I handed them to a major domo. The empress had an expression almost always as melancholy as the black mourning in which she dressed. Unless your ears were alert you might suspect she had not spoken in passing so softly did she say *bonjour*. One room of her hotel suite had been transformed into a chapel and there each morning a mass was said for the empress by the Abbé Rosso from Roquebrune. He was a magnificent looking priest and that magnificence was exaggerated by my small size when I attended him as altar boy. I would put wine in the chalice, move the Book, utter the responses and steal glances at the empress. She sat in a big chair and had before her a stool softly upholstered in velvet which matched that on my arm even to the double eagle. This was to receive her knees when she stooped to pray. Her sister, beside her, had a stool as soft but it was not ornamented.

Once I was present when Queen Victoria arrived and I saw these two empresses embrace each other. The Queen of England was like a grandmother to all the world and her fleet was the greatest on the seas; but the perfume which triumphed when these two ladies came together was the simple lavender of the Empress Elizabeth. I was so sensitive to its odor I could have followed her like a hunting dog when she walked in the woods with her sister. Several men always followed them at a discreet distance, bodyguards. When she was killed by an assassin in 1898 I regretted it almost as if I had been one of her subjects. Yet she was not my favorite empress.

That lady was Eugenie-Marie de Montijo, the Spanish woman who became the wife of Napoleon III. In the successive seasons that I worked at the Hotel Cap Martin she was always there in an apartment on the first floor. She was more than seventy when I first encountered her but you would not have thought so because she had so much élan vital. Yet no extensive suite attended her because she was, sadly enough, an ex-empress.

"Are you a French boy?" she asked me.

"Yes, your majesty."

"How do you know I am 'your majesty'?"

"I learned in school—" For the first time I lacked my customary aplomb. How was I to tell her what I had learned in school? She was wearing a peignoir of lavender silk, gray lace and white, and each movement of her round arms strengthened the air with the spicy perfume of carnations. I began to stammer.

"Sit down."

"But I must not, your majesty. The *patron*—"

"Who tells you?"

"The Empress of France."

Then she smiled gaily and opened a big box of bonbons. When I had eaten three or four my courage returned and I began to talk and, small imp that I was, I knew things about the hotel that not even an empress might find out for herself. I chattered as with a friend. Then when I saw she was restless I prepared to leave but before I did so she said: "Here are the bonbons on this table and whenever you have business here help yourself. The sugar of these confections will make you big and so I will be doing something for France. Eh?" To think she lived to be ninety-four! My friend Jean Devisse afterward was for ten years in her employ and so once, when I was grown, I was permitted to salute her. She had not forgotten me.

King Umberto and Queen Margerita of Italy came that winter, or perhaps it was the next. I remember the regiment of cuirassiers with shining steel breast plates, scarlet trousers, blue tunics and helmets with horsetails, the regiment of Alpine blue devils and the others that paraded when the President of France met at Cap Martin the Emperor Franz Josef; but I must have been completely a royalist by then for I have no recollection of the President, neither his name nor his features.

CHAPTER IV

HOME WITH A FORTUNE

One day as I slipped into the kitchen to see what regal food I might get for myself Jean Camous addressed me. He said: "Henri!"

I gave him my attention and saw him pour a big spoon of curaçao, a cordial made of oranges, into a saucer. Then with a cooking spoon he produced from a freezer almost the precise amount of vanilla ice cream which I could contain. He mixed quickly and thoroughly and then sprinkled this with hazel nuts that had been browned in a roasting pan and sliced thin. "For you," he said.

I began to eat. I smacked my lips. I ate until it was all gone.

"So," he said, "you can eat with enthusiasm still? I think, now, it is time you learned to cook the same way. Anything you do must be accomplished with enthusiasm else it is worthless. The season here on the Riviera is about finished. Next I shall go to the Grand Hotel Frascati in Le Havre. There you will learn about cooking. But you won't make so much money for a time."

I wondered how he knew about my money. I had become a little miser during the six months. I had become also a fox. I had learned how to solicit from waiting coachmen the names of their masters and mistresses. Then, as these departed with comfortable digestions from the hotel restaurant I spoke to them, politely uttering their names, wishing them pleasant journeys home and quick returns to our establishment. Invariably they plunged their hands into their pockets.

Those generous actions were but repercussions of the cuisine of Jean Camous.

Many persons who were to be my life-long friends and patrons were first encountered in that season on the Riviera, Mr. J. P. Morgan, Commodore Vanderbilt, aye, a host of great ones and beautiful ladies, too; and all contributed to my swelling fortune.

Screwed to the bottom of that cavernous trunk of mine was a box which was kept locked as was the trunk itself. Whenever I had possessed enough silver and other small coins to buy a gold coin from the cashier I had done so. Each of these had been wrapped in paper so that it would not betray itself and me by clinking. I had when it was time to return home for a visit in Contes 3,300 gold francs, more than six hundred dollars. It was, beyond question, a fortune. I had, beside, clothing for myself and presents for my friends. I had become adroit in searching rooms after the departure of guests and cigarettes, cigars, perfume bottles, fine gloves with, perhaps, just a tiny hole in them, and all manner of things had been added to my collection. True, the perfume bottle might bear a legend saying it was black tulip when the odor would be saying it was gardenia, but what did it matter? My trunk was full and also my heart on that day when Mr. Ulrick shook my hand and told me to return in September, that I was "hired again."

I carried my gold close to my heart. It was in a treasure chest that I had improvised by ripping out of the box the paper compartments designed for twenty hard, black little cigars called Bastos. This box was fastened inside my coat by four heavy safety pins which fettered it at the sides, the top and bottom. On the train to be safer I forced myself into a compartment reserved for ladies and there were nine of them present. So often did I squirm free of their crowding in order to pat my box of gold that one of them accused me of having St. Vitus' dance. At Nice I hurried to the Place Garibaldi and, sure enough, there was Badou dozing on the box of his diligence. Now for the first time did I realize how thin and famished were his horses; how shabby was that old man. I had brought tobacco for him, a pound tin, but when those old beasts of his turned to look at me with lifted ears, when they recognized Henri Charpentier as a person of Contes, then I knew the emotion behind a secret of the hotel business: that the stranger likes to be recognized. I knew what a feeling it is that makes the stranger glow and tip when you call him by name. So I bought Badou's horses some sweet biscuits, and only then did I awaken him. He embraced me and I kissed him on each cheek, tasting his tears.

When we reached Contes, when I had been kissed by everyone and had kissed everyone, Papa Camous put four bottles of wine on the table. Then Celestin sniffed and Cesarina sniffed. It was my perfume, of violets, from a little bottle abandoned by the Duchess of Rutland. When the meal was finished I pushed the figs from the center plate and with a sudden movement emptied onto it my store of gold. I shall never forget that music, the clink of gold on porcelain, nor the look in the eyes of my foster-mother when I told her the money was for her. She lives today and she is old, but I think some of her vitality comes from happiness generated by that expression of love which I brought back to her from Cap Martin.

In that spring of 1891, when I had returned in triumph from the Cap Martin, much more than I had enjoyed the actual experience with royalty I was enjoying the effects of my adventures upon the people of the village. In that time, while I was a little boy, the Rue Henri Charpentier in Contes was called something less significant to me.

Now, in that village, I am somebody, even a legend; but the things for which they have honored me so touchingly are really growths of the first seeds of pride which those dear people planted in my soul. Because of the emotion I knew then I understand perfectly when Admiral Byrd returns to the frigid Antarctic; it is not the South Pole he loves so much as it is the acclaim of his coming home. Naturally I did not go on to Havre and my cooking apprenticeship until I had enjoyed the full flavor of my return. Ah, it was exquisite emotion!

There I was, aged ten and a half, attracting more attention than anybody in the village and since all loved me none was jealous, not even a little. If I but shut my eyes I can hear again the shrillness of the small girls of the school of the heavily bearded M. Draghui as they clustered about me. *"Mon dieu, Henri,"* exclaimed the first to inhale my aroma, "already the world has put upon you the scent of a violet." They took turns placing above their braids of hair my big gray hat, they fingered the fabric of my suit and squealed when they discovered my gloves. I think there was never a village as kind and gentle to an orphan as was mine. Even my cane, a test of the manners of the boys, excited only admiring comments. Everywhere it was the same and the priest, Don Albini, began to change his former opinion of me. His fingers ploughed my hair, darkened without its sunburn, as we reminisced, the two of us, about the escapades of the nine-year-old who in the previous year had been myself. I confessed to him then that it was for revenge that I had driven into the church the little donkey which had brayed an interruption to the class in catechism and then had guzzled holy water from the *bénitier*. This minute the hair on my neck prickles as I hear the little beast's hoofs rattling on the stones of the church floor as Père Don Albini yelled and started for me with his cane uplifted. But on my day of atonement I acknowledged I had not been entitled to revenge, that the sacristan probably had been divinely inspired when he seized me by the ears as the guilty one that night when the old woman began to scream. When my unholy delight had betrayed me I had actually been standing before the priest in the robes of the thurifer. I was swinging the censer in such wide arcs as to make its charcoal glow and the incense smoke to fill the nostrils of all the congregation with an aromatic fragrance. It all comes back to me now. I remember how thoughtfully I had observed the old men and women dipping their work-numbed fingers deeply into the basin of holy water as if they hoped to encounter a miracle. That was what suggested to me the idea of putting small green frogs into that water. I was spanked with the priest's cane and called "boy" in its worst, its French meaning, that night. But the priest forgave me and through the years until he died in 1932 we were warm friends.

Best of all during my two weeks at Contes were the hours in our ancient house at the top of the village. I who had been eating food prepared for kings anticipated with doglike eagerness the serving of the contents of cooking pots suspended in the blackened fireplace. One day it would be a rabbit they had sacrificed; another time the victim would be some hen that had retired from egg-laying. My Mama Camous would prepare even an old hen so that it would be saluted by Escoffier. She and Papa Camous beamed upon me as twin suns might shine upon a small world. Think of their gratitude! With 3,000 of the 3,300 gold francs I had brought home debts were being paid that for years had been a burden depriving them of food, sometimes of medicine and always of comfort. Now, because of Henri, the orphan, the cramped house was to be expanded in its upper story. Really, I do not brag. It is not of myself that I speak but only of a little fellow who like one of my ancestors is blended into the man I am. In this fact I seek refuge from blame for boasting.

My *maman nourrice* is old now, ninety-seven, but when I have paid visits to her in France always she has remembered it. Never has she failed to tell me how it sounded when my return from Cap Martin was heralded to her. First she heard the whip-cracking of Badou, then, the rumble of his coach and then, faintly, his deep voice, calling, "Alesandrina [her name], Henri has arrived." Then other voices from houses farther up repeated the cry. In that valley a call loudly made is swiftly echoed. Consequently it had been as if many voices were telling that I was coming home to be kissed. But the echoes of that announcement have never ceased to sound in her heart, I tell you that.

They sent me off the second time with prayers for my safety. Havre was at the extreme other side of France! Only a few in the village had been so far. But they knew I would be with my foster-brother, Jean. Certainly when I arrived and went to work in the Grand Hotel Frascati I soon knew it! Jean Camous had in his kitchen a discipline that could not be softened even by Jean Camous, the brother.

There were over twenty cooks in his crew and ten small fellows like myself who were learning and assisting. Each of us was aware that we worked for a kitchen tyrant, a "no-return" chef. Not one course was taken from the kitchen until Camous had tasted and approved; but when he had approved you had adventure in a tureen! Romance in a casserole! Paradise in the sweet!

Once, at the Frascati, Baron Rothschild came to the kitchen to speak with Camous concerning arrangements for a dinner. My eyes were wide to see every detail of this ultra-rich banker, his thin-soled shoes, his striped trousers, his redingote. I did not hear what he said but I heard Camous reply, and at first he spoke softly.

"I admit that you may not like it, Baron; but I defy you to say it is not good."

The Baron made some reply, perhaps not discreet and then I saw the real Camous. His vast blondness, his blue eyes, his goatee and beautiful moustache, his white costume all focused upon the Baron an astonishing amount of indignation.

"With your banks and your wealth," he said, "you are a Baron. But with my art in my kitchen I am a Count."

The Baron tried to soften the rage he had aroused. "But, please, Camous, tell me how you make the sauce I liked so much."

"Baron," he retorted haughtily, "it will never be too inconvenient an hour of the day for me to duplicate it for you; but, Monsieur le Baron, this is my treasure vault you would invade." Jean tapped his head with such vigor as to make it sound as if he were rapping on a table rather than his skull.

Ah, but for me that treasure vault was always open. He taught me everything about cuisine, from the peeling of potatoes to the making of sauces. "Fellow," he would say, "a vegetable is a wonderful but a delicate thing. If he is wearing his skin put him into cold water and let him boil until he is cooked; but without his skin he should be plunged at once into the boiling water." I learned by listening to him instruct and chide all those who were in his company. Once I heard him roar: "Stop it! Animal, are you a cook or a mason? Do not stir thus, roughly, with your spoon. But do it like this: take the butter so:—be gracious." That lesson was a demonstration. First he aped the heavy-handed mixing of the one he rebuked; then he became Camous and each finger that was working stood out stiffly from its fellows as if not only were it keeping respectfully out of the way of the workers but as if it were actually enjoying participation in an exquisite sensation. If Paderewski may do that when he plays his piano why not Camous? Or, Henri?

CHAPTER V

AN ADVENTURE WITH BERNHARDT

What makes a life? I, Henri Charpentier, am not simply a man, a restaurateur in a white apron in Rockefeller Center in New York City. No, I am an essence of all my experience since I was small and helpless. In the timbre of my voice, the shape of me, my response to another's misery or happiness, in my affections and prejudices, my flavors, so to speak, I am like consommé. If we might, by agreement, say Consommé *Petite Marmite* Henri IV, I could support my argument with a most charming lady.

She was all in black, her gloves, her frock and the laces and tulle about her face that was so white. With wide gestures she was entering the restaurant of the Grand Hotel Frascati. So plainly is the memory focussed that although this was more than forty years ago I wish again to be heroic for her. I hear her voice, too, calling as if with a great longing, "Baptiste, Baptiste!" Baptiste was my chief and the best waiter I have ever known, a bald little pelican of a man with spraddled feet and I was one of the least of his assistants, a boy of eleven. With a flick of his napkin he sent me flying toward the kitchen, not dawdling as usual to admire my reflection in that polished mirror of wood, the parquet floor. The message I carried to Camous was an adjuration to prepare to exceed himself; that the one who had arrived was Madame Sarah Bernhardt.

What role was she to play that night? I cannot remember but

whether L'Aiglon or Camille I do recall the grumbles of Camous. How unjust, he complained, that the program which named the couturier who created her costumes should neglect to identify the chef who prepared the fuel for the day's performance. Of one thing I am sure: nothing that Madame ate that day gave her so much nourishment and power as the *Petite Marmite* Henri IV, with which she began her meal. In France for centuries kings and peasants alike have thrived on that rich consommé.

For a family of six you would take about two pounds of beef, and accompanied only by its fat, place it in a casserole after treating it to a few pinches of salt and a few turns of the pepper grinder. This meat is browned over a hot fire for about ten minutes. In another casserole treat a chicken similarly. Keep the chicken moving so that it does not burn. These two, then, become companions in a soup pot containing about six quarts of cold water, along with some beef and veal bones and a bone from which the marrow has been carefully removed. Put that raw marrow aside. It is important. Next, take an onion with its skin intact and allow it to roast over your hot fire until it turns brown and throws off a strong perfume. Now put that onion, maybe two or three, into your soup pot; also two or three turnips, the long ones rather than the round, two or three peeled carrots, a bunch of leeks and the green tops (only the tops) of a few stalks of celery. Skim this broth whenever a froth forms during the first hour of boiling.

Now, never cook your cabbage in your soup. Put it in cold water in a separate pot, add a little salt and boil it. When the cabbage is cooked, rinse it in cold water. Then add to this cabbage a little broth from the consommé pot, and resume the cooking of this vegetable.

After the soup has boiled for an hour remove the meat, the chicken and the vegetables. They have contributed their best to the consommé, which should continue to boil slowly for another four hours, being skimmed whenever necessary. By that time it will contain nourishment to give a dwarf the force of a giant. If you are not rich the beef, the chicken and the vegetables can be the other courses of your dinner. Steam them for twenty minutes in a covered pot containing just a little of the consommé.

Ah, but that Consommé *Petite Marmite* was for Bernhardt. She would want only one or two small pieces of chicken in the amber fluid, with perhaps, two or three slices of carrot.

At the very moment I arrived in the kitchen to receive the con-sommé for Madame Bernhardt, croutons that had been toasted with a covering of grated parmesan cheese were being taken from the oven. That marrow-fat of which I spoke had been sliced as you would slice a banana. It was clear of even a suspicion of blood, proving that the butcher had understood his business. The round slices had been laid in cold water; they required no other preparation. Then the consommé was poured into a silver tureen. Two slices of marrow-fat were added for each portion and on these went a little chervil, not chopped but cut with a pair of scissors, some tiny bits of chives, a few pinches of pars-ley. Then, finally, those little rafts of toast with their brown cargoes of parmesan were launched in that silver vessel and the cover put in place. Within my arms I had a steaming fluid I believed was destined to become the gestures, the tones, the very stage business with which that night Bernhardt would make an audience in Le Havre cry and clap.

I started across the rough cement floor, proud as a soldier. Had not Baptiste told me that always my customer was to be regarded as the flag, a thing to respect and protect? Naturally, with such a zeal to serve, I hurried. I turned my small back to open the swinging door and then eager for Baptiste's commendation I went swiftly, almost running, across the parquet floor of the dining room. I was precisely beside Madame Bernhardt when my feet slipped. But as I fell, I remembered to protect my customer. I pulled the tureen toward me so that as I struck on my back the scalding fluid drenched me with pain and anguish. Even so I could see pieces of white chicken and yellow carrot clinging to the black skirt of her frock; and it was wet. What humiliation!

"Oh, Madame," I exclaimed through my tears as I scrambled to my feet, "will you excuse me? I have spoiled your dress."

"Ah," she said with a voice more tender than she could employ on the stage, "this poor little one! My friends," and with a movement of her fine eyes she commanded the attention of all, including Baptiste, "see him! See, with his fingers swelling and turning white with blisters how he does not consider pain; but only my dress. Gallant fellow!"

She applied her napkin to my steaming eyes. She lifted a piece of chicken from her dress and popped it into her mouth. She recovered another piece from her lap and laid it on her plate. She made her eyes go wide as if with pleasure from the taste.

"Hey," she said, "Sarah has three hundred and sixty-six dresses. What does it mean to Sarah Bernhardt, one dress?"

But my tears continued to rain.

"My little boy," she coaxed, "don't be scared. You know what I think? This is *Petite Marmite* Henri Quatre: I think that king tried to grab Bernhardt's dress!"

That was a fantastic idea at which I smiled and then, delighted, she said: "I think that old Henry Quatre would rather be the charming little Henri [she had heard Baptiste speak my name, harshly] who stands here beside me? Eh?" So she cajoled until I was laughing through my tears and then she opened her purse and for the first time since I had left Cap Martin I was presented with a golden louis.

Again I scurried to the kitchen and when I returned with another tureen of consommé Baptiste was still on his knees at Madame's feet patting her skirt with his napkin and moaning as if the burned fingers were his, but she was busy with a cruet of olive oil. She had saturated her handkerchief with its thick fluid and when I came she wrapped this bit of cambric and point lace around my blistered hand.

No one scolded me for that accident. But when the actress and her party had gone bald Baptiste pretending that he had hair like the mane of a horse, drew his fingers through this imaginary *crinière,* as if in chagrin. "I would be glad to have such a burn," he said, "if Madame Bernhardt would deal with me as she did with you. So much fuss! So many compliments. 'Charming'! 'Sweet'! 'Gallant'! *Pourquoi?* For being stupid." Poor old Baptiste. He loved me, too, and worried over my burns as if he had been my mother and my father.

Ah, but this consommé, this Henri Charpentier, how is he flavored by such an experience. Well, certainly in such subtle ways as are impossible to express in words; yet how little imagination is required to appreciate that such noble behavior by a lady would be an example to the beneficiary until with his own voice and hands he had expressed ten thousand repercussions of her kindness. As a sentimental knight in armour might have kept a guerdon so through many years and many countries I kept the handkerchief of Sarah Bernhardt. I kept it until one glorious day she came to my establishment in Lynbrook on Long Island and I revealed myself and my life of gratitude,—but I must not cross the ocean until I come to it.

CHAPTER VI

LESSONS FROM CAMOUS

There at the Grand Hotel Frascati I was taught the splendid purpose of a market basket. Under the mansard roof was the attic which I shared with Felix, Josef and Dulzot who were like myself, Henri, apprentice-cooks.

Because I was the smallest my bed was close to the wall in the space between the dormer windows where the floor and ceiling came close together so that, even with my insignificant proportions, when I crawled into that nest I had to crouch a little and then be careful to wake up gently lest I rise too quickly and bump my head. Oh, I liked that roof which sheltered me and I liked best of all to hear rain drumming on its metal close to my ears. Yet every morning before dawn I had to leave that languorous retreat to attend Camous on his shopping tour of the Place du Marché. I had to sacrifice desirable moments of sleep because I dared not let it occur that my foster-brother should be first at the rendezvous, the employees' entrance of the Grand Frascati. His apartment was in the annex within the court but he had cautioned me solemnly: "When you learn your craft you wait for the boss; don't expect him to wait for you." He loved me but with his big hand he could cuff like a bear so I was always first to stand there in the early morning shadows as it became five o'clock. I would be shivering a little at the knees because of the thinness of the blue and white checked cotton fabric of my cook's pants. My arm would be thrust beneath the fat handle of my wicker basket of a type which we called a panier. On each of the four corners there was an eyelet of metal and the flat wicker lid was slotted to accept those. When the lid was in place it was bolted securely by two wands which extended the length of the basket and passed, at their ends, through the eyelets. This fastening was important because, as you shall see, this market basket when we returned would be a chef's treasure chest.

In France the market basket is an object of the utmost significance. If it is true that England's battles have been won on her cricket fields, then it is not to be questioned that the greatness of France has been nourished from her market baskets. Not all Englishmen play cricket but with the exception of farmers every French family has as its protective charm a market basket. If I were to design a new flag for France I think I would simply impose upon the tricolor the market basket as the device by which every family exercises economies, accumulates property and, above all else, makes of the dinner table a happily anticipated gathering place.

But Jean Camous was not buying for one family; he was buying for one of the best hotels in Europe, one with a restaurant catering to blasé, luxury-loving clients, to gourmets. Beside my basket the other part of our equipment was the handful of gold and silver coins in the pocket of Camous. He would take to market each day the equivalent of $150 and before our return to the hotel he would have spent most of it. Later in the day the small family marketers would come a-shopping in search of bargains, but we were in search of quality along with other buyers for the good hotels and the homes of the very rich, and therefore we went early; so early that some of the market carts were still in motion as we approached the Place du Marché.

This was Normandy, remember, and so those cart horses were huge Percherons with feet big enough to support an elephant. What lovely animals! Each one was the pet of the family for which it worked. Some were brown and some were black but all were handsome with liquid eyes that saw everything including my small self who in turn saw that those animals were suitable for a race of giants. I knew, somehow, that I was the descendant of the knights who had fought centuries before in saddles strapped to the backs of the ancestors of those same big horses. Ah, we had a great deal in common, the market horses and the little Henri.

Every cart was shadowy under a hood of canvas and at the front of those still moving I could discern the faces, always, of a man and a woman. Sometimes the faces were young and of sweethearts; sometimes they were old and of couples who had grandchildren. The women wore Normandy caps, white and stiff with starch in a design curiously suggestive of the fleur-de-lys. Their skirts were short and of heavy fabrics. The men wore blue smocks and high crowned caps with long shiny visors.

As we entered the salad market Camous would shout: "*Bonjour,* and how is the young lady?" The one he addressed would be a farm woman of such an amplitude as to make her size, beyond doubt, a matter of concern even to the Percheron who drew her cart to and from the market. Romance would have retreated everywhere but from her blue eyes; she would be old, but Camous, that handsome Frenchman, he knew that no woman is ever so old or so fat she is not prepared to hear a compliment with pleasure. Compliments were nearly as important to our enterprise as gold.

"Yes," he would say, "you grow more tempting—" But then, suddenly, he would become interested in a particular one among the heads of lettuce arranged along the market bench like soldiers on parade. "Um, your heads are not nice today, Madame."

"Oh, M'sieu Camous! That is blasphemy!"

"Not blasphemy, but the truth. See this one!" He would lift up that one he had been regarding. Invariably it would be the least desirable head of lettuce in the entire display. "See how its center is yellow and cut by a worm. A worm, Madame! Can I, Camous, offer that one to Baron Rothschild when he comes to the Grand Frascati for dinner? Or to Madame Bernhardt when she appears for luncheon? No! You can see for yourself."

But Madame would not look. She would turn her head with queenly disdain so as not to profane her eyes with a sight of an imperfect product of her garden. She had, always, wonderful merchandise; but Camous had an uncanny instinct for searching out the least tempting object among her wares. He would worry over it, clucking to himself in the manner of a disturbed rooster, until, at last, aroused, Madame would undertake to refute his slander. She would select her finest head of lettuce.

"Your Rothschild, I suppose he would be offended if he were to receive a portion of this emerald for his salad?" She would extend that green head of lettuce in her two hands as if it were the head of John the Baptist and she, herself, were Salome. Against such sarcasm Camous would appear to wilt.

"That one is very beautiful," he would concede, whereupon Madame would select and offer another fit to be its mate; but if she flagged the least little bit in the search for the best of her wares Camous would search out another with imperfections with which to renew her energies. This would continue until he had all the best of her stock after which he would proceed to another stall.

Again he would begin with compliments and then discover the heads with the imperfections. But this time, probably, the imperfections would be of a serious nature. For example:

"This head, Madame, it is soft inside, gelatinous, slippery. How is that?"

"Oh, M'sieu Camous, I think you have wizard fingers because always you pick up the wrong heads."

"Little lady, you plunged your lettuce into water before coming to market."

"Oh, no. Why that would be monstrous!"

"As if I did not know! Perhaps you had bad luck yesterday and did not sell them. But please, for Camous, always have salad severed from its stalks no more than ten or twelve hours before. Today I cannot buy your salad, in spite of my high regard for you and my almost indiscreet admiration. No, Madame!"

"You make me feel very badly!"

"I am desolated, Madame, but today—no heads from you. Although your pretense is unworthy of you and of your fine farm I will buy all your lettuce, not for salad to be served with dressing but to be cooked as a vegetable. Naturally the price will have to be adjusted. You agree?" What he bought was then sent to the hotel packed in flat baskets, called *corbeilles.*

Do not get the idea that Camous was taking advantage of that farm lady. Oh, no indeed. It was too important for him to keep her good-will and the good-will of all the people who brought farm produce to market. But, on the other hand, he dared not allow one of them to take advantage of him. It was after such a transaction one morning that he said to me:

"I spread this business because it is my duty to do so. I buy lettuce from one; dandelions from another; escarole from another; and so on with endive, romaine and other salads. It would be easier to buy from one; it would be nice to buy from friends only, but my duty is to have the best for the hotel and the people we serve."

Naturally he did not have to tell me that it is a deception and therefore improper when vegetables and salad greens are displayed dripping wet. I knew that as any country boy knows it. The poor plants revive a little in their bath but they have ceased to be fresh garden produce. Such things should never be placed in water the first day after they leave the garden. After two or three days it may be necessary in order to give them an appearance of freshness but what is gained for the eye is lost to the palate. That is easily tested with parsley; it will absorb water like a sponge but it will lose its aroma. All green things lose some of their flavor when they are rejuvenated with water. The water, naturally, dilutes the flavor. Is this not simple, common sense?

The memory of man is a wonderful thing! I cannot smell in memory but how plainly I can hear and see vanished things! An actual odor of wild watercress or of a ripe tomato from my own garden is sufficient to make a broken vision of that old market place in Havre come alive. Then it is as though I watched through a tattered curtain in a theatre. I see again the vivid complexion of peaches, the tight spheres of cabbages, the vermilion of tomatoes. I see the wide haunch of a seated market-woman and the shaggy dog that sleeps beside her stool. I see the intelligent calloused hands of a farmer. I hear plainly, too; the voices, the laughter, the scrape of baskets along the stones and all those sounds, all movement, is adjusted to a cadence which does not exist in America. It is the rhythm of clicks and taps from the wooden soles of many sabots, each one made snug for the foot that wears it by a nest of straw. I do believe that if I could contrive to smell the entire harmony of odors of that market place my vision would be a complete thing. Yet that seems to be hopeless because I do not know where to find *fraise des bois.* No doubt wild strawberries exist in America but who brings them to what market? And on what days? Tell me and I shall be there, early!

Fraise des bois were on the index of rarities which when acquired were placed tenderly in my basket. They would have come to market in a small basket, nested in grape leaves and between each layer of these precious berries there would be a cushion of grape leaves. The woman who had found them would have only a few, perhaps a pound or a pound and a half. They would have been picked without stems like raspberries and they would have been picked, moreover, on the very day of their ripening.

Camous would pay at the rate of sixty or eighty cents a pound for such berries. I think, if necessary, he would have paid a dollar a pound because at the hotel there would be avid customers willing to pay ten francs a portion for *fraises des bois* so early in the season. That was the equivalent of two dollars and a half a portion, but it was not too much, I think, for the joy it brought to palate and nose. The customary way was to dip the berries in wine, any good wine, and this treatment developed their aroma so that it enveloped with envious hunger all who sat near the person who ate them. Now the point of this is that what fetched the high price was not the size of the berries, for they were small, but their flavor, their bouquet, something that bewitched your nose.

Sometimes a lady of the market would reveal to Camous that she had a few mushrooms, not domestic ones that she had cultivated, but wild ones, a gift of nature like those *fraises des bois*. Aye, those were the prizes in the lottery of the market, the sort of chances that lured Camous and other great chefs into the open before the light of day. Some wild mushrooms were brown, some were pinkish white and others had the form of eggs. Egg mushrooms sliced and cooked with a piece of roast veal are more odorous than truffles. Right now I seem to see Camous bending to press his nose in a basket of such mushrooms. The mouldy earth and moss in which they had been nourished would have lost none of their humidity in the journey to market. By way of supporting with an affidavit that evidence which his nose had given he would raise with his thumbnail the skin of one of the mushrooms. The flesh would be white and Camous would be happy.

The mushrooms would be placed in my basket along with the *fraise des bois*. But if the flesh of any mushroom offered to Camous showed dark when he lifted the skin with his fingernail he would have nothing to do with them. He knew that when the flesh of that species which he bought turned black it was spoiled.

Another rarity for which we would be alert was watercress of a special kind. That which grows in stagnant ponds is apt to have coarse stems of considerable length; what we wanted was watercress from some cold and lively spring or brook. We wanted watercress with brittle, tender leaves that were so brilliantly green they appeared to have been varnished. If we were lucky we might buy ten or a dozen bunches of this wild plant and when Camous had made certain that not one leaf had turned yellow I would add this purchase to the contents of my basket.

At a certain season my basket was sure to acquire some *calville* apples. The Normandy farmers produced them by a variety of stratagems designed to assist nature to outdo herself. Some of the leaves were stripped away and many, many apple buds were sacrificed so that the few which remained on the tree were extraordinarily flavored. They came to market cushioned on cotton wool which in turn rested on straw. Those apples were of a tender green that threatened as you watched to become either white or pink; so delicate was that hue one hardly dared pronounce it green for fear it would fade. The flesh was so fragrant that when one was cut open in the restaurant the whole dining room was perfumed. For such an apple we charged seven francs fifty in a time when that represented a dollar and a half. And do you suppose Jean Camous would invest in such precious foodstuff without smelling to make sure it was precisely what it should be? I tell you his nose contained an important part of his intelligence.

Consequently, you will understand that I am speaking seriously when I assert that the lady who goes to market should be sure her nose is in good working order. I think, myself, that she ought not to smoke even one cigarette until she has completed her marketing because that mild indulgence might disturb the accuracy of the sense of smell, a faculty which is delicately attuned to if it is not actually a part of the sense of taste. Jean Camous would agree with that.

When one buys eggs one must take them on faith, but with most other things faith is unnecessary. The nose and a fingernail, which should be left unlacquered, are sufficient tools for a trip to market. Are the peas fresh that are offered for sale? The green grocer says yes; he will not be offended if a fingernail is dug into the pod. If sap appears in the wound the peas are fresh enough; if it does not appear then one does not want those peas because then one may be sure they left their parent vines many days before. Vegetables cannot be good unless they are fresh; of course if they are dried vegetables that is another matter, another flavor and a totally different cooking process.

I read the autobiography of an eggplant where the stem joins the purple satin skin. If each member of that junction is firmly attached, if the union between the big vegetable and the segment of vine on which it developed is still firm then the eggplant is fresh; if they have begun to detach themselves the eggplant has begun to spoil. How do I know that? Camous told me but he did more than tell me. He demonstrated.

He took one which he pronounced fresh after indicating to me the firm attachment of vine to vegetable. Then he cut the eggplant in half. All the pulp and seeds were white. Next he showed me one the purple skin of which was not distinguishable from the first. But the green attachments of the stem were loose, like the flaccid fingers of an invalid. That one he cut open too. The inside of that eggplant was spotted with black. Its flesh had begun to mortify. I have never forgotten that lesson. I do not have to split eggplants in the market: I do not have to quarrel with market men. I simply do not buy eggplants unless the stems are firmly attached.

Camous told me: "If you wish to know whether the apples you buy were picked months ago or yesterday split the piece of stem with your fingernail or a penknife. If the stem is soft and sappy it is a fresh apple. If the stem is tough and brittle like an old stick—well, you can answer that one yourself."

Tomatoes? Ask your nose! If they do not have the tempting odor of tomato, an aroma that should capture your attention even when the tomatoes are arm's-length away, then they were picked green and their flavor will make you think you yourself are growing prematurely old and losing your sense of taste. The fault, however, will not be your own or that of your palate, but of a distribution system which requires that most of us should eat fruits and vegetables two or three thousand miles from the gardens where these plants were reared.

A cauliflower? Sometimes nowadays I shake my head with pity as I pass a display of enormous heads of that splendid vegetable. The tops will be as wide as my two hands placed side by side with the fingers spread. Some poor woman will buy one of those and think she is getting a bargain because she gets so much. She will be sadly cheated. Such a big head of cauliflower will be soft and spongy to the touch of your fingers. If you examine it you will see that another process of its growth has begun. The flesh is breaking up into separate lumps no longer clear white in color and by peering through the interstices you may distinguish the slender yellowish leaves which will tell any cook who knows his craft that this particular vegetable has ceased to be an edible cauliflower. If you should cook one your entire household would be aware of the strong, unpleasant odor. But a cauliflower is one of the nobles of the vegetable world when it is in its prime state, the flesh white, tightly packed, almost hard.

Asparagus is another vegetable with the dual character of Dr. Jekyll and Mr. Hyde. If it is fresh and in the Dr. Jekyll state this will be revealed to you by the smoothness of the stem near the cut. That part should be white and pinkish with life like a healthy lady's finger. If it should be, instead, pale, wrinkled, pass to another vegetable display. The green tops also should be considered to make sure that the Mr. Hyde stage of the asparagus has not already begun. To be good the leaves should not have formed; instead the green top should be tightly folded. If you are conscientious you will select asparagus stalk by stalk and before cooking you will cut away that hard skin from the base of the stalk for it contains a bitter substance that will be transmitted by the boiling water to the delicate heads. To cook asparagus properly tie it in bunches and place it in cold water, with salt, to boil. When is it done? When you can press the tines of a fork into the flesh at the juncture where the stem ends and the green begins. When the fork enters readily, remove the asparagus from the hot water and wrap it in a cloth. Asparagus should be served warm but dry. Put the dressing on at the last moment.

Unless one knows these things how is it possible to buy with intelligence?

I have problems that never occurred in the life of Camous. There are, for example, artichokes. When I buy them in New York usually they have been shipped from California. Eight days or so after they have been severed from their stalks those heads begin to look very rusty. The way I satisfy myself how long artichokes have been away from the fields where they grew is to take my pocket-knife and slice off the blackened end of the stem; if what is revealed is also blackened I do not want those artichokes; but if the cutting shows white and moist then they are all right. I wonder often what Camous would have thought if he had been compelled to buy vegetables three thousand miles from the gardens which produced them.

Why, Camous was so set upon having fresh fish that he bought, not from a dealer, but from a fisherman and he was not lenient with him. Once I heard him scold the man for being a little late. "Fellow," he roared, "I want my fish from you tide by tide!"

In other cities of France where I worked with Camous I saw him, many times, apply tests which I still use to judge the freshness of a fish. He would take the tail between his forefinger and thumb and try to bend it. Unless the tail slipped from his fingers he would not have it. But he required also that the eyes have the brilliance of life and that the tongue be as moist as the tongue in his own mouth. When the scales of a fish become sticky it is no longer, in the sense that the word is used by a first-class cook, fresh.

Camous would take oysters and rap their shells together. If they were heavy and sounded like stones he was satisfied. He would do the same with clams. Shell-fish when they are exposed to the air alive keep their shells locked fast; when they die the muscles relax and the shells part. Naturally he would use his nose at such a time also. A fresh oyster (or clam) will please your nose; but if it does not you have no business eating such food.

I am sensible of the fact that Camous, buying for a first-class hotel where some patrons would cheerfully pay four dollars for a portion of out-of-season peas, engaged in transactions beyond the means of most families. Yet Camous used methods and tests that are common to all who go a-marketing in France. And he knew and practiced many stratagems of economy and efficiency. For example if he wanted a strong almond flavor in a macédoine of fruit he would crack one or two peach stones and use the centers which are even more strongly flavored of almond than the nuts which bear that name. His vanilla flavoring was made simply by keeping a couple of long vanilla beans in a covered jar of sugar. The oil of the beans imparts its flavor to the sugar with which it is imprisoned after two days of that companionship. I do that myself, not because it is an economy but because I believe it to be the best way. Yet I know what economy is. If circumstances challenged me to live on a small income, say of twenty or thirty dollars a month, Henri and Philomene Charpentier could do that and still eat excellent food. But that is not remarkable when you think how many times I watched my dear foster-mother make one egg impart its flavor to pancakes for a big family.

Sometimes I enjoy an inward laugh as I encounter on Park Avenue or Fifth a beautiful girl who is wearing a sleek and handsome fur jacket of white or black or brown. She is kept warm by it and she looks seductive but she does not realize, I think, that her lapin coat is a product of the economy of French families. Such coats are cheap and good but the fur does not, generally, come from big rabbit ranches such as would come into existence in America. No, indeed. In France almost every family outside the cities has its pair of rabbits and those rabbits explain why the small-town people and the villagers have no garbage. The discarded tops of carrots, the spoiled outer leaves of cabbage, the peelings, the greens trimmed from cauliflower are fed to the rabbits. All Frenchmen, rich and poor, like rabbits. This is the only meat which you may kill and serve immediately and that meat, I tell you, is splendid. Sometimes we would have it stewed with wine, a few mushrooms, a few olives, potatoes, tomatoes and two or three slices of bacon. Or else it was transformed with a wonderful sauce. It would be cut in pieces like a chicken and then roasted with lard, garlic and onions. Five minutes before it was ready our mother would take the juice of the rabbit and combine it with a glass of wine and perhaps some brandy and produce a chocolate-colored sauce that was entrancing.

In Contes every house without exception had its pig but each household had numerous rabbits. The fur skins of these animals were sold. We also sold our beef bones that came from the soup pot one by one after they had given the last particle of their nutriment and flavor. They were wiped dry of grease on a piece of newspaper and dropped into a bag that hung in a corner beside the fireplace. The greasy paper was squeezed into a tight ball to be used to stimulate a lagging fire. The purchaser of beef bones was an itinerant who came several times a year and paid a few francs for a great many bones. These later reappeared in the world, possibly even in Contes, as buttons and toothbrush handles.

Yes, I think it might even be fun to be poor again since I know how easily simple foods can be transformed into things that kings would delight to eat. Certainly on a very small piece of land in this broad continent I could build a paradise. My pair of rabbits would in a few months become the parents of numerous young. In the late Spring my garden would produce not alone vegetables but flowers, for do not think I would be content to live without beauty and without perfume. I would have bees, too. Possibly in this country where only a few appreciate goats I would have to keep a Mr. and Mrs. Goat in order to be supplied with milk. Obviously my seven hens would have an escort. But I would get along with one pig. If there were potato peelings I would not feed them to him raw. I would cook them. What part of the goat's milk I could not drink I would feed to the grateful pig. Be sure he would thrive. Eventually he would weigh enough to provide me with a pound of pork for every day in the year. But I should deprive myself of some. I would trade one of his hams, after smoking it in my fireplace, for another small pig just as we used to do in Contes.

I am sure I could do that because when I was a little boy and poor I lived among resourceful people. If I were to become so poor again I would have a market basket, oh yes. But I would use it to carry food from my own garden to my own kitchen where Philomene would be on hand to transform it into something quite as delicious as anything we now offer to the richest clients of our restaurant. When I handed her the basket of raw food I would also hand her a bouquet of flowers and I would utter such compliments as would make us both sing while the dinner was cooking.

Camous was a sun-worshipper. Long before scientists began talking about vitamins, fish liver oil and sun-lamps as substitutes for good food and a clean conscience, that fellow had it all set down in his philosophy that the source of healthy animal life was the sun. One day when we were coming from the market in Havre and I carried the basket heavy with edible treasures he had purchased there I guess I must have stumbled from weariness.

"Fellow," he said, softly, "are you tired?"

"Yes," I replied in a weak moment.

"Don't be tired," he roared at me so loudly that I stiffened and was cured of my weakness. Yet when we were in his kitchen he handed me a big tomato, scarlet, fragrant, less than twelve hours from its vine. "That color is the sunlight," he told me. "Eat it and you will understand magic. The skins of fruits and the skins of vegetables are subtly charged with the properties of the life-giving sun. Rob a flower of sunlight and see what a pale, grotesque thing it becomes. It is true of all animals, including ourselves. Eat the tomato. It will give you so much élan I'll put a chain on you as if you were a monkey to keep you from climbing on the ceiling." But he was not satisfied with me. That night he spoke to me again.

"Tomorrow, Henri," he said, "I send you across to Trouville to work for a month in the kitchen of the Rochesnoire under my friend Laboureur. Expose yourself to the sunlight when you can so that I may write to our mother that you are rapidly expanding into a restaurateur."

Trouville was two hours by boat from Le Havre. For a season of three or four of the hottest weeks of the year the most fashionable people of the world gathered there for the horse races. Me? I was lucky if I was in the open air daily for half an hour of sunlight. Nevertheless I throve because, possibly, in the kitchen the range fires were so hot they served me as a private sun. All of us who worked there stood on our bare feet in wooden sabots. The stamp of the chef's sabot on the cement floor was a command like the tapping of the baton of an orchestra leader.

"*Saucier!*" he would say loudly to that important assistant. "Four filet of sole, white wine sauce."

"*Bon,*" the *saucier* would reply. There was a constant shouting of such commands and a perfect machine gun fire of "*bon, bon, bon, bon,*" thundered at the chef.

As a waiter and as a maître d'hôtel I have heard fine ladies and gentlemen complain of the heat in summer and speak fretfully of the necessity of eating. Often I have thought how cool they would feel if they would but stroll through a big hotel kitchen and then escape back to the coolness of their chairs placed at tables covered with frosty linen.

Trouville, Le Havre, Cap Martin, other playgrounds of France were working places for me. Always, though, in those first years Camous kept a tether on me; if I was not under his eyes then I was under the eyes of some dear friend of his, one who could be trusted to give the little Henri the back of a hand if he became impertinent or careless. Oh, this is not a complaint; it is an expression of gratitude to Jean Camous. Some of his lessons linger in my mind with all the flavor of adventure. I would ask you to recall the fascination you could feel as a child as you considered the sweet peril of Hansel and Gretel nibbling at the candy house in the woods where dwelt the old witch. I watched one time while Camous made such a house for Felix Faure, the president of France.

We were at the Grand Hotel Frascati and I was working as a *commis*.

I saw Camous in the afternoon taking from the stove pans of nougatine. It was a compound of figs, honey, sugar and chopped walnuts. The seeds of the figs supplied to the surface a rough texture like stucco.

"These," Camous told me importantly, "are to become the walls of the Elysées Palace and of a smaller house, the one where Felix Faure was born."

I think I invented a thousand useless chores in the vicinity of my foster-brother that afternoon and he who could be so stern was like a boy with me; indeed, I am sure he was glad to see me loitering about, my eyes glittering with a feverish interest in his project. I watched him, my tongue curving up on my lip, as he cut windows into those walls just where they appeared in photographs of the buildings which he was reproducing. I watched him lift the walls and never was a farmer with a barn to raise given more assiduous help by neighbors than Camous received that day from Henri.

The little house he made of cake; portions were of chocolate, others of mocha and of vanilla; but the shutters were of green, of pistachio. But still he was not finished. On the night of the big banquet to President Faure the courtyard of the presidential palace became a pavement of ice cream. That night I was working with Baptiste, the waiter, and so I was a greedy spy observing everything as the President of France, exercising his prerogative, strode up to that magnificent palace of candy and broke off a peppermint bloom from a pistachio shrub and popped it into his mouth. "So," I said to myself, "that is what it means to be great!"

CHAPTER VII

A COOK CAN STARVE

When I was twelve I set out for England to learn to speak English. No one, Camous insisted, could be a good maître d'hôtel who did not speak English. I had just completed my third winter season at the Hotel Cap Martin on the Riviera; I had behind me two summers at the Hotel Frascati in Le Havre where I had been by day a waiter and by night a cook's assistant. For a short season I had been everything at the hotel of Madame Blanquet at Etretat, a seaside resort near Le Havre. I had been page, chasseur, porter, and yes, concierge. For one so young I was extraordinarily experienced in hotel and restaurant work. I had an aplomb that came from contact with emperors, empresses, kings, queens, dukes, duchesses; with such millionaires as J. P. Morgan, James Gordon Bennett and with South Americans who had become fantastically rich through operations in rubber, sugar and cattle. I knew Escoffier. I was the brother of Jean Camous. In short, I think I was the most self-possessed boy of twelve ever seen by Madame Rock of Stamford Hill, a suburb of London. "Very small," said Madame in bad French; except for this concession to my limited understanding her opinion was expressed in the manner and tone with which she would have commented on an undersized carcass of chicken offered to her by a butcher. She was vast around her middle and the sleeves of her frock puffed into great hams at the shoulders. Her stern gaze was to show me she would stand for no nonsense, even from an unripe Frenchman.

London in that time was overrun with boys from the Continent who would accept employment on any terms for the sake of learning the language. What those swarms of us did to the labor market I can not bear to think. I was to be paid twenty shillings a month, I who had been given more in single tips from Mr. Morgan, the Duchess of Rutland, Gordon Bennett, and others. But to Madame Rock I was a piece of merchandise, not a little boy. "Very, very small," she repeated.

"Ah," I said, "but the wage is proportionately small, too."

Madame's grunt of reproof was accompanied by the gesture in which she handed me my apron of blue and white striped ticking; not so much as a ha'pence of the pound was to be wasted in allowing me to recover from the fatigue of my two-day journey. I quickly learned I was to do everything in that house. I was butler, chamber-maid, major domo. I was gardener of a small yard in the rear of this house crowded into a row of similar neighbors. I had so many duties that properly I should have had a secretary to remind me when to switch from one office to another. I was, among other things, the nursemaid of two dogs.

I met the dogs before I met Peters, the cook. To my delight, although one of the animals was a little griffon called Branly the other was a French poodle, a *caniche,* that breed of incomparable sensitiveness and intelligence. Madame, warning me what offenses he must not commit, said his name was Dick. He was a recent immigrant and "Dick" meant less than nothing to him. He did not even thump his tail when Madame called him as if she were a brigadier general and the dog a private.

"Mon petit joli," I said softly. Never have I seen such an explosion of dog. I think he went crazy with delight to hear his own language after days of melancholy experiences with harsh, unsympathetic sounds. *"Joli!"* How he behaved! He licked me as I had often licked the cooking spoon of Jean Camous. But our mutual joy was a matter of annoyance to Madame.

"Do not call him by that French word," she commanded, "call him Dick." Much we cared, Joli and Henri; we were, so long as I stayed in that house, allies, partners, brothers.

Peters was a lovely surprise, too. She was about twenty-one, of an intoxicating English blondness, her head a mass of golden curls, her eyes violets and her pink cheeks sprinkled with freckles. We were the residents of the attic but in my opinion that poor girl did not know how to cook.

Late in the afternoon I made signs to her that I was hungry. She offered me some cheese, crackers and cup of tea. That was all. It was intended in that household that we domestics should eat nothing more until morning. When Peters and I had finished our pantomime and I understood this was the custom I shrugged and went to the ice-box. From it I selected four eggs, two for Peters and two for me. When you are hungry a pair of eggs is never a mistake. I proposed to have shirred eggs and found the proper dishes on a closet shelf.

"No, no," breathed Peters, in an agony of fear, "Madame will be furious."

"Hah," I said fearlessly. I had placed a spoonful of butter in each dish and put these on top of the hot range. While the butter melted I broke my eggs carefully and being sure they were good, waited until the butter was bubbling with eagerness for the eggs. Then I put the eggs gently into the butter. Two minutes was all the cooking they had. A pinch of salt for each egg, and then I took the pepper grinder, giving one little twist over each dish until the eggs had as many black freckles as Peters had brown ones. I was making tea, too. It was a quick meal, but a good one.

I plunged my bread into the yellow egg and Peters breathed in a whistle as if I had stabbed Madame Rock. Since Peters would not participate in my crime, I ate, when I had finished my pair of eggs the two I had fixed for her. She drank, timidly, one cup of tea; I drank three.

This was not a mutiny, as Peters thought; it was a revolution. I turned that household upside down and for its own good. In the morning when Madame Rock called me to account for the eggs and explained that the servants were given bacon, eggs, bread and coffee for breakfast; liver, potatoes, tea and occasionally a pudding for luncheon; but only cheese, crackers and tea for their third meal, I listened respectfully. Then I told her what I could do. I persuaded her to let me buy all the food and to allow Peters and me a shilling each per day for our own food. So, every day thereafter I set forth with the two dogs and a big basket. At the butcher shop when I had the meat I would demand, as in France, the soup bones free. At the grocers, chattering French, I would pick up a turnip and a carrot and shake my hand in vehement negation when they proposed to charge. "But, no! It is for the pot au feu!" What sacred custom is this? they would wish to know. I would tell them about France. Before long we all were friends and I know the market basket of Madame Rock never before had been brought home so crowded with good things bought for so little money. I saved the family from ten to twelve shillings a week; besides which Peters and I lived in our kitchen like lords. We had chicken at least three times a week. We had hors d'œuvres always and sometimes double chops. And every day I had from Peters my English lesson. It lasted six months and then one day Madame got into a tantrum when she looked into the oven and saw the chicken cooking for Peters and Henri.

Despite the fact that everyone in the household was eating better food, prepared as if by Jean Camous himself; notwithstanding the improved temper of Mr. Rock over the changed conditions, Madame was scandalized. Think of it, roast chicken for domestic help.

"How do you manage to do this?" She thought I was cheating, I suppose. I did not speak enough English to make clear to her the whole variety of my schemes.

"Well, I flatter the store keepers. I talk French to them."

"I forbid it. Talk English to them."

"Madame," I said, taking off my apron, "I speak enough English to tell you I am finished. I quit."

Peters quit, too. She could not bear to go back to a cheese and cracker existence. When Peters broke a plate in the old, the pre-Henri days, the price of it was deducted from her wages; but after I came we had replaced broken dishes out of Henri's economies. Certainly that was just.

We did not talk much, Peters and I, as we drove into London in a cab. We were too sad. When we were parting she embraced me like a big sister. We kissed each other, cried and waved farewell. What, I often wonder, became of Peters? Especially when I knew what happened to Henri.

I sought out the hotel where Escoffier was chef. When I mentioned Camous he remembered and welcomed me. Six years before when I was only seven that little man with soft brown eyes and hands like a surgeon had lifted me to a table in his kitchen in the Grand Hotel in Monte Carlo. He had placed upon my head his chef's cap as if in a ceremony of magic and commanded me to become a great restaurateur. Now, when I stood before him in his office in the Hotel Savoy he said he would help me get a job. I became forthwith a broom boy; in a week or so, a bus boy and then an assistant waiter; but the maître d'hôtel did not care for me and soon gave me the little red check of dismissal. It would have been unethical to appeal over his head to Escoffier.

Then began for me a period of misery. For two months, thanks to my foresight in paying sixteen shillings rent in advance, I had shelter in a room in Commercial Road. For food I ate bread and golden syrup, continuing on this diet, until, after weeks, I had literally nothing. There was no work to be had. That was my first depression, in the winter of 1893. It was December when the landlady put me out on the street. I had pawned until I had nothing left, not even a coat.

There was a little park on the bank of the Thames under the Waterloo Bridge. That was where I went to live, a boy of thirteen. The Thames was my lavatory. I had two towels and no other baggage. When the cold and darkness of night came I looked enviously at the open fire of other, older waifs clustered in a semi-cylindrical recess in the stonework of the bridge. This group warmed itself at a fire held in some kind of battered tin receptacle, the flickering glow twisting their faces into evil expressions that made me sure with a wisdom beyond my years that I ought to avoid them.

The first hours of that first night were the most dreadful. After watching the helmeted silhouette of a gigantic policeman beating the seats of other benches with his truncheon to make sure no homeless wretch took advantage of the darkness to sleep off the damp, cold ground, I crept under my bench. I was then lonely beyond comprehension. Gray fog was blowing from the surface of the river in wraithlike wisps. Without a coat I was shivering. My hunger was an acute ache that touched my thinking processes. Perhaps I was an absurd boy to ascribe what happened to the cause I did; and yet in mature philosophy I can find nothing more rational to explain his sudden, providential appearance. It was alarming for an instant to feel his cold nose against my face and hear him snuffling, but the odor told me it was a dog. He began to lick me. He frisked about in the cold as if to tell me to cheer up. Then he crept beside me under the bench and we kept each other warm. Marvel of marvels, he was a French dog; I discovered that by his ecstatic response when I talked to him. Although he was not barbered I could tell he was a poodle, a *caniche*; he might have been the very brother of that one I, illicitly, had called Joli at Madame Rock's. But this one, I believed, had been inspired to join his low fortunes with mine. I believed that somehow my dead mother had made him an instrument of her love, and, if you must know, I still believe that. Had it not been for that dog I should have died.

I slept some of the night. I saw in a dream all the preparations for a luncheon digested more than a year before by Queen Victoria at the Hotel Cap Martin. I think it was not really a dream. It was as if in some manner my memory became the present and through the power of wishing a former experience repeated itself in a weary brain that lacked power to invent a dream. I tell you this: I saw the old lady in her widow's bonnet with an edging of stiff white fabric. I saw her suite of ladies and gentlemen attending her as she entered the little salon reached through the left entrance of the hotel. I saw the Swiss maître d'hôtel, Cassut, bend at the waist. I heard again the clapping of his hands as he commanded Gustav, the waiter, and Ambrose, the butler. I saw and smelled the mounds of violets and the sheaves of pink roses in the big vases.

Then from the terrace I went into the kitchen, as I really had the year before, and saw Jean Camous take into his own hands the preparation of the filet of sole, Queen Victoria style. I saw his knife cutting the filets. I saw the remains of the fish, bones and scraps being placed to boil with a little onion, a little carrot, chopped in slender strips. I saw the slices of parsley root, heard the hissing as he poured cold Chablis wine into the boiling broth. I watched the golden hairs on the back of his hand as he pinched a bit of salt and added pepper. I think my dream or vision did not hurry by one second the entire process; the thirty-five minutes of boiling, the addition of Chablis and the spoonful of brandy, and then the spoon of gelatine-like fish stock. I saw the teaspoonful of butter stirred into the pot; likewise the two tablespoons of double cream. I heard the chop, chop, chop of his knife on the truffle that was added. Then I saw this sauce poured into a double boiler to be kept hot.

I saw the filets of fish meat dipped into cold milk and saw them drying on a plate while the butter in which they were to be cooked was melting in the pan. I watched those filets turn a light brown and saw them placed, each one on a piece of *feuilletage*, puff paste, lighter and richer than pie crust. I saw again his finger counting the pieces on the platter and I heard his voice telling me, "See, Henri, these little fish have benches so they can sit down before the queen." I saw the sauce poured and the final touch, the sprinkling of the filets with crumbs of grated parmesan cheese and powdered truffle. I watched the platter go beneath the blaze of the salamander to give the sauce a skin, thinner than the queen's, so that the aroma would not be inhaled by unworthy nostrils as the dish was carried to the table. I say again it was not a dream. A dream is a wild invention. What I experienced was the repetition of reality, without regard to time and space. It was a cooking lesson. You could reproduce the filets as they were made for the queen more than forty years ago by repeating those processes as I have described them.

In the morning I was weak and famished but I laughed until tears streaked my face at the comic appearance of that unbarbered ugly gentleman of a dog. We were a pair of silk hat fellows who had become tramps. He went foraging at dawn, but would not let me follow. It is my conviction that dog was afraid we would find the same piece of bread or bone and he would have to bite me. For the whole month he never hunted for food in my company, but sometimes he brought a bone into our nest of dead leaves under the bench. The bread and scraps of food I found I washed in a fountain; I, who short months before had shared the bonbons of an empress.

I was not made to beg; I could not beg; and some sense of failure, some Quixotic sense of pride kept me from appealing to those who would have shared with me anything they had. Some days I was too weak to wash myself at the river bank. With my stick-like fingers I could have played the *Marseillaise* upon my rib basket. I was day by day losing strength without knowing what the process was that was occurring to me. I was dying. The dog knew. One night he withdrew from my arms and sat outside the shelter of our bench. Twice I saw him lift his nose into the air and open his mouth halfway. Perhaps I did not hear the first howls. Then a policeman roared: "Shut up." I was too weak to answer but I saw the thin yellow ray of his oil dark-lantern suddenly spread to a dazzling radiance. Presently I was being put into an ambulance and when I heard something again it was the doctor chiding a nurse.

"This boy? Nothing's the matter with him except he is starving to death." He was right. My stomach was too flat to receive nourishment; but they are ingenious in hospitals in ways not permitted to restaurateurs. They fed me.

When I had a little strength the doctor, Dr. Tunnel, came to hear my demands for my *Joli*. "That dog?" he said, laughing. "I have him safely at home. Tonight, or tomorrow I will bring him here to see you." But when he kept his promise I did not recognize that dog. I swear he looked like a real Frenchman. He had been cleaned and clipped and barbered. He was strong as a lion, his beautiful black eyes were full of soul and when he saw me, hospital or no hospital, he jumped right onto the bed and tried to smother me with kisses.

"Hey," said Dr. Tunnel when I had spent a month in the hospital getting fat and was starting forth to take a job in the Café Royale, "why, you crazy boy, did you starve with a five franc piece in your pocket?"

How could I explain without French phrases my sentiment for that coin? Papa Camous had given it to me when I first left home and it had become my talisman.

CHAPTER VIII

THE PRINCE OF WALES
AND MADEMOISELLE SUZETTE

Well, I speak six languages, but that is how I learned to speak English. In the following year when I was fourteen I talked in English with the son of Queen Victoria, with Edward, the Prince of Wales, when he came for luncheon to the Café de Paris in Monte Carlo. I was striving to hold my position as *commis des rangs*, a kind of assistant waiter against the growing hostility of the maître d'hôtel. Day after day the Prince came to the Café de Paris for his luncheon. Often I had helped serve him and then, through a series of fortunate circumstances it fell to my lot to wait upon him and his party.

"Good morning, your highness," I said and the maître d'hôtel scowled with his Arab-brown face, for he had forbidden me to speak first.

"*Bonjour,* Henri," said the Prince gaily. "What are we going to have for luncheon today?"

"Sir, today it will be a sweet never before served to anyone. I have contrived out of something—"

The bustling of seating began; and that day, in the party of eight gentlemen, one place was kept for a little girl, the daughter of one of these gentlemen.

Often I had experimented with what are called French pancakes. Many times in Contes Mama Camous had made them, using one egg to much flour. Her way was to prepare thin strips of lemon and orange peel with sugar syrup and then cook the cake and the syrup together. As a *commis des rangs* I believed I could improve on that. I was not hampered by the poverty of Contes and I had the advantage of my training under Jean Camous.

All French chefs know how to make pancakes *française*. Let us say they are to be served two each to four people. That would require three eggs, two tablespoons of flour, a tablespoon of water and a tablespoon of milk; a pinch of salt. Stir this smoothly until the paste is of the consistency of thick olive oil. My test is to lift a measure of it a foot or so above the mixing bowl. When it falls back, or rather when it pours back, silently, then it is ready. Really it should be like velvet when it falls, not a thick cream, a thin cream. Remember this is a French pancake. By comparing a French pancake with a German pancake you may discover for yourself why the two nations will always be toward one another as they are.

Now, put into a small round-bottomed frying pan a piece of sweet butter as big as one joint of your thumb. When this bubbles pour in enough paste to make a cake that will cover the bottom of the pan. Be quick in moving the pan so as to spread the paste thinly. As it cooks it will look almost like the white of an egg. But keep the pan moving for it is a tender substance, that paste. A minute of cooking and the job is three-quarters done. Turn it upside down. Now again, and again and again. It has become nicely browned. Now fold this circle in half, and again so that it has been reduced to a triangle like a lady's handkerchief. You are going to make eight of these. They are to be cooked a second time. Since this is a smoky operation it is performed in the kitchen. But the rest of the process occurs in the dining room right where a prince or a princess may watch how it is done.

Now for the sauce, which should really be made in advance since it keeps without spoiling for many months. Cut a thin piece of lemon skin of a size big enough to put a patch on the ball of your thumb. Be sure not to include any of the white pulp; only the outer skin which contains the strong oil. Do the same with a piece of orange skin. Cut these two pieces of skin into thin strips. Now add these to a spoonful of vanilla sugar (that is simply made: put a vanilla bean in a mason jar of sugar). In the space of a day or two the sugar will absorb satisfyingly the pungent flavoring oils of the lemon and orange skin. This preparation should be covered so it will not lose its aroma.

When you are ready to make the sauce take about a quarter of a pound of sweet butter and melt it in a thin silver pan. When it starts to bubble pour into it three ponies of a previously prepared blend of equal parts of maraschino, curaçao and kirschwasser. This will catch fire and your pan will become a mass of blue flame above a mass of light brown bubbles. As the fire goes out the bubbles begin to subside and that is the time to add the sugar and lemon and orange peel.

For years I have kept gallons of this Suzette butter on hand ready for use. But on that day when I worked to please the Prince of Wales I had not cultivated the invention to its present standard. It was quite by accident as I worked in front of a chafing dish that the cordials caught fire. I thought I was ruined. The Prince and his friends were waiting. How could I begin all over?

I tasted it. It was, I thought, the most delicious melody of sweet flavors I had ever tasted. I still think so. That accident of the flame was precisely what was needed to bring all those various instruments into one harmony of taste.

Graciously, in a manner to win approval even from Jean, I plunged my supply of folded pancakes into the boiling sauce. I submerged them. I turned them deftly. And then, again inspired, I added two more ponies of the blend of cordials. Again my wide pan was alive with blue and orange flame and as the colors died from the pan I looked up to see the Prince of Wales.

He was dressed all in gray that day, with a cravat of light blue. There was a carnation in his button hole. His gray beard was faultless. But now his chin was up and his nostrils were inhaling. I thought then and I think now he was the world's most perfect gentleman. He ate the pancakes with a fork; but he used a spoon to capture the remaining syrup. He asked me the name of that which he had eaten with so much relish. I told him it was to be called Crêpes Princesse. He recognized the gender was controlled by the pancake and that this was a compliment designed for him; but he protested with mock ferocity that there was a lady present. She was alert and rose to her feet and holding her little skirt wide with her hands she made him a curtsey.

"Will you," said His Majesty, "change Crêpes Princesse to Crêpes Suzette?"

Thus was born and baptized this confection, one taste of which, I really believe, would reform a cannibal into a civilized gentleman.

The next day I received a present from the Prince, a jeweled ring, a panama hat and a cane. And after that how would a maître d'hôtel dare to give a red check of dismissal to little Henri?

CHAPTER IX

How to Feed a King Named Leopold

Camous never scolded me for skipping about from situation to situation; he encouraged me because he was so sure that in each restaurant that was new to me I would learn something of value. At Ostend, for example, I learned how a king pays a compliment to a lady and I learned, too, that a gourmet king does not annoy himself picking at cold food in hot weather.

Do not wonder if I cherish an equivalent of that belief in sympathetic magic which impels black savages to eat the hearts of lions. If you would become a king, I say, eat the food of kings and drink their wines. Many migrations taught me that the rich and powerful of Europe no matter what language they might speak at home, generally desired food prepared in the French manner, and, usually, by authentic Frenchmen. This was why my fellow artists of cuisine and service were migrant birds. We followed the seasons.

This was true in 1890 when I emerged from my chrysalis into grand atmosphere on the Riviera. It is still true, I find, whenever I go back. Naturally, then, I did not get my education (as a restaurateur) on one campus as do my children; I learned all over Europe, in gay places as well as in grand ones. I sometimes worked in establishments where kings often went incognito and without their queens. Sometimes I went hungry and sometimes I lived, literally as you shall see, like a prince.

In the late Spring of 1895 I was a part of an institution which was the very capital of the world of bons vivants. I was at Maxim's. It is impossible, I think, for the average person to be so thrilled by the name of that rendezvous as I am. Consider, I was only fifteen when I was projected into its intimate coziness. The carpets, the curtains, the upholstery and the gilding on the furniture were as French as the state coach of Louis XIV. Yet the place was the reverse of imposing. Indeed, all the thoughts of its creators had been part of a scheme to contrive the utmost in fascination. It happened that some of the exciting charm of the restaurant grew out of chance blendings of the loveliness that came there. For example, the chairs: each one had acquired from its successive occupants a special perfume, as I knew, I who often helped to stack them up when the gaiety of a day at Maxim's was finished.

What an apprenticeship! Could there be anything so tantalizing in all the world, anything more diabolically calculated to arouse ambition in a young fellow than such an atmosphere? Is it wrong of me to say that as I have filled a glass for Cleo de Mérode I have inhaled the perfume of her hair? Blonde Venus! Dark Juno! I stop here and now. It is too much to expect of me, a Frenchman, that I should discuss the wonderful visitors of Maxim's with the restraint proper to letters; therefore I shan't even try. I shall, instead, and discreetly, tell you what it was they ate, those favored mortals who began a day with luncheon there; especially the elderly gourmets who looked about them in that Paradise and wished to be immortal, or, anyway, youthful; they ate *escargots*, snails.

All over America these creatures of delicate flesh fastidiously eat their vine-leaves in complete safety, for they dwell in the sanctuary of a gustatory prejudice. But think of it, four hundred dozen were eaten day by day at Maxim's. I could tell here precisely how they should be prepared (always alive) for the cooking pot but what is the use even though the shell-snails of America are as edible as those of France? Instead I will tell about the *Court Bouillon* in which either *escargots* or *écrevisses* may be cooked and about the Sauce Provençale which is equally pleasing with oysters. Oh, well, forget the snails; remember *écrevisses*.

Ecrevisses are those miniature lobsters of fresh water streams, the armored, pincered fellows that your bass fishermen sometimes use for bait; crawfish to all who were born in America. In France crawfish are easily taken at night. A bucket is submerged to the brim in brook water or sunk in marsh land where these creatures have built their towers. A red lantern hung above this trap lures them and in the darkness they stumble, one by one, into the bottom of the bucket. For them it is the pathway to the boulevards. At least they arrive alive and they are alive when the cook puts them in a pot of cold water. As the water grows warm they go to sleep and die relaxed and tender. I think they meet their fate gladly, aware that in the original scheme of things it was not planned for a creature so pleasing to the human palate to pass away in a green state; no, he deserves to finish brilliantly, with cuirass, helmet, gauntlets, all his armor, brightly red.

Ah, Americans, you of the hinterland, who have destroyed the wild pigeons, the buffalo and other delicious natural foods of the continent, why have you for centuries ignored the tiny fresh water lobsters of your brooks and rivers? Louis Quatorze and all the splendid ladies and gentlemen of his court ate crawfish even though they called them *écrevisses*. Sometimes that king leaned forward at his table to receive one from the fingers of a marquise, on the theory that the sauce was thus improved, and his queen could not tell when he slyly nipped the fingers that fed him. I can't produce for your banquet the people of his court but I can make the sauce and so might you.

Into the cold water where the crawfish have their last swim toss a little celery, a few grains of pepper, salt, an onion, parsley and bay leaves. Permit them to boil for five minutes. As this process goes on, prepare the butter.

The proportions are these: to one pound of the best sweet butter, a piece of garlic. Mash that clove of garlic on a plate, then throw away the solids; the oil on the plate is ample for your purpose. Sprinkle it with salt and pepper and then add a few sprigs of parsley cut fine with a pair of scissors. This is the substance that you work thoroughly into your butter. Simple enough, surely, for a result so wonderful. With *escargots* some of this butter is introduced into the empty shell, then the solid part of the creature is returned and covered with more of the butter paste. That is the way they go into the oven.

I do that for myself, sometimes, with oysters. Leave them on the half shell and cover them with the butter paste before they go into the oven. When they are ready to serve sprinkle with finely chopped shallot. Incidentally, another excellent way to treat oysters on the half shell is to bake them briefly after drenching them with sherry and cream, or Chablis instead of sherry.

From Maxim's I moved on to a position as assistant waiter at the Restaurant Paillard which was a very small, intimate rendezvous of Epicures on the Grands Boulevards. The Grand Duke Alexis, the Prince of Wales, King Leopold, the gourmets among the great merchants, the bankers, the military, all such came to the Paillard when they had a special occasion to commemorate or a close friend to gratify. When I sigh over that place I remember something that will astonish and shock most Americans. The cost for dinners there averaged twelve or fourteen dollars a plate. This is something people from the United States have never understood, I think. Often when an American tourist has supposed he was being outrageously overcharged nothing more nor less has happened than that he has wandered by mistake into a restaurant conducted for gourmets. These first-class restaurants are never able to serve food at a low price. It was commonplace for those who dined at the Paillard to order a bottle of Chateau Yquem of the vintage of '70 or '78. The price was 250 gold francs and the gourmets knew it was not too much. I used to wonder then when I watched some old graybeard smack his lips over a single drink of fine champagne for which he would pay the equivalent of five dollars. But now, I think, for the sensation he enjoyed of a half-hour of youth, it was not too much.

Surely you will admit that such a bon vivant as Leopold, King of the Belgians, would have known all the wisdom of living graciously, comfortably, yet I know he did not adjust his appetite to the weather as so many do. First he would have some oysters. In Europe close to the seashore we paid no attention to a rule that applies in America, that oysters should be served only in months containing the letter R. Personally, I believe that rule is nonsense. After his oysters at Ostend Leopold would eat very often Lobster Américaine. It was prepared with a sauce of tarragon, garlic, tomato and brandy. But it was a quality of the King's mind that kept him cool.

When he sat at a table on the terrace of the Kursaal in Ostend he could see only the creamy beach and the sea, blue to the horizon. I know, because when my duties as assistant waiter brought me behind the King's chair I shared his Majesty's view. Sometimes his eyes would gleam with a sudden quickening of intelligence as he saw on the surface of the sea a ship or on the beach a team of plodding horses and a curious vehicle, a bathing machine. The ship meant trade, international politics, the development of the far-off Congo; but the cabin on wheels meant that within some lady was changing her clothing, preparing herself for a plunge into the ocean. Even though it was a Belgian ship that competed for his interest I think it was always the bathing machine that held the attention of the old King. He was a connoisseur of everything and on a hot day it was, I believe, a pleasure for him to forget his responsibilities; I know at least that he would forgo a privilege.

At Ostend when a dish was presented to him first as is the custom with a king he would do a very lovely thing. Usually there would be half a dozen ladies and gentlemen in the party. The King would lift his chin a little and then incline his head toward a lady, usually an elderly one, a princess perhaps or some English noblewoman.

"Madame," he would say, *"je vous 'en prie."*

Then that lady was served first and long afterward, I think, she would be cool on her skin but warm in her heart. That is what I mean by finesse.

In spite of what I say I realize there are persons who insist upon cold food for hot days. For such, I think, French cuisine offers nothing so appropriate as jellied consommé. There is no mystery about it and only slight expense.

A piece of calf's head, a veal bone and a small piece of meat should be boiled for about two hours along with a whole carrot, a whole onion, a clove of garlic and a piece of celery. Season with salt, freshly ground pepper and Worcestershire sauce. When you strain the contents of your soup pot into a glass dish you have a fluid that becomes thick when it cools. That, if you please, is jelly consommé. Stiffen it, if you think necessary, with some packaged gelatine; I would not myself, but then, I am a restaurateur with strong prejudices, some of which are, perhaps, unreasonable.

For the second course of the meal arrange on a big platter carrots, peas, potatoes and any other decorative vegetables which have been boiled. Accommodate in the vegetable designs six or eight poached eggs and then cover the eggs with hot jelly consommé and put a border of this gelatine around the edge of the platter. Do not put the gelatine on the vegetables. When such a dish has cooled it will be fit for almost anyone. Anyone, that is, but Henri. I would request you to go back to the kitchen and bring me a plate of hot soup even if we were dining in a desert.

Another time, until his wife made trouble between us, I worked for Camous who had newly become the proprietor of a restaurant in Sainte Adresse near Le Havre. I remember that a gentleman of distinction in the community strode into our dining room there breathing out clouds of tobacco smoke from a pipe held in his mouth. To me this customer said: "A *bisque d'écrevisse*."

Jean, attired in his white jacket and apron and with his natural dignity augmented by the high crown of his cap, starched stiff and white, was standing in the doorway of the corridor that led to the kitchen. I saw that he was scowling darkly at that tobacco pipe.

"A *bisque d'écrevisse*," I repeated.

"No," thundered Camous so that the customer heard him.

"For what reason do you refuse?" asked that man with great indignation. "Is this not a public restaurant."

"Come back tomorrow before you have started sucking your pipe," said Camous coldly, "and I will make a *bisque d'écrevisse* that will entrance you, Sir. But today, it is useless. I would not waste my efforts. You could not appreciate my cuisine so soon after smoking that strong tobacco. With what organ would you taste? Your tongue? Your nose?"

"Ha," protested the customer, "so long as I pay what do you care?"

"Sir, I am a chef," said Camous swelling his chest. "When I cook for you I risk my reputation. The greater your distinction the greater my risk, for if you say I am not a good cook many people will be foolish enough to believe you. But I know you are not a liar and I know you will appreciate what I cook if you have not barbarously destroyed for the day your capacity to enjoy. Return tomorrow, Sir. Henri! Serve m'sieu a glass of wine with our compliments."

The last place I worked that year, before I returned to London to grasp more English words, had a specialty which made me sorry to leave it. Leopold left his capital sometimes, I do believe, for no other purpose than to eat in Paris at the Tour d'Argent Frédéric. On the menu it was printed: *"Canneton Rouennais à la presse."* But the King only had to appear for the preparations to begin.

The young ducks were a special breed, a cross between a wild species and a domestic duck. They were never beheaded; each one died like Desdemona. Sometimes, now, I fancy that M. Frédéric himself supervised their strangling. With his black skull cap, his fine beard, and his delicately formed hands he was more like a surgeon than a restaurateur. At his place a duck was roasted less than ten minutes, four minutes on one side, four on the other, something less than two minutes more on the breast. The skin was removed and then the meat was cut into small thin slices, *aiguillettes* as we called them. These were kept on a warm silver platter during the remainder of the preparations which occurred in the dining room right where His Majesty could observe with eyes that rolled with eagerness.

The liver, in a pan containing a little sherry and a little brandy, was mashed to a purée. The carcass of the young duck was squeezed in a silver press until it had yielded the last drop of its red juice into a glass. A duck of the right species should produce about half a pint of that which because of delicacy I call juice.

I discovered that no true gourmet no matter how beautiful his companion nor how interesting the conversation ever could keep his eyes off the cooking of his duck from that moment forward. Into a silver pan directly over an alcohol flame I would put a lump of butter. When this began to bubble I would give to it one quick shake of the cayenne pepper can and then pour in quickly a pony of port and a pony of brandy. The vapors of these catch fire immediately. But as soon as the flame vanished I would pour in the duck juice, stirring, stirring, steadily. Next the liver was worked into this sauce and during two minutes of cooking it would receive a pinch of salt and a sprinkle of black pepper. By that time the boiling sauce would have the consistency and the color of heavy chocolate sauce. Bubbling with its own heat it was poured over the thin slices of duck.

I have seen Leopold, screened by his napkin, use the end of his tongue to recover one little drop of that dark sauce from his whiskers. One of those ducks at the Tour d'Argent was sufficient for a party of four or five. And it was from such food that I went back to London and another period of trouble. How narrowly I escaped disaster!

CHAPTER X

ME, A THIEF!

No. 55 Commercial Road, where eight of us were reduced to a hive of one room, is a long penny-ha'penny bus journey from the Hotel Savoy. But if the two addresses, my London residence and the scene of my employment, had been as widely spaced geographically as they were socially I never could have linked them by walking, as I did, twice a day. I walked because we needed every farthing of the few shillings I could earn. We were trying to avoid starving to death.

I was the only one of the eight who had a job. One by one the others, Edouard, Jules, Prosper, Charles, Auguste, Jean and the Alsatian Dulzot, had lost their places. Because I had starved one winter the knowledge that my companions, who had become to me as brothers, were hungry, made me wretched as a thin cat with a litter of mewing kittens. Their sad plight, and my own certain knowledge that death by starvation was one of the recognized exits from life in London, are my excuses for what I did.

The Hotel Savoy's main entrance on the Strand was forbidden to hotel servants; we used a door on a side street. This opened into a corridor that was haunted by the ghosts of rich sauces, of roasted pheasants, or *patisserie*, of cooking butter and all manner of gustatory temptations. This passageway was guarded by a scowling giant of a watchman. He was authorized, nay, he was required, to open all bundles carried from the building.

Supper follows a theater party in England as certainly as if it were an epilogue written into the performance by the playwright; this is a tradition of the upper-class world and a part of that tradition prescribes for the meal cold meats. The one who carved the cold meats at the Hotel Savoy each night was an assistant maître d'hôtel, Antoine, a tall heavy-shouldered, olive-skinned native of Marseilles. He was a fellow who might have handled an executioner's sword without changing the expression he focussed upon his work at the hotel.

Without being aware that I was his pupil he taught me all I know of carving. Oh, how sharp he kept his precious knives! Cold meats should always be sliced thinly and this it is not possible to do without keen-edged blades. Antoine could carve from a roast pork a slice so thin and white you might use it for a cigarette paper. In my memory I can see him now starting to work on a big ham. He would insert his fork deeply into the meat on a slant that was contrary to the direction his blade would take; such a slant that the handle of the fork would be close to the meat when it was driven to the guard. Consequently, when he carved his hands moved apart as he put pressure on his blade.

Whether he carved a ham or a leg of veal it was the same. He would cut from the hip of the joint toward the knee. First he would take long slices from the least prominent side until he had an entirely flat surface. The joint would rest on his flat surface as he proceeded with his carving. Always he would begin to take round slices from the large end and finish near the small end of the joint, winning each time an even, smooth-textured slice. When Antoine finished with an ordinary-sized joint of beef, a leg of veal or a ham he would have exposed a clean, shining bone without enough meat on it to interest a famished dog. But I must remind you Antoine worked on the edges of his knives as if he had been a barber, and the blades razors. Indeed, I have always told my new waiters: "Carve a ham as if you were shaving the face of a friend."

Never have I known one like Antoine for he could carve a slice of ham so thin it would seem to vanish when laid upon a rose colored plate. My scheme for feeding my hungry friends embraced a little of the activity of this great carver, but I regretted his skill. As I approached his sideboard he was clashing a big knife on a sharpening steel with such flashings of light and noise as to suggest that Antoine was dueling with Antoine.

"Monsieur Antoine," I said with business-like mendacity, "cold meat, party of ten. And please: not transparent." The look he turned upon me then was sharper than any knife in his collection, but he set to work. When I received the platter it contained slices not so thick as some parchments I have seen. I knew that any one of my poor friends could eat it all. However I managed, unseen, to twist the meats into a napkin which I pushed to the bottom of the wicker hamper in which soiled linen was stored. At the end of each night's work I was the one who counted that linen before it was surrendered to a laundress. Before long I returned to Antoine. This time I said:

"Poulet, party of six."

Antoine glared at me but not because he was suspicious; his dirty look was simply the sincere expression of a disappointed artist. He enjoyed carving when it was a major operation; the minor surgery of cutting a chicken in half was, in his eyes, work for a bus boy. Long afterward he chided me in a voice deep as Chaliapin's, tender as a father, "My foolish boy: if you had told me the meat was for hungry boys of France I would have carved slices of ham so thick as to make them believe they were receiving pieces of elephant."

I was the last employee to leave the Hotel Savoy that night. I shuffled past the time-keeper and the doorman in the manner of one who is too tired to lift his feet. I was trying to keep them from suspecting I was an ambulant Savoy banquet. I wore Antoine-slices of meat like a shirt. Halves of chickens padded my biceps and thighs until I had the shape of an athlete. For once the hasty wind of winter did not chill my marrow as I crossed the Waterloo Bridge. What I wore was warmer than a fur coat!

My friends were so hungry, poor devils, they picked me to pieces in no time and with such happy shouts that I do believe, if they had had the implement they would have squeezed me for my juices under the wheel of a duck press.

For six weeks I fed my friends in the manner I have described. Then, a few days before Christmas, I, too, got that thing which the British call the sack; but not for stealing. Ah, no! Those undetected crimes of mine I afterward confessed to foppish, brown-eyed Cesar Ritz himself and heard him laugh until I thought paint would fall from the ceiling of his office. I was dismissed with others simply because we could be spared. Is it, then, so extraordinary that my skin becomes like goose flesh at the thought of London? Yet my recollections of London nights without shelter were more terrible than my memories of my hunger and so, with most of the shillings I had saved from tips and wages I paid the rent of our one room to the middle of April. I bought potatoes, tea and salt. And there we were, a band of young adventurers as likely to starve in the midst of the world's greatest concentration of humanity as though we were mariners stranded on a desert island.

The night before Christmas we had one candle to keep company with our little stove. We sang that song with which the French receive the first hour of Christmas, a song which begins *"Minuit Chrétien—"* We were singing it when a voice at the foot of the stairs roared out the Cockney notion of "Charpentier." It was the postman responding to the magic in that holy song. He had a heavy wicker basket, a gift from Mama Camous. There were cakes, big ones and little, rich with butter and country nutriment. There were dried grapes, each one as sweet as a piece of France; there were dried figs which I salted with tears.

In a few weeks when we had nothing left I was the one who proposed we find vegetables for our pot au feu by visiting the Italian women stall-keepers in Covent Garden market and offering to buy a ha'pennyworth of potatoes or carrots or onions. It would be as foolish to try to buy a cent's worth of food in an American market; foolish that is, except for the understanding which told me women have soft hearts. That mean little scheme worked until, I think, we wore out our poor ha'penny.

When we could satisfy our hunger in no other way we pawned garments until some of us from nakedness were prisoners in the room. We took turns with the clothes when some of our curious errands into the streets had to be performed. Sometimes it was tobacco we required for our pipes. Cigar stumps in London, I can tell you, are short and soggy. Eventually we discovered a better way. Being short I would approach a tall Briton who had a pipe in his mouth.

"A light if you please, sir."

As matches were costly he would bend over and place his pipe bowl, upside down, to contact mine with its cargo of gray ashes. I became expert in giving a quick suck and an apparently accidental knock to the implements during their brief kiss. In this way there would fall into my pipe some of the tobacco as well as fire from the pipe of the Good Samaritan. Do I blush now? Fortunately my conscience remembers that I reserved such tricks for men who appeared to be well fed. I had in me at least a seed of the Robin Hood instinct: I did not rob the poor. You see, the little Henri who had starved silently another time now was in danger of allowing his character to take its shape from the matrix of the world.

Then one day when it was my turn to wear the only remaining pair of trousers I stood in a crowd seeking work at the Hotel Cecil. That morning I had been almost ready to surrender, to appeal to my poor foster-parents. Fortunately, in the crowd of unemployed waiters, bus boys, cooks, pantrymen and others I had enough alertness to grab a chance; probably because I represented eight appetites. So I was hired for the night, to serve at a banquet and receive three shillings, my food and, if lucky, tips.

I passed the maître d'hôtel's inspection despite trousers with six inches of excess length pinned inside the bottom of their black cylinders. Perhaps he excused the elephantine sag in their seat as something compensated by the fine white sheen of my shirt bosom and cuffs. These had been fashioned out of a carte du jour of the Hotel Cecil. When I could, I stood with collapsed chest to keep, as long as possible, from perspiring against the printed legends of food and prices that confronted my skin. Yet I cannot believe that any gentlemen were served with more zeal and politeness than the nine who sat at my table and listened to flattering lies. I addressed them as noblemen and nobly they responded when I passed (I swear it) toothpicks at the end of the meal. Each gave me half a crown. Again I knew the sensation of being a millionaire. But my friends would be hungry.

As if in answer to a prayer I saw in the kitchen a long table burdened with gigantic hams intended for supper in the ballroom later in the evening. Each ham was decorated with truffles, cherries, aspic jelly and other media of kitchen artists. These were no ordinary decorations. The great Costa himself, chef of the Cecil, had conceived the designs and etched in the brown skins deep patterns with a sharp knife. Officiously, boldly, I seized one of the silver trays and bore it off with its burden precisely as if someone had said, "Waiter, bring me an entire ham!" The windows of the ballroom on the fourth floor were open. I stood before one of these. I calculated a trajectory that would end far below within the circumference of a small garden protected by a tall iron fence. Then like a human catapult I heaved a ham. I was poised with the silver platter overhead at the expiration of my follow-through when a solid hand grabbed me by the neck. I heard the whistle of breath through teeth and then a fierce voice transformed that inhalation into as terrible a denunciation as ever I heard.

I squirmed about and confronted, of all people, the chef, Costa. "What," he said again, "are you doing?"

"Sir," I said with practically no presence of mind whatever, "I am stealing a ham."

He groaned at this confession of iniquity.

"Sir, for seven poor French boys who are without work, without food, I steal this ham."

I felt the talon-like fingers relax and become tender. But suddenly they tightened again as, sternly, he said: "Don't lie to me!"

"Sir," I protested, "I am a Niçois. We of Nice do not lie."

Then he spoke in our patois, saying, "I am of that town. If you are not lying speak to me as a Niçois." Appropriately I answered. Shouting, "I believe you," Mr. Costa then seized my hand and shook it. But for the tender structure of my shirt bosom I would have embraced him then. Later I reported to him in the kitchen. He had prepared a huge basket, filling it with cold chickens, cheese, cake, wine, cigars, French bread, sausages and other luxuries. "For the hungry boys," he explained. Then without regard to the carte du jour shirt I flung my arms about him. Both of us cried.

Mr. Costa accompanied me as I carried the basket past the inevitable guard out of the Hotel Cecil. When I put down the burden and vaulted over a fence he exclaimed: "What's this?"

"Sir," I replied, "I am getting my ham."

It was long after two in the morning when we arrived at No. 55 Commercial Road and when my friends heard the strange voice of Mr. Costa they thought: "Henri has been arrested," yet they had determined, they told me afterward, that they would go to jail with me. Imagine how they felt when Mr. Costa, seeing we had no chairs, sat with crossed legs on the floor and whisked the napkin from the food in the big basket. Think of the appetite hungry boys would bring to Chicken *Galantine de volaille!* You make that with ham, white meat of chicken, with pistachio nuts inside and perfume the whole with sherry, barding it with lard and then steaming. Costa that night in a London tenement ate with us his own food and cried and laughed. I tell you that is why the French are a great people. They live! They feel!

When we had finished eating Mr. Costa said he would see that all of us were given work at the Cecil. "But we have only one pair of pants," I said. "I will put pants on you," he promised. He kept all his promises, too, that great heart of a man, Costa. He was killed in the Tokio earthquake after the war, but I'm sure the day he died he had not forgotten us nor lost his silver cup inscribed with words that spoke of our gratitude.

CHAPTER XI

MACÉDOINE OF FRUIT

FOR TWELVE

London on a summer afternoon can be oppressively hot. As in New York, it is the humidity that makes the atmosphere difficult to endure. Worse than this discomfort on an occasion I remember was my homesickness. I, the little Henri who worked as a *commis des rangs* in the Hotel Cecil, I was wretched. I yearned for a sight of the face of my dear foster-mother, my Mama Camous. Something within my soul commanded my nostrils to find and inhale the summer fragrance of Contes, our home village in the South of France. So I tried to obey the compulsions of my nostalgia by working a sorcerer's trick in a salad bowl; and I succeeded. I cured my homesickness.

Into the kitchen went little Henri affecting the manner of one in a great hurry to serve important guests. Those who overheard must have supposed they were at least of royal blood, the persons for whom I boldly ordered: "Macédoine of fruit; twelve people." That vast order will reveal to you what great ambition resided in my small stomach.

They were in readiness for such an order at the Hotel Cecil in the summer. The pineapples had been brought from Africa, the figs from the valley of the Euphrates, the peaches came from my own France, the oranges from Spain, the bananas from America. These were all peeled and sliced and the juices caught in separate dishes. Nor were the fruits mixed then. The next operation was a most important part of the sorcery: the creation of the flavor.

Two peach stones were cracked, like nuts which, in fact, they are. The small almond-shaped kernel of a peach stone possesses an intensity of almond flavor. These two kernels were pummeled in the salad bowl until they had surrendered all of their oil. Then sugar was added, several tablespoonsful. Next, deftly, a lemon was robbed of a piece of its skin, the size of the ball of my thumb and as thin as it could be cut. This was shredded and mixed into the sugar and after that a piece of orange skin was added. The order is important, first the peach nuts, then the lemon, then the orange. Sugar has an affinity for the strongly flavored oils that inhabit the interior of peach stones and the vivid fabrics in which nature wraps her citrus fruits. So we had a strong, appetizing flavor that was entirely natural and not in the least bit a manufactured chemical thing. Oh, no; this was at once splendid and subtle; even puzzling. This sugar was distributed fairly over each of the fruits in the ice-box. Then the juices were mixed and to them was added a big spoon of kirsch, one of maraschino and another of curaçao. This fluid of the combined cordials with its tempting aroma at the last minute was poured over the fruits which had been mixed with their sugar in the big bowl where the work of art began. Sometimes I add cherries and corinths, which are dried seedless grapes, to such a macédoine. On this occasion they were not included.

I shouldered my tray and departed from the kitchen, ostensibly to serve the hungry customers who had ordered twelve portions of a macédoine of fruit. Nobody paid any particular attention to me and I was at ease in my mind because Mr. Gui, the maître d'hôtel, was nowhere around. The heat, I decided, had vanquished him. That settled my fears and as for my conscience that was not involved since my benefactor and friend, Mr. Costa, was no longer the chef; he had returned to France. This new chef? What did he matter to Henri?

Upstairs on the east side was the terrace along which I approached the Blue Room, a cool, quiet, darkened chamber in which small parties were sometimes served in privacy. It was an harmonious atmosphere in which to deal with nostalgia. So, I was eating, filling my mouth each time with the serving spoon. I think there must have been half a pint of juice and cordial. For twelve people it would have been a delicious flavor; for one small boy in an oversized costume of a waiter, it was like a double cocktail. I ate and talked aloud to my macédoine of fruit.

"Yes," I said, "I eat you because I love you. You were twelve portions and now you are no more than five and I love you just a little less, but I remain grateful." I did not speak English nor French. I spoke in the patois of Nice in which even today I think—in my own soul. But suddenly on that occasion I was hearing French. A voice, the voice of Mr. Gui, was speaking from above me, for he was tall. *"Petit,"* he said, in the manner of a member of the Inquisition, "you must eat it all."

I rolled my eyes. He moved not at all. So I believed him and crowded into my unwilling mouth another piece of pineapple.

"All of it, *Petit,*" he said. "Do not think it strange that two of us like the privacy of this Blue Room on a hot day. Go on, little one! EAT!"

I ate it all and what was left I drank. Consequently I needed so much sleep afterward that I reported late for work the next day and discovered my small job had been given to another. I was fired. That meant I could go home, and I did.

CHAPTER XII

BLOOD RELATIVES

Despite my previous sad experiences I returned to London a third time. Again I worked at the Hotel Savoy and every day for many weeks it fell to my lot to wait upon a tall, slender, gray-eyed gentleman with a brown Van Dyke beard. He was in appearance one of the most distinguished men I have ever known; he was a Russian, Prince Alexandre Pariasdensky. For such a connoisseur I outdid myself. I made Crêpes Suzette. I managed to transform a duck before his eyes into one like those served at the Tour d'Argent. He was grateful with gold, that Russian nobleman, and when he asked me if I would enter his service I had difficulty in accepting in a tone of voice that was less than a yell.

I thought in the beginning I was to be his butler, but, no, for in Paris he asked me to employ a butler. His staff while we were at the Hotel Continental included two attachés, gentlemen; a valet, a footman, a butler, a secretary and Henri. What was I to be? "Henri," said the Prince after a month during which I had performed all manner of errands for him, "you will be my taster. So, you will sit at the table with me. The more I see of you the more I appreciate you."

Well, for sixteen months every corpuscle in my blood whether red or white responded to an existence which I am sure was more natural to all parts of my being than the peasant life in which I had been reared at Contes. We traveled all over Europe in the Prince's coach. Horses were a big part of his life. The coachman was Telas, a lean, sun-dried Cossack with muscles tough as steel wires. The Prince told me an astonishing story of his competence. A sleigh team got out of hand when one of the reins broke. Telas vaulted the curved and painted dashboard to the back of one animal, grasped the broken reins behind its bit and then brought his fist down with a crushing blow between the ears of the frantic mate of the animal he bestrode. It dropped, kicking and quivering in the traces and the runaway was ended. Telas could drive eight horses like one. We went everywhere in Europe with six, the interior of the coach crowded with trunks and servants. The teams were hired by the day and were matched as to color at a price which ran about three hundred francs a day.

We crossed the Alps, going from Mentone to Rome in a couple of weeks. Sometimes the Prince drove and when he did I sat beside him on the box, our legs kept warm under the same rough textured robe, our lungs expanded to contain extra measures of the thin, cold mountain air that could intoxicate one like draughts of Napoleon brandy. Every night's stop was a fresh sequence of adventure.

Once we crossed to Africa to visit the estate of a wealthy man in Morocco. How shall I ever forget the enjoyment we had from a native dish, a meat delicacy which had the flavor of chicken and had been stuffed with bread crumbs, eggs and green herbs? The next morning in the plaster-walled lean-to outside the kitchen I saw another of the creatures being prepared for the oven. It was a lizard as big as my leg. "Never," I counseled our host, "tell my prince what he has eaten for if you do be sure he will return your luncheon."

The Prince loved music and was himself accomplished with the violin, the flute, the piano. He could sing. He could speak the language wherever he went. He was generous beyond all my experience. Once I calculated that he was spending at the rate of a million and a half roubles a year. I myself handled bags of gold. I paid the bills, I dealt with the tailors, the hatters, the bootmakers and other tradesmen when we were in Paris. But I was more than a steward. At night when he would smoke a last pipe before a fire I would sit with him. That philosopher never said a word that failed to impress me, his neophyte. His pipe was a monster, a German thing of painted porcelain with a tasseled stem of cherrywood. He had a trick of making rings of white smoke emerge from his bearded lips in an astonishing succession. When I spoke of these one time as haloes he glanced smilingly at the gold and silvered icons on the wall, holy relics, of which ordinarily he did not seem to be aware. "True, Henri," he said, "they are haloes and my pipe is my saint."

Sixteen months I was in constant association with that Russian gentleman and he tutored me in all his notions of courage and honor as if I had been a son. Slowly, slowly he erased from my mind the influence of the miseries which I had suffered in London.

Now I come to a moving part of my story. Whenever I display to friends one of my treasures, an enlargement of a photograph nearly half a century old, a picture of the group of my schoolmates in Contes, something happens which is significant. None ever hesitates to identify in the first little row among more than fifty round little faces the alert visage of little Henri. Why is that? It is not because of a resemblance to the man; no, it is further proof that blood tells. My prince used to say to me that I ought to seek a reunion with my relatives. While I lived with him I was content but when circumstances, not involving any unpleasantness between us, forced me to leave his service I went on to Munich. I was eighteen. I got a place as waiter at the Hotel Vier Jahreszeiten (Four Seasons Hotel). Thanks to my association with the Prince I was dressed in my leisure time like a Parisian boulevardier.

One day I wrote a letter to the Mayor of Cannes asking if he could give me news of my dead mother's father. I did not reveal why I asked. His reply was a cautious suggestion that I might make further inquiries in Valluries, a little town linked with the one called Golfe Juan. That mayor was a friend of my grandfather's and he had given me deliberately but discreetly a thread to follow. I sent a registered letter to the Mayor of Valluries who did not reply to me. Instead, I received a telegram which read: "Thanks to God at last I am going to meet my grandson. Forgive us. Letter follows. I embrace you. Your grandmother, Elizabeth."

When the letter came explaining they had believed I had died in infancy, leave of absence was quickly arranged with Mr. Fritz Reiser, the maître d'hôtel. I returned to Contes, impatiently waited while Papa and Mama Camous put on their Sunday costumes, and then the three of us set out for Valluries and the Golfe Juan. The Chateau Robert is still there but my family no longer possess it. Even then they had been required to move into one of the small chalets.

I passed along a graveled drive bordered by mimosa, palm and pine trees, hearing the heavy treads and the embarrassed breathing of Papa and Mama Camous. Then I saw, standing on the verandah, the old gentleman; blue eyes, pink skin, a white moustache and beard in the style of Napoleon Third. Beside him in an armchair was an old lady all in black, with hands almost transparent, a face like marble. She was my grandmother. That was when I began to run, when I realized who she was.

How can I explain how it felt to discover she had as much elegance as the Duchess of Rutland? or how unutterably sad I became as even my tender embrace revealed to my fingers the touch of her bones through her frock at the back. She was so very frail. The rustling sounds I heard came from the newspaper, *L'Éclaireur de Nice*, which had dropped from my grandfather's hands to the floor. The noise was made by his tears. He had been hard; he became hard again; but he could weep! My emotions swing back and forth between love and anger when I think of my mother's stern and dictatorial father; but for her little mother, my grandmother, I feel only love and sorrow. I remained for a visit of weeks but when I departed she began to die. I came back from Contes for her funeral. I met again the aunts, my mother's sisters; I spoke to cousins who had been well educated but I did not feel any trace of inferiority. I had their blood and besides many superior advantages; I had above all, my Papa and Mama Camous.

Soon after I returned to Munich the maître d'hôtel, Reiser, died. Herr Obermyer, the proprietor of the Four Seasons Hotel and of the Hotel Russe, spoke to me about taking his place. I mentioned everything in my training from Jean Camous to Aix-les-Bains and the Prince.

"Still," he said, "eighteen and a half is young."

"Sorrow matures one early," I replied. "If you will exchange the staff of the Four Seasons for that at the Hotel Russe my youthfulness will not be a handicap."

CHAPTER XIII

THE SCHNEIDIGER FRENCHMAN

Something had happened to my personality through the contact with people of my own blood. It was as if I had escaped from a sheath of glass that previously had divided me from other people. I seemed to expand. I took on dignity without surrendering one little piece of my tenderness. I grew a moustache and so it would be as fiercely masculine as those of the German mode I trained the hairs as patiently as if they were pets to curve upward above my nostrils. When I could not trust them I waxed them. When I emerged for a walk in Munich I placed upon my head a silk hat. I enjoyed myself in the beer gardens that are attached to all German breweries and the best of which are in Munich. What had happened? Henri had discovered he was a man!

One time during that period in Germany I delighted a large picnic gathering with an original arrangement of the salad. It was a party in a grove on a river bank not far from Munich. A lady who always called the young boulevardier, Henri, the Schneidiger Frenchman, she invited me.

At the picnic grounds I was fascinated by an artificial cavern of rocks and mud with the outward shape of an Eskimo igloo. That place was packed with ice and contained the kegs of beer. The structure was a permanent feature of the resort. During the morning the men scattered along the stream, fishing; but the ladies were expected to arrange the meal for midday. The food had been brought in baskets, except my contribution which was stored in the same icy atmosphere with the beer. What I had brought was a *Salade Fleurie.* I will tell you precisely how it was made.

At the hotel I had required the carpenter to saw a wine barrel in three parts. The bottom and the top each became a shallow, pungent-smelling tub; the middle section we threw away. Into those tubs I had placed, upright, assorted salad greens. I arranged romaine, endive, lettuce, escarole, watercress, dandelion and *barbe de Capucin.* That? It is pink and white with long leaves. At an outdoor market in an Italian neighborhood they are sure to have it. Anyway, I massed my two tubs with these various kinds of salad stalks. Here and there to support the pieces in upright positions I fixed a peeled cucumber sliced at the end to a helpful bluntness. Be sure to realize that all this salad stood packed in the tubs like flowers in a vase. Aye, but the contents of each tub were to be blended into one big flower, a gigantic blossom.

By choosing the salad stalks for color I had created an illusion of petals and in the center I had made a shallow, circular depression by inserting a head of lettuce. This I filled with crumbled hard-boiled egg yolk. It was the pollen of this flower! It was the center of a series of concentric circles made of chopped tarragon, parsley, chives and a white one of chopped egg. I had two of these flowers. Then, when the luncheon was proceeding my tubs were carried out of that cool cavern and shown to the hungry guests.

That was when I rose from my place beside the lady who called me Schneidiger Frenchman. I pulled up the sleeves of my double-breasted frock coat. Then walking very erect I strode to the head of the table and made the salad dressing while the Germans sang. In a big bowl I mixed a quantity of purple wine vinegar with four times as much olive oil, adding salt, pepper and English mustard. Then when I had beaten this into an emulsion I tilted the tubs, one after the other, so that I could scrape the hearts of the flowers, the egg yolk and the egg white, into the dressing. After that with dexterous gestures I proceeded with the serving of the first few plates. Only then did I begin to hear that the Germans were singing "*Ja, das ist ein Schneidiger* Frenchman." I was very proud.

Well, that salad does not need to be served in tubs. It has become a specialty of mine and when one wishes the table to take on a fresh and restful appearance bring on a *Salade Fleurie,* one of suitable proportions for your table companions.

In my position of authority I ceased to be a waiter and became a restaurateur, a gentleman of the hotel world. Then the great ones who patronized the hotel were glad to have my friendship. I met there all the royalty of the small German courts, of Bavaria, of Saxony and of Prussia, aye, the Kaiser himself, although I was not important enough, perhaps, to speak to him. But I did speak to his brother, the splendid, warm-hearted Prince Henry.

There was a strong resemblance between that prince and his uncle, the Prince of Wales. When he came into the hotel he spoke to me in German. My reply revealed I was not German.

"Ummm," he said with a rising inflection, "now we shall have in Munich a small Paris."

I can recall to this instant a dinner I arranged for the Prince soon afterward. There was caviar served in its tin cylinder fixed in the back of a favorite German bird, a stork fashioned of snow with a carrot beak. Then a *bisque d'écrevisse, Filet de Sole* Victoria, saddles of baby lamb, *Salade Impériale,* a sweet, a special coffee of Prince Henry, blended of slightly roasted mocha for aroma, of well roasted Maracaibo for color, and of medium-roasted Java for strength. These dishes were passed down a corridor of wine bottles. Finally, there was some Napoleon brandy that raised my temperature as a Frenchman when I did no more than think about it. It was, they informed me, a part of the loot of 1870. Prince Henry, like his English uncle, was a gourmet, a bon vivant, a perfect gentleman. He was so pleased with the Eiffel Tower I had reared out of flowers that his compliments caused the red hairs of the beaming Herr Obermyer to stand apart with joy. When it was over the boss and I drank together a pint of the best champagne from the marvelous cellar of the Hotel Vier Jahreszeiten.

I had the honor of receiving Prince Henry a score of times, I think, while I worked in Munich. A check was never presented to a personage so distinguished. As maître d'hôtel I would make out a bill which would be forwarded to the controller of his household. But the Prince never forgot the people who had served him. He would lower his voice and say to me: "Add a thousand marks for service." That would mean a tip of twenty-five dollars for each of ten persons in his party. This money would be divided among all who had participated in the service; the maître d'hôtel, of course, excluded.

All the flowers sold to patrons brought a profit to me. I had other perquisites and a salary so that I was making three thousand marks a month. I paid many debts of the old folks in Contes. I was extravagant with my own gratifications. But even so I accumulated a fat bag of gold between 1898 and 1901. Why should I abandon anything so fine? Because of my patriotism.

I started back to Contes before my twenty-first birthday to draw my number as a conscript.

CHAPTER XIV

THE ADMIRABLE HENRI

While in passage I visited in Normandy and there I helped the people of a village from an awkward predicament by my skill as a maître d'hôtel. I first heard the problem from my friend, Leseigneur, in whose house I was a guest. He was the driver of the omnibus horses of the Hotel Blanquet at Etretat, not far off.

"In this place tomorrow," he told me, "we are going to have a picnic banquet for nearly two hundred people and he is not equipped to serve so many, the man who keeps the auberge." An auberge is a village inn. At all such places in France, no matter how small, the food is well prepared.

"What an insignificant problem over which to fret yourself," I chided my friend. "Take me to this auberge proprietor and I will show you how to turn his frowns into a big smile."

"His name is Feuro," said Leseigneur, "and we will go there." We found this one in a painful discussion with his wife who was around as big as she was high.

"Fellow," I said to him, "cease to cry because I can show you how to do what is to be done."

"You are clever," he said in disbelief. "I have two hundred to fill with food and usually I serve no more than eight, or, maybe, twelve at a meal. I have eighty plates—"

"And forty knives and thirty-eight forks," said Madame.

"What does it matter?" I spoke with as much authority as if I had been in Munich at the Four Seasons Hotel.

"But the mayor is counting on us to do this with a gracious manner. The president of the council of Etretat will be here and others of consequence. It is not so easy—"

"For me," I said, with finality, "it is easy even with your poor arrangements. The first thing I observe is that you have no suitable table. I will contrive one. We go to your forest early in the morning."

Well, at dawn we took possession of a tree which had been condemned because of a blight. We cut off the robust branches and preserved the living leaves. Then with axes the branches were pointed and hammered into the earth in a pattern that formed three sides of a rectangle. Then a few slender young tree stems were fastened with nails to those uprights. Upon this framework we built the top of our table, using stout branches, available boards and finally, instead of a cloth, we covered this rough surfaced structure with a thick layer of smooth leaves, packing leaves into the depressions until the green surface was as smooth as though covered with linen. The auberge-keeper, I tell you, had begun to feel much better after three hours when the table was finished and equipped with a strong bench along the outside of the three sides. You see he no longer was troubled by worry over inadequate furniture and linen.

"But the plates for the soup?" The auberge-keeper's wife put all her bulk behind that cry. "We have no more than forty soup plates and as many soupspoons."

"Madame!" I spoke in an injured tone. "We will divert some of the guests while others are eating their soup. It will be easy." So I arranged another square table, a strong one and covered it with sods most of which had peeping through their grasses little pink and blue wild flowers.

"But how will this help?" demanded Feuro.

"On it," I told him, "we will place a buffet, including canapés, fruit, cold meat, the salads. While some look and nibble the others can, as quietly as possible, eat their soup. Presently your boys will be able to wash the soup plates. Three times each plate will have to be used; for any others the soup will be served in cups. I have seen a Russian General drink soup from a cup as he sat on horseback, reviewing troops. It is, I tell you, suitable."

I, myself, supervised the preparation of the buffet and its enticing canapés. I confess they were not made in the country manner but in the way taught to me by my foster-brother, the great chef, Jean Camous.

"A Frenchman," he told me when I was just high enough to see over the top of the table in his kitchen, "should not eat a sandwich. That is an English invention and terrible. It is fit only for people who cannot see or who lack appreciation. We Frenchmen must see what we eat and for a commonsense reason: when we watch our food, secret body processes function. I will convince you."

He took a lemon and with a flourish sliced it. At that moment something occurred in my mouth.

"Comme ça!" Camous spoke with triumph. Then he resumed quietly: "No man can say what happens beyond the palate in response to stimulation of that kind. But I can tell you what is the consequence when nothing happens at the sight of food: the result is a terrific indigestion. Therefore a man should always see what he eats. In that way when hungry he plays upon his digestive apparatus as an inspired musician manipulates a great organ. It is true: the eyes and the nose give the signals for the release of the chemical fluids which are secreted in the body by an intelligence which is of tremendous significance in the philosophy of a chef, the intelligence of the inner man."

He was right, that Camous.

Well, I made those canapés with such artistry that I think no two were quite alike and each one was tempting. To begin with I had plenty of good country bread which I sliced and trimmed until I had a supply of two hundred five-inch squares that were half-an-inch thick and without crusts. I was not making those foolish things with which women beguile themselves after an interval of bridge. These were for hungry people. They were toasted just a little, not to dry out the moisture but to keep it in so as not to destroy the effectiveness of the slice as a disappearing platform on which to mount good food.

Then I had dozens of hard-boiled egg yolks crumbled with a fork and placed in a big mixing bowl; in another bowl the whites of those eggs; in another chopped green pepper; in another chopped tomato. I had a supply of parsley that had been finely cut with scissors, not chopped. I had a bowl of anchovy fillets, another of shrimp, one of crabmeat, one of lobster and one of fine red radishes. That array was the palette with which my digestion-exciting pictures were to be painted, my colors, yellow, white, brown, green, scarlet, vermilion. Now, you see? That is the way in which to approach the making of canapés. What more does a lady need to know?

My lobsters became handsome scarlet ringed discs of white. Some of these segments contained, each one, a little spot of scarlet that was roe. My radishes became thin red circles with white centers. My anchovy fillets were in my eyes brown stripes to make handsome patterns. Aye, but everything I used had a further purpose, that of sending exciting signals to the eyes and nose of every beholder.

But those things were in the field of tactics. My big scheme lay in the realm of strategy. I knew I had to convert a rushing mob such as only gendarmes might control into a slowly moving, deliberate body of contented people. With such a group a maître d'hôtel, with finesse, can deal. Consequently I worked hard over that buffet after devising the canapés. A big fish had been boiled for me, a very big fish fresh from the sea which was close to this village. And while he was transforming himself into an edible thing in the blackness of the pot, the village carpenter who was also a ship-builder was fashioning of wood a trencher in the shape of a boat. As the fish came from the pot I removed his worthless eyes and gave him a glamorous expression simply by placing in each socket a big, bulging cherry. And then with shredded cabbage I gave him an ocean in which to swim. Consequently, imaginative people saw that my big fish was not merely something to eat, but an edible legend, a presentiment of the great sea-monster which the fishermen of that region believe is accountable for the vessels which do not return to port.

Well, then I arranged my canapés, each on a lettuce leaf, on the grasses of the buffet. My fish was there to win what admiration he could but I provided also a big wooden tray that was covered with thin slices of ham, of *mortadella,* of bologna. Still it was not enough, I thought, to keep the crowd occupied. So I planted mushrooms in the grasses along a pathway bordered by such tiny daisies as commonly grow in the places where mushrooms abound. Each of my mushrooms was fixed by a toothpick to the camouflaged potato which served it as a pedestal.

There were such other foods on the buffet as were available at the auberge; an enormous *corbeille*—a flat basket—packed high with fruit;

also melons and other fresh garden produce, bunches of the yellow cylinders of carrots, the spheres of red cabbage, green and white cauliflowers, globular purple eggplants, all things of exquisite beauty. They were not there to be eaten but to create a picture and an emotion. I wished for the two hundred guests to be persuaded as they came that none need hurry in the presence of so great an abundance of food. That was a part of my finesse. And I had told the keeper of the auberge to stay in his kitchen with the fat mama and keep things moving once the guests were seated. But I did not mean to seat them all at once. Oh, no indeed, since that was impossible.

I have forgotten now the occasion of the celebration of that community but I can see in my memory the approach of the procession into which they had formed behind the flags and the dignitaries. There was a small group of musicians playing as they marched toward the tables and I knew that the crucial moment would come when the music stopped. Consequently, I stood beside the buffet and at the very moment the man with the flute took his instrument from his lips I spoke:

"For every lady and every gentleman," I said, "this buffet contains an element of surprise. Choose carefully. If lobster does not agree with you, nor crabmeat, then pick yourself anchovy. If you care not for red take green and yellow or what you admire!"

Did they grab for the canapés? You do not know people, if you think so. They became as indecisive as if they had been selecting pastry at the end of a meal. They ceased to be a crowd. They became individuals, each one aware of preferences. They clustered around the table making selections. They fell into conversation with each other and alert on the edge of the crowd was myself, the trained maître d'hôtel, ready to pounce on those who had been prompt to select and eat their canapés. These I seated where the soup places had been laid. And then the few waiters that we had began the busiest period of their day. They ladled soup. They carried off soiled plates and quickly returned with them, clean. My strategy was so successful that we had the whole array of soup plates and spoons on the table available for service before the last two-score at the buffet had made a choice among the canapés. My stage management had been perfectly timed.

Moist grapevine leaves were used as plates for the course after the soup; three leaves for each plate. Then the farmers' boys and girls who served as waiters paraded inside the open quadrangle of tables, carry-

ing enticing baskets. Frenchmen understand the necessity of that ceremony: in the same way that a wise rider shows a horse the obstacle
over which he must jump, and allows him to measure the difficulty
with his eyes, so a maître d'hôtel appreciates that the interiors of the
customers must be advised of the chemical processes to be prepared.
But this day we displayed things to make the mouth water! Fried *goujons* and something else that was fried! Aye the brown and green signals
that flashed to avid eyes and the tempting odors that stole into dis-
tended nostrils created eager appetites.

Goujons are tiny brook-fish like the white bait which are served on
the sea coast in this country; but to watch a Frenchman with an
untrimmed beard as he devours schools of *goujons* is an experience.
The crisp brown fish, each about as thick as a pair of kitchen matches
are often dropped to become entangled in the meshes of a beard. Even
then they are not out of bounds and it is in keeping with even royal eti-
quette to recover such vagrants and eat them. Why, one time at Le
Havre I saw the King of—on second thought, no! On that day His
Majesty dining beneath a sunshade on a terrace was incognito. It
would be wrong of me to disclose that a personage so high could miss
so many *goujons.* You do not have *goujons* in the United States but I dare
to say that any minnows of the size of cigarettes or smaller are as delicious as *goujons.* Simply fry them in deep fat like potatoes. On the day
of that picnic our inexperienced waiters laid before each guest on the
grape-leaf platters all the fish that could be lifted with a pair of asparagus tongs; then a piece of lemon.

The garniture served with the *goujons* was fried parsley. You never
heard of it? Then it is time you did. It should be cooked like French
fried potatoes in deep pork fat boiling hot. Four or five seconds in such
a bath is sufficient to transform parsley into a vegetable crisp as straw
and with a flavor that cannot be described except with a motion picture of a Frenchman's eyes rolling in ecstasy. Fried parsley is not a dish
for the undernourished; it is something for epicures who delight in
surprising their palates.

The next course, too, began with a ceremony. A waiter entered the
space inside the tables proudly bearing a basket that contained six
whole roasted chickens perfectly browned and comfortably nested in
the varnished green of watercress. They were part of a flock of chickens that had been alive and feathered two days before. Forty had died

to make this feast. They were of an age, not like automobile tires in their flesh, but tender. None had been sluiced with water but instead had been cleaned inside, after drawing, with a dry cloth. Then a lump of butter and salt had been introduced into the interiors of each. In the cooking, the basting with butter and with juices of the birds had been performed almost ceaselessly. So the procession of six chosen birds in a basket left in the nostrils of each guest an incense which was the beginning of digestion. During this pageant most of the other birds were still cooking but when my ears told me that the chef's cleaver was cutting through tender bones I gave the signal for the service to begin. The leaves, the few traces of *goujons* and neglected bits of parsley, not many to be sure, were brushed into baskets and fresh leaves were placed. Then came the carved chickens.

Actually, the first of the carved chickens was being carried to his doom before the last dozen of his fellows had been taken from the oven. We were having a picnic served with restaurant efficiency. In the kitchen as the auberge proprietor with single well-aimed whacks of his heavy blade carved the chickens, the mama of the establishment was cutting slices of country bread. Each slice was plunged into the sauce in the roasting pans just long enough to varnish one side. Then the bread in pairs of slices, sandwich fashion, to preserve that varnish, was placed in one basket while the pieces of chicken went into another. At the tables the waiter with the bread preceded the waiter with the carved chicken. Each slice of bread in that way became an edible plate on which the following man placed a piece of chicken.

The only part of our meal that was less than excellent after the soup was the salad. Again we had to use the limited supply of china and forks; but when a Frenchman reaches the salad he is resting and in no hurry. He eats the salad to prepare himself for the cheese. That day, after the salad, we served Camembert; for the ladies each cheese was cut in six segments, for the gentlemen each one in four parts. Again there was bread because cheese is the partner of bread and not of crackers. For knives that time we depended on the fact that every Frenchman is a soldier and carries as a souvenir of his years of patriotic service the pocket-knife of his army days. A man could pass such a knife with its open blade to a lady and if she looked unhappy he might say in raillery, "If you require better we must go to Paris."

When that meal was finished the important people of the village surrounded the auberge-keeper to drench him in compliments but he said: "Mon Dieu! It was not me at all; it was that young fellow, Henri." And then I heard my friend, Leseigneur, the omnibus driver saying: "Why, I knew him when he was just a page boy at the Hotel Blanquet and now he is a great maître d'hôtel." Those expressions of admiration and wonder were my reward, and completely satisfying.

At Contes I received my number and then after some precious hours with my Mama Camous I went back to Germany for the few months of liberty that were left to me. I had found the German people, I confess it, very *gemütlich*. But their food I could not even be polite about. They are colossal eaters, the Germans. At noontime they would have a meal which began with hors d'œuvres and proceeded leisurely through courses of soup, fish, entrée, a roast with compote of fruit; then the vegetables separately as a course; there would be at least one and sometimes two desserts and inevitably an assortment of cheese with pumpernickel. Then coffee in a big cup with plenty of cream. They would come back for a hearty supper at seven, too. No, it was not astonishing to me, the pre-war shape of Germans; they had earned their *embonpoint*. The *charcuterie* is very good in Germany and one dish I added to my repertoire, a roast beef made with a cream sauce mixed with horse radish and served with salt dill pickles.

One day we had the Kaiser for luncheon. There were Army manœuvres near Munich, but he came in a gray suit and we prepared for him, you may be sure, with great care. For instance, I gave the waiters instructions to change the napkins after the soup that had followed the melon. Then there was a trout of a species which is plunged alive into boiling water. Next a chicken stuffed with *paté de foie gras* and flamed; fresh truffles, endive salad, a *soufflé* Alexandra, coffee and champagne. To think that with the energy generated from that meal served under my aegis he was contriving future troubles for France! Aye, but it was only a little later that I said goodbye to Germany and reported to my regiment at Marseilles.

CHAPTER XV

CONSCRIPT

We hated each other instinctively, me, the conscript, and Sergeant Major Orsatti, a Corsican, who sat behind an ink-stained table in the battalion office. He looked upon me with disfavor; from my shiny boots to the waxed points of my soft moustache I was objectionable to him.

"Huh, huh," he sneered, "you go to the opera?"

"Maybe." With one finger I touched my moustache ever so softly by which gesture I made him to realize as well as if I had spoken that I held him in contempt.

"What's the matter with you?" This he roared at me.

I studied a fingernail which had only the day before been polished by the buffer of a blonde manicurist in Nice; then I breathed upon that glossy surface. Slowly then I replied to him:

"France called me, did she not? I came promptly, did I not? Is it an offense because I did not go to the rag picker for an appropriate costume in which to report for service?"

Now the sergeant major had become like an expectant dog at a rat hole. "I will teach you, my pretty one," he said, "what it means to be in the army."

"Probably you will teach me nothing," I said. "You are a sergeant major but in civil life I have been already a captain accustomed to command. I have learned to be gracious in six languages while you can be rude only in one."

"Shut up," roared the sergeant and I could see that the juices of his ego were running out of him. "Shut up and remember you are speaking to a superior!"

"I do not know what it is, superior. In fact I do not know what it is to be a soldier; that is what my country promises to teach me."

"Shut up," screamed the sergeant.

"Maybe tomorrow," I said.

All others in that room were listening and whispering and I heard some of their words. One said: "By God this fellow is not a greenhorn." Another conjectured: "He must be the son of an ambassador." But the sergeant major's conjecture which I also heard was not so flattering. Then he snapped at me:

"Attention!"

I did not budge; in fact, I forbade my eyes to blink.

"You hear me? Attention!"

"Sergeant," I said, "you must first instruct me how to be at attention."

Suddenly he took control of himself and became icy and from that moment I was less comfortable. I realized it had been a mistake to make this non-commissioned bully think less well of himself. Always that is the high crime of human relations.

"Fill out this form, soldier," he directed and handed me a long document on which I was to write crisply the banalities of my life. I answered most of the questions but there were a few to which I did not commit myself writing merely "personal."

When I handed back the paper the sergeant rejected it and gave me another which I wrote upon precisely as I had upon the first.

"Fellow," said Orsatti, "I shall make you sweat. When I lack the money to attend a theater I shall have you to amuse me. You are not fat but I will find something to melt from your bones."

I laughed at the sergeant then and spoke to him in English, obscenely but smilingly.

"What did you say?" He was truculent, that soldier.

I spoke some German elaborating my original idea of his ancestors, and in such a way as to suggest that I believed completely in metempsychosis.

All the others, my twenty-five fellows, looked upon me with wonder when I entered for the first time our barrack chamber, a long room, a bare floor, plain hard beds. One who had served most of his three years looked me up and down and then expressed his mind:

"I feel sorry for you, my young greenhorn; you will be tasting the flavor of your impertinence for a long time."

I was wretched. There were four floors of men all as much alike as the army could make them; there were human odors; there was no concession to the former living habits of anyone. It was, I thought, dreadful.

The next day we young recruits went to a storeroom of the barracks to receive our uniforms. My sergeant major was waiting for me and when he saw another about to hand to me some clothing he interfered. "For this dandy," he said, "we must provide something special." What was then tossed into my arms was a pile of dirty garments that filled my nostrils with indignation.

"Put it on," ordered the sergeant major.

"When I have washed it," I said.

"So you won't wear your uniform?"

"When I have cleansed it, I shall wear it with pride."

"It is an order: put it on now."

"Yes; the instant it has been washed and is dry."

"Enough of this," said Sergeant Major Orsatti and breathed upon his hands. Then he spoke to three uniformed peasants who stood near, grinning. "Undress this one, my boys."

I did not resist then but when they had me standing in my bare skin and one stood before me holding for my legs a filthy pair of drawers, I knew I could not submit. One big fellow behind me reached his arm about my throat. That was when I squatted and kicked back and up, striking him in the seat of his maleness. I heard him roaring with pain as I went through the door and onto the parade ground. Running like a rabbit all naked as I was I came to the door behind which was the desk of Captain Roux and he was there to open his eyes wide at me.

"Don't you know better than to present yourself in such a way?" Bald he was and very tall and as he glared at me he bit on his long moustache. I gave him the first salute of my life and chattered of my wrongs. Then the captain rose and escorted by him I passed before the most of two regiments, the captain chagrined, Henri quite wretched.

"Orsatti," said Captain Roux, "give this soldier what he is entitled to have, a uniform for a second-class soldier." Orsatti was frightened for his *galons* then and obeyed scrupulously but next day in my clean uniform it was my job, and no escape, to bring the water in a heavy metal carafe with double handles to our chamber on the fourth floor of the barracks. I did not enjoy the work one little bit more because the signal to do it was sounded by a bugler. But the sergeant was not satisfied with a revenge so mild; he imposed on me the task of sweeping the room and of washing the staircases to the ground floor; but I ignored the steps.

I was called before the sergeant, subordinate to Orsatti, who had put these tasks upon me.

"What about the steps?"

"Sorry, I called the steps by various names but they did not answer me; I guess we are not acquainted."

"What reason do you give?"

"I have been reading the regulations and I see that it is forbidden to make one soldier do the dirty work for a battalion."

"Ho, a barrack advocate? That's what you are, eh? The steps don't know you? Now I'll tell you a secret: of trouble you shall have sacks full to the top."

Well, there were so many complaints about the *soldat* Henri, that slowly, slowly the captain ceased to have any patience with me. To maintain my nerve then I began to ridicule him when there were only private soldiers' ears about; but of course there were spies to tell him of my bad manners. Then I was forbidden to go out of the barracks; for two months I was a prisoner there and anyone with the slightest trace of authority felt in duty bound to add to my woes, to bend my spirit to the desired shape. One day the corporal of my squad threw at my feet his pair of boots.

"Here, *Russe,* clean those." Because I had returned to France from a foreign country he thought it was humorous to pretend I was actually alien, not French.

"I came to serve the French army; not to clean boots for a corporal."

"Do you refuse?"

"No, my corporal, I don't refuse but I fear nothing will happen to your boots."

One of the company sergeants came to remonstrate with me.

"Why not forget everything that has gone before? Make a new start and then could you not determine to adjust yourself?"

"Sergeant, I cannot allow Henri Charpentier to be scared into good behavior. My soul would turn sour."

Saying that I was a bewitched fool he left me after imposing some further degradation. Every day I wrote in a little diary the various injustices that were inflicted on me by the non-commissioned officers. There were two months when I drilled with the others but when they had small liberties Charpentier must clean the latrines and at night when they slept in their beds I slept with the others who were being punished, on sloping boards in a white-washed bin-like roost. This punishment was being inflicted when the captain sought to induce me to prepare for an examination to test my fitness to be an apprentice-officer, non-commissioned. What else could I do but to continue to be unruly? Yet all the time I was hoping, like a little boy at Christmas time, for forgiveness. I put into the basket kept for such things a written request for permission to spend an evening out of the barracks, at a theater. It was refused. Ten times it was refused and then the captain had me before him again.

"Tomorrow you are to be examined and I want you to pass it; you have the intelligence, if you will obey, to become an officer."

"Since the time of Napoleon it has been the privilege of a soldier to regard himself as a human being."

"Charpentier," said the captain pulling at both ends of his moustache, "I have some privileges, too. I can send you, if you do not obey, to Africa."

I knew I was in genuine difficulty but I did not know how to compromise; this fellow Henri was most unruly and even I could do nothing with him. However, in the morning my bayonet was shining like a silver chafing dish. My shoes were lustrous. My uniform was as smart as I could make it with earnest brushing. But I was starved to a thinness dreadful to contemplate. With sticks a drummer might have fulfilled his office on the tight skin that stretched across my ribs. In my four months of tantrum I had eaten without enjoyment.

At the morning inspection as the major stopped before me I brought my rifle to the position of present arms while I myself stood with the rigidity of a soldier sculptured in stone. I shouted my name, my number, my company, my battalion, my regiment. I wanted the major to know I was not mad at France; only at a stupid little officer. Then there was an oral examination before a gentleman who sat relaxed at a table; at his elbow was his *képi* and the pattern of its gold braid was looped in five lines; he was a colonel, great in wisdom, in chivalry, in humanity. I introduce him with pride and gratitude; Colonel Coulloux of Regiment 141 at Marseilles.

He began by asking a simple question which any soldier might have answered but I was still stubborn.

"A thousand excuses, my colonel, but I do not know what to say."

"Oh, ho! I think I have heard of you: a soldier who will do only what he wishes to do."

"My colonel, it is not accurate. Four times I have sought permission to put my case before you but always I have been denied. I came home to France to give my service leaving a position as maître d'hôtel, a fat post in which I might have become rich. I was afire with patriotic fervor but with stupidity I was insulted—" I plunged ahead with my story, I began to cry and I was most convincing. I told him of my childhood, of Mama Camous, of my misery in London and suddenly he extended his hand to me and I saw in his eyes that the colonel had become my friend. That was when he sent for my captain.

"Regard this one," he instructed him. "He has been fighting single-handed a regiment. Would it not be superb if we could have a million soldiers like this Charpentier; but would it not be better if we turned such spirit against our enemies rather than against ourselves?"

In his confusion that captain polished with the heel of his palm his bald pate. Life was better for me from that moment. I became the tutor in German of the colonel's children. I got permissions as readily as my fellows and then I got a letter from Jean Devisse, the one who at the Cap Martin had introduced me to the porcelain miracle of modern plumbing.

CHAPTER XVI

MY COMPLIMENTS TO
THE GENERAL

Jean Devisse, too, was in the army, in Paris. His service was nearly complete; he was the butler of General Bazaine Heyter and what he proposed was that I should succeed him in that officer's Parisian apartment. It was all made simple by the general. I was transferred to the 76th regiment which was stationed in Paris at the Caserne du Prince Eugène in the Place de la République.

I well remember that day when Jean presented me to the general. I was feeling that if corporals were mean, if sergeant majors were bullies, if captains were, in my experience, brutal, that surely a general would be a monster. I was in my uniform; Jean wore semi-livery, a linen vest of transverse green and black stripes with sleeves of solid black. He knocked hard on the door of the salon of the apartment in the Parc Monceau. I was almost sick with anxiety and Jean was not helping me to calm myself. "You better put yourself at attention before the door opens," he cautioned me; then he knocked again and from within came a roar: *"Que est là?"*

"You heard?" Jean smiled slyly, as he whispered.

"A giant nine feet tall at the very least."

"But wait," said Jean and then spoke loudly: "Jean, my general."

"Avant!"

Jean pushed open the door and I nearly fell down in surprise. A quite small general sat there at a desk. He was wearing a *robe de chambre* but embroidered upon it were the stars of his rank; that one was a general even in bed. I stiffened as I saw him push a monocle behind the bones around his eye.

"My general, this is my friend Henri, the one who is to take my place."

Looking to see me better the general relaxed his squint and Monocle Number One of that day shattered on the hard wood floor. Jean nudged me as a caution to keep my face solemn; it was needless for I was much aware of the general's stars. Afterward I became accustomed to the breakage of his monocles. Even though he broke three or four a day he would not concede himself the handicap of a supporting cord.

"Let him prepare luncheon," said the general.

So I attired myself in white and took command of the kitchen. I cooked for the general for that first meal a wonderful soup, cream of chicken; there was a trout *meunière;* a chicken casserole with *Cepes* Bordelaise which are large brown mushrooms never to be equaled outside of France in my opinion. I made their sauce with double cream and sherry and, of course, an onion. Jean served that meal and brought me bulletins from the dining room.

After the soup he reported: "You have been appointed to the job."

After the trout he returned to say: "The general thinks that one who prepares a fish so gloriously should be at the very least in rank a corporal."

But when the general had devoured the first of the mushrooms Jean appeared again in the door of the kitchen. This time he saluted me with mock respect:

"I think you will be made an assistant general. But listen closely and you will hear Madame Bazaine smacking her lips."

After that meal Jean brought to the kitchen a fine, long cigar, an Havana of costliness.

"See what I have stolen for you," he said. "It is one of the general's best."

As we began to smoke in a little cubbyhole Jean chuckled quietly; then he said: "I do not know whether to address you as chef, general or damn-fool."

"Never mind what you call me," I told him, "so long as you help me wash the dishes."

In that apartment I had all the rest of my military career. They were days of mingled ease and glory for the people to be served were the best in France. Madame Bazaine was very sweet, very gourmet, very big. Her lovely daughter was an essence of gentleness. The general was a loud voice attached to a kind and generous heart. At the barracks I was still a private but in the kitchen of the apartment in the Parc Monceau I was at the very least a field marshal. I commanded three maids and two orderlies. Every day I went scouting with a market basket, a pocket full of the general's money and my head filled with schemes to entrance those people through their appetites, their palates.

And my rewards? They were numerous. I did not begrudge the general his medals, his handsome uniform, his vast authority. I, too, was learning what was best in the existence of a general. You see, I ate his food, drank his wines and his fine champagne; I smoked his cigars and, on occasions, I wore his linen. Every month-end the general summoned me into his presence. Arriving I would salute with an arm that quivered like a metal spring; then the general would hand me my wages, eighty francs, but always what he handed me was a hundred franc note, dismissing me when I gestured as if to give him change.

But it was in the night-time that I could really appreciate to the uttermost the delightfulness of my military service. At the barracks, at the Caserne du Prince Eugène, the men of four battalions would be retiring; but the bugle which gave them the command was heard by Henri only in fancy. In the American army there is similar trumpet music but we had French words for the notes: "Ta, ta, ta, ta, ta—ta; count, count your men well corporal and if none are missing say so, ta ta." If a soldier was outside the barracks gates when the last notes sounded he was in trouble. But Henri, as the general's cook, was relieved of all such regimentation.

I slept upstairs above the general's apartment in a garret that was one of the happiest regions in all Paris. We who served in that luxurious apartment house had our own society and we were, I know, much gayer than the people who lived below. As I passed along the garret corridor from one half-opened door would come the notes plucked from the strings of a guitar; from another the music of a mandolin; from others pleasant voices. It was a place of romance, of adventure, of glamorous excitement!

I participated in everything but the gossip. There were fourteen young women in our society and four men. Up there we knew what was going on in all the apartments below; only the general's was immune. "Young ladies," I would say when they pressed me to reveal something interesting to the gathering, "I am dumb, mute; I hear nothing. But if you would like to hear me sing an English song—" Oh, yes we were quite happy in our garret and for my part I think there was never a soldier who served France more willingly than Henri Charpentier when he was the cook and major domo of General Bazaine Heyter. Why, I was even permitted to appear on the boulevards in my hours of leisure wearing my best civilian clothing, including a silk hat; and in my buttonhole always there was a flower, one to which I had helped myself from the choice blooms sent to the daughter of Madame. The colonel of the 76th Regiment met me one time in that costume and in my surprise I saluted so hard as nearly to break the brim of my silk hat.

"I suppose you are on your way to market?" The colonel wrapped a sun-browned hand around one handlebar of his moustache and wove it into a rope; his expression was blank so that his temper was concealed. I decided to make my play on the chance he was a good fellow.

"My colonel has eaten of my cooking at the general's table," I said, "and I am sure he appreciates that I am allowed to wear the uniform of my craft."

"But you are a cook, not a boulevardier."

"Pardon, I am a restaurateur; we have as many costumes as a Prince of Wales. In the kitchen white is appropriate; in the market a work suit, but in the dining room it becomes one to appear as a gentleman in order to grace the role of maître d'hôtel."

"But, soldier," said the colonel menacingly, "you are not in a dining room."

"But my colonel, I go to one now, to get for the general some— ideas. Three times a day I must please him if he is to be kept in a good humor and not everlastingly to be putting hand grenades of reproof under his subordinates."

Now the colonel exposed the grin he had been wearing all the while.

"Ideas, hey?" He began to smooth both sides of his moustache, thinking furiously. "One begins to suspect you would not know how to behave in a good restaurant beyond the kitchen doors."

"I have never before been challenged by a colonel," I said daringly. "If in some future state of being we were to meet I could prove my case; now I am but a private soldier."

"If you did not have to cook the general's luncheon today, now, this thing could be put to a test."

"Sir, the general, the general's lady and their daughter are afar off, in the country at the chateau of the Minister of War."

There is a splendid democracy in the army of France. A colonel, aye, a field marshal does not feel that he has demeaned himself if he sits in comradeship with a soldier; it is not precisely a habit but it is by no means rare. My colonel and I fixed the terms of our contest. It was simply required that the people of the restaurant should show one of us the most deference. We were to take turns ordering the food and the wines.

The colonel failed at the fish; a salmon with cream sauce had been ordered and he told the sommelier to serve us a Meursault.

"But pardon, Colonel," I said and in sportsmanship waved out of hearing the wine waiter. "Chateau Yquem or Barsac would be more gentle because of that cream sauce."

"*Bien,* after all, I am a military man."

"Certainly! one of the first." And as the order was changed I continued to explain my point, that if a fish is broiled or fried or prepared with butter its flavors are intensified by taking a sip of Chablis or other dry white wine, such as Pouilly if one does not wish to be too extravagant.

The sommelier and Joseph, the head waiter in that restaurant, brought their heads together frequently during that meal. Once I raised an eyebrow as Joseph looked my way. He came as swiftly as though on roller skates. To the colonel I explained: "Should the general return early I might be embarrassed." To Joseph I said: "I have scribbled here a message to be telephoned." There was no message and the colonel was too dreamy then to care; a small envelope was in my hand but its only message was a fifty-franc note which Joseph, I knew, would realize was an expression of appreciation for him; a little tip in advance.

I have been many years in America; I have raised my sons here and so I anticipate that many will say I had with that act been unsportsmanlike, cheated on a bet; but that is entirely wrong because of the character of our contest: we were there to decide which of us could establish himself as most exquisite; which is precisely what I did with complete fairness; half the value of a tip is contained in the manner of its presentation; never, never should the exchange be made in a manner to lower the esteem of the waiter for himself. You see?

As we walked forth from the restaurant it was for Henri that the lowest bows were made; the *vestiare* produced first my black cylinder and then gave to the colonel his gold encrusted *képi*. And when we stood on the sidewalk that noble officer called me "son," told me he was proud to have me in his regiment so that I went back to my kitchen in the general's apartment, with tears in my eyes and happiness in my being.

My only problem with the general was, for me, no problem at all. He was frequently in a hurry to be fed and sometimes at inconvenient hours; but no matter under what circumstances I always satisfied his appetite. Sometimes he would return from some wearying military exercise, a review perhaps; again he would be summoned away and wishing to eat quickly as a matter of course would open his mouth to roar: "Henri!" I never let him yell twice.

"A melon is on the table, my general," I would tell him. "Before you have eaten half of it there will be supreme of chicken just as you like it."

Once when he complimented me on my swiftness he said: "The old Napoleon had a chef who put a chicken into the oven every five minutes so as to be sure to have one precisely when it was desired; yet you who are so economical, so careful of my funds, you never make me wait for chicken. This delicious breast, for example: can you explain to me the wizard's way you produced it?"

"Certainly! Camous showed me and he learned from Escoffier. It is called *Suprême* of Chicken but actually it should be called 'The racing bird for the customer in a hurry.' You put a big piece of butter into a small, a very small copper casserole without a cover. While this is melting, season the breast with salt and ground pepper; then put it into the casserole. From that instant cook with a full fire, for your intention is to boil that tender little breast of chicken in oil; but always be sure the piece of chicken has been completely submerged in the hot butter. Four minutes of cooking in that boiling bath and the trick is done. Aye, four minutes, my general."

When I had told him that much the general had finished eating and was looking about for one little tot of brandy, which was ready, too.

At other times on the spur of the moment I gave him scrambled eggs. Never, never did I put them in a frying pan. Eggs scrambled in a frying pan can never develop into anything better than an unsuccessful omelet. Break your eggs, one by one, so that if there is a bad one he will have no chance to contaminate the others. Then beat them until they are as smooth as cream. Indeed, if you think best add a little cream to the mixture. Then, into a double-boiler already boiling and containing some melted butter, put the beaten eggs. Continue to beat slowly; first in the one direction, then in reverse. Again add a little butter before the eggs can stick to the pan and when they have a granulated appearance they are ready to be eaten. At that very moment you may mix into them some crisp little pieces of bacon, or almost anything that happens to be available; jelly will do and just to make it more desirable add a little whipped cream to the center of the dish when you take it to the table.

Sometimes the general wanted meat in a hurry. I could give it to him in about four minutes after his first yell. Usually I kept on hand for such emergencies a slice of sirloin about one-quarter of an inch in thickness; the full length of sirloin but without bone. This I would put into a pan containing a very little but very hot olive oil. Two minutes for one side; then turn for two more minutes, but I would use a part of the fourth minute to put the steak on a plate, to strew along the top a handful of chopped shallots, finely cut parsley and chives; and then to deliver it fuming to the place between the general's elbows. No matter how hungry always he would pause to inhale the bouquet of those hot herbs.

Many years have whirled around since those days in the Parc Monceau and never do I see a customer in a hurry without smiling him into a calm. To myself at such times I always whisper: "My compliments to the general." When one wears a general's stars on his nightshirt then one is important enough to have his hurry respected; otherwise, I think, one should be leisurely.

CHAPTER XVII

WHAT TO DO FOR A BRIDE

Twenty-one, twenty-two, twenty-three; those were my years in the army. For me, for all sensitive people, I think, a part of existence is suspended under regimentation. I emerged when I was celebrating my twenty-fourth birthday. Had I changed much? I had a fiancée. Do not tell me this is not a funny, funny world: wearing my uniform I had gone one day in Paris to visit a friend from Contes. A girl entered the house, a fine-looking brunette. Ask yourself if Henri Charpentier after years in the finest hotels and restaurants in the finest cities of Europe would know a fine-looking girl when he saw one. Such was my enthusiasm that I sprang to my feet and stiffer than a Prussian saluted with a gesture so violent that I nearly knocked from my *képi* its red pompom.

"Mademoiselle Philomene Spinas," I said solemnly, within an hour, "I would ask you a question. Are you promised to marry anyone?"

She laughed. "What do you think about that, soldier?"

Well, I told her; and one month after I took off the uniform we were married in Aix-les-Bains. But once more I was just a waiter. The positions for maîtres d'hôtel are not so numerous. Then my grandfather died angry with me because I had ignored his wishes when I married. I inherited from him only a bad taste in my mouth. The situation made me quarrelsome, I suppose. I remember how I lost my temper one sultry day in the kitchen of the Restaurant Paillard in Paris. The hungry man who awaited my return to the dining room was Mr. James Gordon

Bennett, a true gourmet but a crank. I did not want to excite him because he did not object to making a scene. He had ordered stew and I had entered the kitchen in complete sympathy with that desire because a stew, to me, is one of the most appetizing dishes; but I want it served in keeping with its fine old traditions.

"One portion stew," I said to the chef.

"One portion stew," he repeated loudly for the benefit of his assistant. Then that fellow in his turn called out: *"Bon."*

Everything was fine and dandy until I saw that assistant chef carelessly holding a plate and dipping out of a casserole a dripping ladle of stew. The imbecile was not watching his work at all. Instead his gaze was directed out of the window where I could see that he was concerned with the outlines of a girl bent over some task in the yard. I became furious. I snatched up an onion, for want of a hand grenade, and hurled it with good aim. It hit that fellow in the neck and he roared like a mad bull. He was reaching for one of the big knives shining just behind him as he kept repeating: "What's the matter with you?"

"Did you see what you were serving, stupid?" I said to him. "No! You put stew on a plate in the manner of one who works in a kennel. Never mind that knife; when the luncheon rush is over I'll be glad to fight with you and if you are tender enough I'll cut you up in little pieces and—"

Well, then it was the chef who interrupted me to tell that assistant to vanish from the premises. That chef knew he had more to lose by the slovenliness of such an associate than anyone else. We both knew and the assistant as well how stew should be served. With a long spoon you should select two or three pieces of meat, making sure that one piece is attached to a bit of bone, that another is lean and another fat. Place these pieces in the center of the plate and then put beside them some potato. Next lift from the pot some onions, carrots and peas and arrange these around the meat. Then it is the turn of the sauce, the gravy as you say it. With a cloth to protect your hand, tilt your casserole or stew-pot. Measure out sufficient sauce to cover the meat but not such a quantity as will drown the vegetables. If you do that with gracious hands and genuine interest the plate will seem as pleasing to gaze upon as a bouquet of flowers. Aye, if you have in you the instincts of a real chef or a real maître d'hôtel you will make sure before it is placed in front of the one who is to eat it of a further decoration. You will take a pair of scissors and some parsley and snip, snip, snip a little fragrant green onto the nourishing food. I tell you, whether the day be hot or cold, such an offering of stew will be acceptable to anyone of good sense. Many times I have seen Mr. James Gordon Bennett irritable, but served with finesse even such a man becomes gentle of manner.

This rule applies not alone to stew, of course; it is true of all food. If you serve *petite marmite* you must select from the pot. If you think the one to be served is unworthy of so much trouble, why then, as I do, pretend the one you serve is yourself. Take from the pot the morsels that appear especially tempting. If you can smack your own lips as you approach the dining table you have a right to look for similar reactions from those who are expected to eat the food you bring. Finesse to me is everything. It is the beginning, the end, the soul of service; but I include in my definition of finesse a quantity of thanks from the one who receives. For those who do not thank you—well for such ladle out the stew with your eyes closed. That will be, in the American phrase, serving him right.

In those days I felt the world was not being gentle with my Philomene. From the Restaurant Paillard, dissatisfied, I moved on to Monte Carlo and there I did a thing as terrible to restaurateurs as it would be to army officers: I struck my superior. I was feeling pretty badly, I tell you, and while I was thinking about depressing matters one day while I carried a steak in the restaurant the maître d'hôtel became angry with me. He did not like the way I was slicing the steak which was long as your arm and as thick. There was a rich Sauce Paysanné Bourguignonne, which I can tell you how to make. First you put a soupspoon of butter in your pan. When it is hot but not quite boiling toss in a shallot chopped fine. In this way you handicap the strong shallot so that the butter wins the struggle to dominate. As it changes to a golden yellow you add chopped mushrooms, including four or five whole ones. Then you begin to add a little Burgundy wine but only after reducing the flame of your fire to one-third its former size. When the mushrooms are nearly cooked you should be ready to add a glass of wine, one-fifth at a time. Now you must open your fire so that the wine perfumes your entire kitchen. In another pan have two peeled tomatoes cooking in butter beneath a cover. When these are reduced to a purée add them to the other sauce along with the final fifth of that glass of Burgundy. By this time your steak is broiling and so the fire under the sauce is turned down; it is cooked; it needs only to be kept hot. The platter is prepared, of course. Place the steak on it. Place the whole mushrooms along the top, one, two, three, four, five. Then take a tablespoon of olive oil, to which you have given the oil of about one-tenth of a piece of garlic, black pepper and a pinch of salt and complete your sauce with this. Then drench your steak and serve.

As I told you, that maître d'hôtel was scolding me and suddenly he tramped upon my foot beneath the serving table. He tramped many times. For one terrible instant that maître d'hôtel was the compound of everything which I did not like in this world. I seized that steak by one end and drew it back-handed from the plate as if it had been a sabre. Then I struck him across the face, drenching his white shirt front with the Sauce Paysanné Bourguignonne. I did not even wait to say "I quit." I just strode out of the dining room which had become, I tell you, a place of confusion. Well, Madame Charpentier and I soon after that sailed from Le Havre for New York, but do not think my adventure stopped when I left Europe; oh, no.

———

I did not fight often. When other men would use knives, guns, ferocious words and other violence to fight their way out of difficulties my most dependable weapon has been, nearly always, a saucepan with, perhaps, a few buttered words. So it was on the ship on which we sailed from Le Havre, determined to make ourselves important in a new world. We were in difficulties on that ship; Philomene and I found ourselves at dusk lifting and falling in the sour, oily shadows of a third cabin bunkroom, a place that if honestly named would have been called the steerage.

All about us were seasick fellow passengers; poor devils like ourselves bound for another land where the miseries of the past could be forgotten, hoping, each one of us, to erase with an ocean of water the stains of humiliations, of failures.

Each mealtime was an affront. Two men who carried between them a tub were the stewards of our company. They regarded themselves as policemen rather than as servants and were bloated at all times with harsh words of authority and cheap cognac. I looked in that tub they brought. It was half full of a gray stew of potatoes and meat and flour. None of us could eat it and after a while it was taken away to be dumped over the side. That was when Philomene and Henri became the good fairies of that pitching, tossing place of misery.

We had, thanks to our friends in Le Havre, big baskets of such things as the people of the restaurant craft give along with their wishes for a good voyage. We had an abundance of oranges, of dry little cakes and bottles of sherry with which to wash them down, enormous bunches of raisins; we had lemons, bottles of kirsch, of maraschino, of curaçao and other cordials. Now you see what sort of things I would wish for were I to find myself a Robinson Crusoe; not hatchets nor saws nor nails; but things for the kitchen, and, above all, a Philomene to keep me snapping my fingers at the world. I had promised her a first-cabin passage to the new world and now, when all of her nausea was not from seasickness, I was almost failing her; almost but not quite! In those heavy wicker baskets were the substances of kitchen magic. In the intelligence of Henri there was everything else, literally.

Out of my politeness, my finesse I conjured a kitchen. A savage fellow presided as chef over the galley in which was prepared the food for the people, dimly realized in our bunkrooms, who traveled to America first class. I, myself, do not think they ate well. I approached that chef, whose lip was hung with hair like the tail of a horse. He had a knife in each hand; was rubbing their edges together with much flashing and the noise of steel on steel. Him I told a little of my history, mentioning Camous, Escoffier and other chefs of great caliber; but I only made that fellow realize his shortcomings. He scowled and told me to get back in my cage. After that, of course, I had to humiliate him.

So I went to the smaller place of one big stove and a big wooden sink where the terrible food was prepared for us of the bunkrooms. That chef was a sorrowful fellow who was not really a chef at all, but a former dishwasher. I complimented him on the food we were getting. I sympathized with him over his excessive labor and I invited him to clink glasses with me, producing a bottle of fine champagne that had reposed deep in one of our bon voyage baskets. In practically no time that fellow was my friend; he was kind-hearted but stupid. I offered to assist him and after his fourth glass of brandy he said: "But why not, my friend, Henri?" So I got my kitchen.

Into that place I moved with a basket of selected things and when the first luncheon was prepared and sent under escort of four chosen men of the bunkroom to our company of hungry voyagers you should have heard the cheers that made me blush and made Philomene proud she was my wife. One of the treasures sacrificed to transform the third cabin into a place more desirable than the first was a little box of two dozen eggs. With that I had contrived something that even the toothless old ones and the smallest children could enjoy and digest. Yet, anyone could make it with three eggs, because three will be enough to make *sabaillon* for a small family. While water in a saucepan is heating, stir together in a small, deep casserole the yolks of three eggs, slowly adding one tablespoon of sugar flavored with vanilla for each yolk. Beat until the sugar has dissolved and then mix with it a pony, or perhaps a little more, of sherry. Next place your casserole in the boiling water and beat the mixture with an egg-beater until it has thickened. Then scrape it out with a clean finger and serve in glasses. I guarantee you can serve that to the Prince of Wales, to your youngest child or your old grandfather.

If I reveal that I feel myself to be an artist of cuisine I must in fairness hasten to say that any intelligent woman may, in her own kitchen, become equally an artist provided only that she is equipped with enthusiasm. I would be very ungrateful if I did not say that, I who am the husband of Madame Charpentier who is herself a great cook, and who did much to help me establish my reputation as a restaurateur among the multi-millionaires of Long Island. Yet Madame Charpentier had to learn, and not from books; from me. Every bride should be taught to cook. In this country where there are all manner of extraordinary appliances designed to abolish drudgery and scullery work from the kitchens I insist we are entitled to have a revolution. I, who am the father of two daughters, wish to see swarms of women leaving offices, shops, factories, stores and making their careers in places where no man can hope to compete with them. I must keep myself under control now for this idea is a great hobby of mine. The American lady has a machine to suck the dirt out of her carpets and rugs, she has another to accomplish her washing, another to iron, another to wash the dishes. She makes her own ice without giving it a thought. Her food cannot spoil. She turns a switch or lights a match and has instantly a hot fire without worrying about fuel. Why should she be reluctant to exercise what remains of cooking? That is, the pure art of it.

All that I am saying now is brought home with special force when it is once more a simple matter to supply a kitchen with wines and brandies. Frankly, French cuisine is not possible without wines, brandy and liqueurs. Lest you be prejudiced against such things as beverages I tell you now that when they are employed to develop or enhance the flavors of food they cease to be alcoholic. Alcohol is the most volatile of substances and vanishes quickly when subjected to the heat of your kitchen fire. What remains is the flavor, a flavor preserved perfectly by alcohol until you are ready to accept it.

I think myself that a most appropriate wedding present for a young bride would be a basket—a market basket of course—containing a piece of garlic, half a dozen onions and a bottle of sherry. With such a basket I could set up housekeeping. You see, sherry is the soul of the kitchen. No family in America, I think, is so poor that it cannot afford to have one bottle of sherry from time to time. A small glass, a penny's worth, of sherry poured into a pan will transform a pair of greasy pork chops into a wonderful dish suitable for the most discriminating.

But if I really cared about that young bride and groom I would add other bottles to the sherry, such bottles as we had on that ship. Next in importance would be a bottle of brandy; if not cognac from France, then a bottle from California. Properly made brandy is a distillate of wine. Brandy is used to enforce sherry in cooking. If you were to pour a glass of brandy into a sauce over a flame almost instantly the alcohol would form a little cloud of gas which you would not see. What you would see would be a blue flame spreading over the pan. That flame would devour the humidity of what you cooked, thereby greatly intensifying the flavor. When the flame expired you would know that the alcohol had vanished with the fire. But I would want more than sherry and brandy in such a basket given, let us say, to one of my daughters. I would want the basket to contain a bottle of sweet Sauterne and a bottle of dry Chablis for the light sauces, for fish. I would want a bottle of Burgundy for the enrichment of sauces for beef and game. Then I would certainly add a bottle of curaçao with its rich orange flavor. A thimbleful of curaçao will, I promise you, transform a pint of drugstore ice cream into something exciting. A few tablespoons of it poured into the syrups of three or four fruits will make you wonder why people can be so stupid as to employ mustard or vinegar in dressings for fruits served as salad.

Now I will tell you an interesting fact: one of the surest ways to arouse a lively interest in cooking, either in yourself or in someone else, is to place in the kitchen a full assortment of wines and liqueurs. The very sight of such bottles seems to create the desire to experiment and when that desire exists in one it is the proper time to go to market. That is when marketing ceases to be a species of drudgery and becomes, truly, adventure. Even though your market be the corner grocer whose stock has, perhaps, grown monotonous in your sight I can promise you a change. Be sure that your eyes will discover fresh marvels in his stock if you approach it with the knowledge that at home, in your kitchen are the magic substances, in bottles, with which the miracles of the finest chefs are wrought.

That third cabin galley cook, stupid, kind-hearted fellow that he was, he learned from me how to cook during days as my helper, and whenever he tried to transpose our positions I put down his revolution with another drink from one of my bottles. And how was it in the bunkroom after that day?

As I went forward from the galley, carrying my basket which could not safely be left in the galley, I heard voices singing. Our fellows had brought from the bottom of their bundles and bags some musical instruments, a zither, a guitar, a violin; others acknowledged they could sing, and thereafter until we could see the Statue of Liberty we were happier and better fed in the bunkrooms than those other passengers of the first and second class; and all because Henri could cook.

CHAPTER XVIII

Cooking in a New World

There were but two tables in the Henri Restaurant which I opened in our home in Lynbrook in 1910. The former Mademoiselle Philomene Spinas was the chef, one who as she stood in white before her range was often interrupted by a kiss on the neck or the ear from the maître d'hôtel, who was I. The motive for this adventure was a creature able to stand upright, as he walked beneath the tables, as easily as a ship passes under the Queensborough Bridge. This motive was Camille, our year-old son.

In the kitchen of Philomene you might have divined from what slender resources the place had been created by observing the sink where the dishes were washed. It was a pair of basins, each a half of a wine barrel. I was its architect and it remains in service today. I am such a sentimental person I have never dared to dispense with whatever part of my luck may have attached itself to this original plumbing. Sometimes I am informed by salesmen of the superior advantages of a great trough of porcelain or stainless steel or other metallic substance, but their memorized arguments become weak and fumbling when I ask, "But can your sink raise in the throat of its owner a lump of emotion?"

Out of an original six hundred dollars for the creation of the restaurant we had in the bank on the day of opening twelve dollars and a half. However, all the bills were paid except for an encumbrance on the small premises. A thousand dollars paid down on an obligation of $7,000 had left a mortgage of $6,000 to be amortized somewhere in infinity through the payment every month of sixty dollars. I have seen Gibraltar and taller mountains, but nothing has ever loomed so high on my horizon as that mortgage. Nevertheless when it seemed to be getting bigger I would interrupt Philomene with another kiss or pursue Camille under a table.

There was a garden of flowers and vegetables outside the kitchen door; there was a chicken run and a pigeon coop. Consequently there was in the ice-box, habitually, one chicken and two squabs. There was also one steak and one rack of lamb. If customers did not come before those things should be eaten we of the family ate them with a virtuous feeling of economy. It was very fine and very French. The food reserve was of eggs laid by our living hens.

There were weaknesses in our equipment, but never in my finesse. One day after a period in which the Charpentiers had been eating too well for the health of the mortgage two automobiles stopped outside and when I saw how many occupants there were I began to feel trepidation. I counted those ladies as they emerged, one, two, three, four, five, six, seven, eight! Eight customers all robed in costly furs in one luncheon party led by Madame Roche. I had encountered the lady with her husband during the four years when I was working as an assistant head waiter at the Café Martin, at the Hotel Plaza and the Knickerbocker. She had come to look us over and when I should have been rejoicing I was thinking of the vacancies in my set of blue willow china!

I think I worried so much about the lack of two soup plates—we had only six—that I must have conveyed telepathically to Madame Roche the idea of having soup for luncheon. Certainly when she smiled upon me from her place at the table she spoke about it immediately.

"Purée Mongole we must have," she said. "My husband has told me how well you make it!" Madame spoke archly and I dared not show the least concern! Well, it is good soup made in this manner: you cook in one pot string beans, lima beans, peas, onion, a little celery with some white navy beans. When these have been reduced to a purée you pass it through a sieve. Then you boil a mixture of two-thirds milk with one-third beef or chicken consommé and add this to the purée. You also prepare, by boiling, a purée of fresh peeled tomatoes with onions, salt and pepper. Now you unite in one pot a mixture of two-thirds of the purée of vegetables with one-third of the tomato purée and boil these together for about twenty minutes. Now you place in the tureen about half a cup of heavy cream and a tablespoon of sweet butter. Pour your boiling hot soup on top of these and stir thoroughly before you serve on hot plates.

Ah, that was my big problem, the hot soup plates!

Philomene began to chide me as I gave her the order.

"But we do not have eight soup plates!"

"As if I did not know! But those broken plates that we put aside as private dishes for the cat and dog, have you those? Never throw away a broken plate!"

"Madman, I have the broken plates all right; but what will you do? Show me how eight people can take soup from six plates."

"You listen and you will learn," I said and took into my arms a load of broken china. In the cement-floored passageway between the kitchen and the restaurant I paused to breathe a prayer. Then I dropped those pieces with a crash that startled all the ladies out of their chairs as I could see through the little square of glass in the swinging door. Then I hurried into the presence of Madame Roche.

"Ah," I said in a tone of regret, "I hope a stupid blunder has not disturbed your conversation. That terrible fracas of breaking china means that I will not have sufficient soup plates to serve you. Will you forgive me if I serve the Purée Mongole in cups?"

"Why certainly, Henri," said Madame, lifting her head to capture some of the fragrance I permitted to escape from the big tureen, "only hurry."

Well in that whole summer of 1910 the total receipts of the Restaurant Henri were five hundred dollars, just two hundred dollars more than I had paid out on the mortgage. Yes, I know all about economy; but I am not one who understands how to be economical with food. The food must be of the best. Philomene could see that I was working feverishly with my brain.

"Are you going to close the place?" she asked.

"My little sweetheart," I said, "no! We are going to make the best restaurant there is on Long Island. I am sorry to make you suffer but it is a contract we have. Fifty-fifty. Since I cannot give you jewels I will give you more kisses." So that is what she got and I climbed on a train that day, October 1, 1910, to go to New York.

I had spoken to my wife in a tone braver than I really owned. Riding to town I thought hard upon ways by which I might defend my little estate. Rootlets from my heart were thriving in its soil along with the maples I had planted. I will tell you about those trees.

There was a forest near Lynbrook which seemed to belong to nobody. I asked a man and he did not know any owner so I went there and took about sixteen little maples no taller than my malacca cane. I carried all of them on my shoulder in one load and my neighbor who, I think, was part Indian, he said: "Why do you plant those sticks?"

"Sir," I retorted, "I plant umbrellas to keep the rain off my house!" When he laughed harshly I continued: "I will bet you that before you pass from this world my trees will be higher than yours which now have a handicap of forty feet and thick girth. You do not take care of your trees. Each of mine shall think that Henri is its father."

For each of those young things which my neighbor had sneered upon as sticks I had created a hole of dimensions big enough for its mother. I had put rich, black earth in the bottom, then a layer of stones, then more earth, then another layer of stones, more earth and on top of that a cushion of dead and porous wood, then more earth and on that structure each baby tree was planted to be supported and nourished by further layers of rich earth and manure well rotted. For the winters each of my trees wore about its base a muffler of straw and fertilizer. The base is the throat of a tree since it stands on its head with its mouth to the earth and its limbs waving in the breeze. Consequently, because I understand that, my trees never catch a chill in their heads, that is, in their roots. That is why in twenty-five years they have become sixty and seventy feet tall and why people think there is no sign upon my establishment. In letters two feet high along the ridgepole of the house the legend reads "Original Henri Restaurant" but my trees hide this boast I no longer need to make and they themselves look down upon the older trees of my neighbor.

I had begun the process of making myself an American citizen by that time also; in fact, since 1909, when I was working at the Hotel Knickerbocker nineteen hours a day. Those hours plus an hour each way from Lynbrook left me three hours each day to sleep and dream if I hurried. I had not intended to become an American citizen. I was born a Frenchman and I expected to die a Frenchman. So when my son was born I arose early one morning in order to make a visit to the office of the French consulate, to have the name of Camille Charpentier written upon a register so that he, too, would be French.

I risked the loss of my situation at the Knickerbocker where I was due at nine, by going instead to the consulate which opened at that hour. But it was not until ten o'clock that the man for whom fourteen of us waited entered the premises. He strolled into the consulate with a tall black cylinder of a hat upon his head and he was wrapped in a fur coat. It was cold that morning and his breath came out like smoke as if he were a baked potato wrapped in a hot napkin. He walked very slowly, he took off one glove, then the other, he removed his hat and admired its sheen before he laid it away. He disposed of his cane and his fur coat. He paid no more attention to the fourteen who waited than if we had been Chinese. I said: "*Bonjour,* Monsieur Consul!" He did not answer and I was insulted. I took fire like brandy poured into a saucepan. I pounded on the desk to receive his attention.

"What," he exclaimed out of the window, "is the matter with that fellow? Has he no manners?"

"You," I roared, "you don't act like a Frenchman. You are a man who represents our country without intelligence. You are without the least qualifications. I work nineteen hours a day. I sleep three. Yet I come here to declare the birth of my son but by your insults I am changed completely. I don't want him to be a French citizen."

"Don't shout that way."

"What! Before you speak to me you apologize! You are my servant; I am not your servant. You are such a stupid waiter I shall not wait to be served. *Allons mes amis!*"

Out we marched, fourteen of us and every one became an American citizen. You may be sure they heard about that in France and were slow to forgive me because that small-minded official told his story first.

No; there was no retreat for Henri. Lynbrook had become my village; the Stars and Stripes my flag. As I left the train in New York on that October 1st, 1910, I knew what I must do. I would again become a waiter. So I went to see my friend Louis Martin. The brothers had split up. The Café Martin in Twenty-sixth Street was being conducted by Jean Baptiste, but Louis, at the crossroads of the world, Broadway and

Forty-second Street, was presiding over the Café de Paris, the former Café de l'Opéra. After a summer gross in my restaurant of two hundred dollars plus mortgage money I thought some tips would look like moons.

The Café de Paris was a place of elegance and its proprietor was a lovely gentleman. Louis Martin's cheeks were a network of tiny veins, his eyes dark and kindly. There was a curl of moustache on each side of his lip and his eyebrows were like brushes. It was an animated face and when he smiled or laughed eyebrows and moustaches moved up and down and from side to side.

"Surely, Henri, there is a place for you as captain."

My wages were $75 a month, enough to meet the mortgage and buy my railroad ticket; for the rest I would have to get tips. I will show you how that is done.

CHAPTER XIX

Diamond-Sapphire-Ruby-and-Pearl Jim Brady

Some months after I went to work at Martin's Café de Paris I observed one night a man of great corpulence squeeze himself through the door. His heavy features might have been sculptured with a hatchet but I think, now, his wide face with sagging lower eyelids, high cheekbones and deeply lined skin, was a symptom of glandular disturbance. This fellow glittered with emeralds that were set in rings on his fingers, as studs in his enormous shirt-bosom and on his black jacquard waistcoat as buttons. An astounding personage, truly, but I observed the other waiter captains were by no means eager to have this rich one and his party of half-a-dozen seated at one of their tables.

One of these assistant maîtres d'hôtel, Tony, an Italian, nudged me, saying: "Henri, take that party. The big fellow, he's a customer for Lynbrook." By some subtle sixth sense I knew this emerald-studded goliath was one who thought an assistant maître d'hôtel was too big to receive a tip.

"Regard my friends," I challenged the other captains as I started forward, "and you will see how one who is accustomed to treat with kings and queens makes this big, big eater grateful!"

"He eats but little," said Tony, thinking I did not see the wink he addressed to the others. "A few crackers, a little milk."

"That great belly," I said, "never took its bulge from such food. This one is an eater!"

How right I was! That big man was Diamond Jim Brady, who just as appropriately might have been called "Turquoise Jim" or "Ruby" or "Pearl." He had complete sets of jewels and seemed to wear a different one each night in the week. He had the biggest belly I have ever undertaken to fill; but he had to match it in size, I insist, a heart of gold.

"*Bon soir,* monseigneur," I said when I stood before him.

"Hey Jim," said one of the ladies, "the funny Frenchman has promoted you."

"Whatd'e say?" asked Mr. Brady and I answered for myself, in English.

"In my country the kings of old first had to be princes; but the prince was called monseigneur and a monseigneur, also, was a prince of the church. You know we believed that such persons devoted themselves to eating and to prayer. They ate well in order to have plenty of power to pray."

A mammoth grunt came from the depths of Mr. Brady. "If you could cook the way you talk," he said, "I would get tonight the finest meal I've ever had in this place."

"Is that your order, sir?"

"What?"

"The finest meal you have ever had?" I made a gesture as if to put my stub of a pencil in my coat pocket by way of accepting a carte blanche if he were disposed to grant it.

"All right," said Diamond Jim, "but if I don't like it—"

I went down the stairs to the kitchen almost in a jump. I knew that if I were to elevate Mr. Brady to the highest plateaus of satisfaction I should have to time the creation of his meal according to the *pièce de resistance.* That, I knew would take at least forty minutes; maybe forty-five if the chef were hostile.

A great one, that chef, a real Gascon. From constant tasting he had become in his white apron a thing of perfect symmetry, forming from chin to ankle one magnificent curve. But he could have tantrums, too, and he began to have one when he heard me speaking, in the tone of a field marshal, commands to his cooks.

"Who," he roared at me suddenly, "is the chef? Me or you?" When he said "you" he lunged across the table with a cooking spoon so that I had to leap back to preserve the immaculate bosom of my shirt.

"Monsieur," I implored him, "you who are known in Europe to Escoffier, to Cesar Ritz, and, yes, to my brother Camous, be patient! Hear me! If you will collaborate with me tonight you shall have all the credit of victory. If there is disaster I shall take all the blame. Lynbrook shall become my St. Helena and you will never be troubled again by Henri Charpentier."

If you had listened without understanding French you would have supposed we insulted one another. But no; my flattery was a part of the meal which Diamond Jim Brady was to eat that night. I continued to beseech him: "This customer is dressed like Ali Baba. He's no coachman. His belly is covered with emeralds like the Malaga grapes I want cooked with the *poularde*."

The chef did not wear his eyes in focus. They were not crossed; on the contrary, each gazed outwardly. So when he turned upon me the friendly look of one eye I knew my flattery had smoothed the way. I think if all the diplomacy used on cooks were barded on the world's dictators there would be fewer wars among the nations.

Beluga caviar in the flat canister in which it had traveled from Russia came first; then a Crême Royale, but the other dishes were in preparation even when Mr. Brady and his guests began to engulf the caviar. It would be impossible to relate sensibly the manner in which I gave instructions in the kitchen of Martin's that night. You may be certain I did not have to tell much to those wonderful cooks; just little touches that I had picked up from Algeria to Russia. The mushrooms for example, prepared in a way that I call today Mushrooms Henri. It is a harmony of flavors and the precedence of the ingredients is of the utmost importance.

Put a little butter in a saucepan. When the butter begins to bubble with heat place in it some chopped shallot. Cover the pan so the hot moisture will prevent the burning of the shallot. When it has turned brown and soft add your mushrooms, whole ones. The mushrooms should not be covered while they are cooking because the process is supposed to reduce them through the evaporation of some of their moisture. When they have cooked for seven or eight minutes begin to add little by little a glass of sherry and a half pony of brandy which will catch fire. As the flame expires add a cup of heavy cream, stirring it into your sauce. When this has become thick, as it should, about twenty or twenty-five minutes after the start, it is done. Serve half a dozen mushrooms in an individual dish with some sauce. Mr. Brady devoured his mushrooms and then ate those of one of his companions who was foolish enough to have a prejudice against mushrooms. Then he looked about for more between drinks of orange juice.

As I watched him quaff the juice of one orange after another I grew a little fearful that he would have no capacity for what I had in store for him. Oh, but I was then as unacquainted with Mr. Brady as you, perhaps, are unacquainted with the *poulardes* of France. The finest come from Le Mans and Bresse; they were regularly imported by restaurants of the incomparable excellence of Martin's. Such flesh! I think they arouse in me much the anticipation that would water the mouth of a cannibal who found himself confronted by a white man as fat as Diamond Jim Brady. These chickens, too, are gorged.

When a young hen of the country region surrounding Bresse is dedicated to the table her life henceforth is as carefully governed as if she were a Vestal Virgin entered in the service of a temple of Rome. She dwells in a box-like pen so small she cannot use her tender muscles. She may stand up or sit down, but that is all. She may put forth her head from a small window and receive the meal which is brought by her attendant, but she does not peck it like ordinary fowls. No, the man takes her by the neck (tenderly for her flesh is both delicate and valuable) and with a spoon made for the purpose crowds into her craw all that it will hold of a ration of corn meal, sour milk, bread and molasses. Five or six times a day she is fed in this manner and the more she has to eat the more she wants. She becomes among ordinary hens a Thaïs and her white meat acquires an extraordinary tenderness. Were she to waste energy in the creation of an egg it would be more than a barnyard scandal; a miracle!

It was such a chicken—she began her career at Bresse—that was prepared for Mr. Brady. Now, the way to draw a chicken is to make in the neck an incision large enough to admit two fingers. With these you can detach organs and entrails; make another incision slightly larger where her thigh joins her body. Draw out everything, but do not cleanse the fowl with water; do this with a clean dry cloth and then sprinkle a little salt and pepper inside the carcass and put in there also a tablespoon of butter.

So many who begin the ruination of the fowls they cook by sluicing water through them, complete the ruin by placing them on their backs to cook. A fowl should rest in the roasting pan on its side, with one leg and one wing down, one leg and one wing up. A tablespoon of butter in the pan keeps the tender flesh from burning in the first three minutes during which you, the cook, are spooning over it the bubbling hot butter. Then you turn it over and baste the other side. In France it is often said that a bird in an oven should behave with as much animation as if he were alive, that the cook ought to lend him vitality. If a fowl is turned back and forth and basted faithfully and with graciousness the skin will not crack or split and the breast will remain juicy and tender. That one for Mr. Brady weighed seven pounds. She was turned more than ten times during the forty minutes she was roasting. The finishing touch was the final five minutes she spent on her back in the roasting pan, drenched constantly with her own bubbling hot juices; that was what gave her a golden brown color which meant she was ready.

The artichokes were prepared by a preliminary boiling of twenty-five minutes. Then the leaves were stripped from the hearts which were cleaned of their beards. These were turned with a spatula in a way designed to season them with salt, pepper, and, very delicately, with a clove of garlic. This had been given a slap by the fingers of the cook. It was recovered and laid to one side during the five minutes the artichokes were being browned in a frying pan after which the piece of garlic was again called into service by being turned two or three times among these delicious vegetables, after which it was thrown away. Jean Camous used to say in jest that there was sufficient garlic flavor when the cook chewed a piece in his mouth and then breathed on what he prepared.

The potatoes cut in the shape of fingers were washed and then dried thoroughly. Dry, they were put into a saucepan with butter and covered. At intervals of two minutes they were turned during a total of thirty minutes by which time they had become brown, but inside they were soft enough to be chewed by a baby's gums.

Aye, cooking is a great deal of trouble! For half an hour a double handful of Malaga grapes had been cooking first, and slowly, in water, until they were swollen, and then furiously with a glass of Malaga wine and butter. Finally they were sprinkled with grated truffle and then, when the *poularde* rested on her back in the big casserole, supported on her right by the button artichokes, on her left by the fingers of potatoes, those Malaga grapes, like the emeralds of Diamond Jim, adorned her breast. The final touch was the addition of a pony of brandy with which that bird was flamed. As the last traces of alcohol were consumed and the blue flame ceased, circular paper ringed with flour paste was laid over the dish and the cover placed on that. The wonderful incense was imprisoned for those who had bought it.

One of my waiters carried the tray into the restaurant and placed it on a rolling serving table, but it was Henri who arranged the decorations into a kind of edible nest for that *poularde*. There were beets, carrots and potatoes that had been carved into the likeness of roses; there was watercress, parsley and celery with a crispness and a true aroma of the kitchen garden. I twice adjusted a single carrot-rose as if that hen were a Venus to be judged by Paris and then I pushed the table beside Mr. Brady, now avid for further nourishment. With a precise circular flourish of a carving knife I cut the seal of paper on the casserole and then, with my left hand, I lifted the lid. A small compact cloud of steam arose from the hen who was now to meet her destiny. Mr. Brady inhaled and sighed. His guests inhaled and sighed. Then I served for fear my large customer would faint with desire.

There was a salad afterward, of escarole, peppers, radishes, endive, chopped egg, parsley, tarragon, chives and with a French dressing not too oily and seasoned to a point. In America salad dressings are served so generously as to spoil the intention. They should never be greasy; there should never be an excess of dressing in the bowl. When I had completed my jugglery of wooden fork and spoon there was not a complete drop of dressing remaining in the bowl.

After that I revealed a *Soufflé Parmesan;* then a wonderful *bombe* of ice cream, covered with sugar like raveled silk and all disposed amid refreshing green rocks cunningly devised out of sugar colored with a paste of pistachio nuts.

More than his fair share of that meal was swallowed by Diamond Jim Brady along with the juice of, I swear, seventeen oranges. I think by then his skin was tighter than ever before but he was a mass of contentment as he sat there munching chocolate bonbons and digesting that *poularde* into a noble impulse. First he commanded me to call the boss, Mr. Martin. He approached, expecting, I think, some kind of trouble for the coil of moustache on each lip was in movement, his brown eyes were shadowed with concern. Rarely do the guests call the boss to praise. To save embarrassment I retired toward the kitchen. Repeatedly during the meal I had caught glimpses of the apron of the chef; but now I met him face to face.

"Has your big one dropped any emeralds into my casserole?" he asked.

"No," I said reprovingly, "but the bones of your *poularde* are all that remain in the casserole and you should be proud to wear them as a decoration." He retired then and I stepped forward to hear Mr. Martin, who beckoned.

"Henri, I am sending you a bottle of apricot brandy to Lynbrook." When it arrived a few days later that bottle had littered; it had become a case! It was sold, drink by drink, thereafter to those who found their way to my quiet establishment.

Mr. Brady, having risen unaided to his feet, offered to shake hands with me; it was his nice way of secreting in my hand a reward. Without looking I put it in my pocket and bowed the party from the scene of my triumph. Then when they had gone the other captains, jealous of that gesture they had observed, began to tease me. First came Tony, saying, "I'll bet he gave you a quarter"; then another said, "It was no more than a dime, be sure of that"; and another expressed an opinion that I would not be able to buy a glass of beer for all my pains. "Oh yes?" I said. "Well then, we shall see." I took the bill from my pocket. To my complete astonishment it was a bill of $100. Suddenly I clapped my hand to my forehead! Surely Mr. Brady had intended me to bring him change. So I rushed to the cashier's window, ignoring the queue of waiters with dinner checks in their hands.

"In line," snarled the cashier.

"Shut up," I retorted violently. "Change this hundred dollars. And you waiters—back."

Those fifty men moved like a single being because they saw in my eyes that I was aroused. The cashier was swollen with indignation but I pricked him with such sharp words of authority he quickly handed me the money. I caught up with Mr. Brady and his guests on the sidewalk as he was about to enter a carriage.

"Sir," I said, "excuse my stupidity for not bringing you change. Had I looked I should have known not even a king would make a gift of such proportions. Please—"

"Henri," he said, "that is all for you. You are an honest little gentleman. It was not a mistake. I intended it."

I could not speak and I could not move because I could not see. Then Mr. Brady said: "Are you married? Have you any children?"

"One, sir, and another one en route."

"Here," he said, handing me another hundred dollars, "this is to be divided half and half among the children and in case of twins let me know."

When I reached home a little before daylight I placed on the pillow beside the head of the sleeping Philomene the fortune I had received. I think now upon reflection that I was a little premature in announcing to Mr. Brady the prospect of a second child because our daughter Josephine André was not born until 1913. But Mr. Brady was not one to challenge the household accounts of a friend. Thereafter until his death he came almost every Sunday to the Henri Restaurant in Lynbrook. He was never without his appetite even on the most torrid days. After he had eaten soup he would devour pieces of imported French cantaloupe, grown under glass, until the crab cocktails appeared. Often when he came to Lynbrook he escorted the beautiful Dolly sisters. So he would whisper to me:

"The ladies must not know, but be sure to put a piece of garlic in the rack of lamb."

A rack of lamb is ideal food for those who wish to enjoy the flavor of meat and at the same time reduce the quantity eaten. Some people never learn to distinguish between saddle of lamb and rack of lamb. The rack of cutlets, the part of the rib basket nearest the grass when the lamb browses, is quite lean and the small treasure of meat which clings to the ribs must be roasted until it is perfectly brown; as it comes from the oven it is seasoned with salt and freshly ground black pepper. Then it cools on the kitchen table. And, please, do not spoil it by placing it in the ice-box.

Mr. Brady, with his elbows lifted by the expansion of his great belly, would devour six, seven, eight chops, keeping one gentle eye at all times upon his guests. The Dolly sisters only nibbled and seemed to nourish their loveliness on compliments. Then when the rack had become bare bones Mr. Brady would say, "You have another one?"

"Yes, Mr. Brady."

"Cooked the same way?"

"The same lamb, the same oven, the same chef."

"For whom did you cook that?"

"For myself, Henri."

Then he would groan with the despair of one who was starving.

"Never mind, Mr. Brady, I will eat something else; I will provide you with more racks until the bones make a picket fence around your middle."

"Fine, my boy. Proceed!"

After that he would eat a cucumber fresh from the garden, peeled and sliced like a banana. On it I would put just a little dressing of salt, pepper, a spoon of oil and half a spoon of wine vinegar. But even on a hot night Mr. Brady would not be finished then. He would say to the Dolly sisters:

"You will become weak and feeble and wrinkled if you do not eat." After he had consumed more than a quart of ice cream in some fanciful form devised by myself he would begin to eat bonbons, trying generously to feed them to the ladies. But they would resist. Well, they have kept their figures. Mine, of course, became nothing to brag about many years ago.

CHAPTER XX

A Surprise for Mike,
the Gateman

I had another faithful gourmet in the person of Mr. William Castle, an importer of olive oil and canned goods. Even through my first summer as a proprietor he had appeared with Mrs. Castle at least once a week. By what means could I attract such people to come to my little place?

Louis Martin was a true friend. Each Saturday when I was preparing to go (actually it would be early Sunday) he would remind me to take some things with me. Sunday was the day of big chance in our place. So from the storeroom of Martin's and from the ice-box I would select such things as I might require for first-class customers.

"May I take a *poularde*, Mr. Martin?"

"Certainly, my Henri, take what you need. Anything you do not sell bring back Monday. Pay only for what you sell."

In consequence, when I stretched out on the bench in the Long Island railroad station about quarter-to-four on a Sunday morning I would place beneath my head an astounding piece of baggage. It would contain a trio or maybe a quartet of rustling live lobsters navigating the darkness of that portmanteau among objects never to be encountered on the floor of the sea; a ripe and creamy Camembert, a *poularde* with flesh soft as butter, fresh truffles, a can of Beluga caviar, a bottle or two of some rare vintage wines, and, possibly, a box of bonbons.

For three years, from October, 1910, I had only on rare occasions more than three hours of sleep in bed. I left the house in Lynbrook at 9:30 to catch a train leaving at 9:45 and which reached New York in time for me to enter Martin's by 10:30 A.M. By eleven, appropriately costumed for work I had to be in the dining room ready to greet the advance guard of that host which would appear for luncheon. At 3:30 the following morning my day's work at Martin's was finished. The next departure to Lynbrook and beyond was a newspaper train which left, as I recall, at 5:27 A.M. Oh, that was a cold and grisly light in which to start home from work! Yet it was warmed for Henri by the kindness of an Irishman.

There were almost two hours, certainly an hour and forty minutes, in which one as tired as I could sleep on a waiting room bench. On the first few nights, fearful of missing the train, I woke automatically every few minutes and would rise up to stare with bloodshot eyes at the clock. Then a blue-uniformed gateman came to me and said:

"Where are you going, huh?"

"Lynbrook."

"All right then, my boy. Your train goes at five-twenty-seven. You sleep with an empty mind. At two minutes before your train goes I'll wake you up."

His name was Mike and thereafter during three weary, weary years he was my faithful alarm clock, but always his touch on my shabby shoulder was as gentle as if he had been one of my mothers. "Time to go, Henree," he would say and I would return from some fantastic dream of the past through a fog of blurred feeling into a shivering present. So it was with me in 1910, 1911 and 1912.

How can I measure the gratitude I owe that railroad man for leaving his barricade morning after morning so that I might catch my train refreshed by his kindness? Oh, no, my friends, it is not such a bad world!

Before I tell about the surprise I gave Mike I will have to recite the circumstances which made that surprise possible. Things began to improve; indeed, by tenfold in one year. In 1911 the gross receipts were $5,000. Be sure to understand I do not say the profits; no, the gross receipts. All the previous winter I had been creating a mouth-to-mouth propaganda among guests of whose gentleness I could approve and at Martin's I had a wonderful selection as the richest people of the world were drawn to that establishment. Colonel John Jacob Astor found it to his liking; many of the Vanderbilt family, the Belmonts, the Goulds, and countless men of power from Wall Street. Each afternoon we could tell when the racing was over at Jamaica or the other tracks by the throng that swarmed into the restaurant for cocktails. Then they would order dinner.

It was from among these people that I selected my customers. Suppose there were a lady and a gentleman whose behavior and understanding I admired. In such a case I would go to the florist and for fifty cents receive from him an American Beauty rose for which he would have charged anyone else a dollar.

When I would hand this to the lady with an appropriate bow I would say: "Madame, a compliment from Henri. Perhaps next Spring when the roads are dry you will come to my place in Lynbrook?"

"Oh, you have a restaurant?"

"Yes, madame. Not big. Very small, very nice and when you enter it you are going to be its queen." The card I would present then was of a sort printed for me at a price of twenty-five cents for a hundred.

I gave Mr. J. P. Morgan one of my cards after serving him one night. I watched him eat his oysters in silence, a full dozen. Then as he sighed with comfort halfway through his steak and with the bottle of Pommard two-thirds empty I became attentive. We had first met when I was at the Hotel Cap Martin, a boy of ten. He had remembered me because, with the exception of my three years in the French army, there was never a year in which I did not catch his eye, smile and wish him health. Oh, yes, he knew Henri.

So this night when he had quite finished and was in an excellent humor I dared to tell him about Lynbrook.

"What?" he exclaimed. "You have a restaurant? Where is it? Lynbrook?"

From his tone I felt he did not know where it was.

"On the road to Long Beach," I said and retired in hope.

I had no liquor license in my first years. When it was necessary to provide drinks for customers I would telephone an order to a certain one of the five dealers in the village who was authorized to sell it. This dealer was a mile away but he had a horse and buggy and a shaky old automobile. So my customers never had to wait long. After more than two years I got a license. Such a document cost $250 and the available ones were all in use. Consequently each one had acquired an increased value. A Frenchman I knew, a maître d'hôtel in New York, said he would get me one. It would cost, he said, $9,000. I was still a greenhorn. I signed papers and soon discovered I had compromised my control of the Henri Restaurant. Eventually he calculated my debt to him at $10,000. But one who came to my rescue was Mr. Jules Weber, a wholesale dealer in groceries and delicacies. An Alsatian, corpulent, with blue eyes, a gray moustache, a noble disposition, he stood between me and the maître d'hôtel.

"You don't owe that fellow anything, Henri," Mr. Weber said to me one day. "I have taken over your account. I made him cut the debt in half; it is five thousand. He only paid two thousand for the license. Sorry I could not do better."

Sorry! Why, he had saved my restaurant. Thereafter I paid him every Monday a little money. One week I would take him twenty dollars and the next week thirty dollars and then, perhaps, forty dollars. One day when I said: "Here is fifty dollars, Mr. Weber," he looked at me carefully and I was aware when he saw the mended place at the knee of my trousers.

"My boy," he said, "you forget to pay me this fifty. Go get yourself a suit of clothes."

All through that period I had a generous credit with his establishment for such goods as I required for the restaurant.

Then, of course, I had to have a wine cellar. I began with a few bottles. I would have one quart of champagne and one pint. If I sold the pint I replaced it with two pints; similarly with the quart. I kept turning all the money from wines back into the stock of the wine cellar until I had cases down there. But of the rare vintages, naturally, there were no representatives. But I was not compromised, not Henri.

The scene would be the Restaurant Henri on a Sunday during its infancy. Felix, our boy waiter, would be scampering between the restaurant and the kitchen. Armand, a regular Camous who had taken the place of Madame Charpentier in, I hasten to state, the kitchen only, would be occupied like a one-man orchestra. Then I would hear one of the few customers command my presence.

"Henri!"

"*Oui*, Monsieur. What is your pleasure?"

"Chateau Yquem, eighteen seventy."

"One-half minute, sir."

I would return stricken with regrets but carrying an authentic but empty bottle which for forty years and more had actually contained some of that rare wine.

"The last bottle on hand. I am sorry. I did not realize it had been served."

It would be the same with a Romanée or a fine old Pommard. My collection of empty bottles was as complete as the richest and most discriminating customers of Martin's, the Knickerbocker and the Plaza could make it. Night after night I carried home in that old portmanteau of mine a choice bottle which retained only the fragrance of its wine. But while I slept on my bench in the Long Island railroad station this bouquet like a gentle ghost would leave its bottle and steal into my nostrils so that I might dream again of the days when I was the companion of a prince or myself a richly rewarded maître d'hôtel in Munich and able without guilt to drink such precious fluids.

One pleasant day in 1912, when all I had to worry about were debts and empty shelves in my wine cellar, I looked out-of-doors and saw a big Renault car. You can well believe I would tremble at the sight of a mechanism made in France but I was delighted when Mr. J. P. Morgan stepped out. He seemed quite, quite old.

"Henri," he said, "there will be ten of us tonight at seven."

It was then half-past-two in the afternoon and I knew I could produce everything I needed easily; if only I had had a little more money I would have bought that day new furniture, I assure you. I sent Armand to town so that each fish would be selected by the lifelike expression of its eyes; so that the vegetables would be perfection, and so that everything would be of the standard I had set for myself.

My own errand took me into my garden. When I had completely de-flowered it I invaded the gardens of my neighbors. The chairs I had were poor things for which I had paid a dollar apiece. I made of each something so well concealed with flowers that you might have offered it at a funeral as the floral design from the chief mourner. I make light of it now but I do insist I wove every flower into its place with a feeling that this day was a chance to show whether I was a restaurateur or the proprietor of a lunchroom.

At seven Mr. Morgan strode into my house followed by his guests. I personally received his cane, his hat and coat. Then I led the way into the transformed dining room. You might have supposed my place in

Lynbrook was in Aix-les-Bains on a gala night. Mr. Morgan looked at each chair in turn. He observed the chandeliers, the mantelpiece of brickwork above the fireplace. Not one piece of ugliness was exposed. Then Mr. Morgan looked at the chair where he was to sit. His guests, five gentlemen and four ladies, were standing too. Then he said: "My friends, please see the way a Frenchman covers his poverty with flowers." And there were tears in his eyes!

I served them caviar, *pot au feu*, Sea Bass Henri, *poussins* (very young chickens) casserole, vegetable *panaché Salade Monte Carlo*, Crêpes Suzette and coffee. It was several hours past seven when the last pancake Suzette was gone and the final drops of enticing sauce spooned from the plates.

I heard many warm compliments and then Mr. Morgan spoke: "Henri, send the check to my house in Thirty-sixth Street. And here is something with which to buy new chairs."

Politeness kept me from looking to see what that piece of paper was I held in my hand. To avoid the temptation I pushed it deep into my pocket. Only when my guests were out of sight did I look. The same Mr. Morgan who had once handed me a gold piece when I was a page boy had given me $500. I displayed this the following day to friends who said the piece of paper was just a banker's advertisement. They almost convinced me but I went to Barth's and bought a few pans, a few plates and other utensils. The bill was $40. I had such an amount in my pocket in bills of a denomination with which I was familiar. But I took a chance: I tendered the big bill and Mr. Barth did not shoot me. Instead he said: "Henri, with so much money why don't you equip your place right?"

"Mr. Barth," I said, "you keep all that money. I'm taking two dozen chairs and other things."

What actual wines I could buy came very often from Mr. Jack Grubman. I went to his place one day in 1913 and selected a few cases of Bordeaux wines. Precisely five, just what I could pay for. But the next day a large van arrived at Lynbrook and the men began carrying into my cellar about 500 cases of a carefully chosen assortment of wines, cordials, of everything that might be necessary to satisfy the most discriminating palate. I was never so confused, I think. I called Mr. Grubman on the telephone.

"I ordered five cases and you send me five hundred."

"That's all right," he said, "it will keep in your cellar as well as in mine. Pay me when you feel like it. I know you, Henri, O.K.?"

I went upstairs and looked upon the tiny Josephine André and I said: "Infant, I think you have brought some luck."

My friend Mike, the gateman, realized I was somewhat better off when on my weekly trips to town (I had left Martin's) I would bring him a pair of freshly killed chickens but it was not until 1915 when my place had expanded to a park of more than five acres with an imposing brick gateway, that I arranged a Sunday dinner party for Mike, his wife and five children.

All day the flowers remained on the table and slowly they wilted as I did, who had picked them, for Mike had disappointed me. Still I held his table even though our usual crowd of two hundred and fifty patrons were pressing for space. In the park outside I often had scores for whom there was no possibility of regular service. For these I provided a light buffet supper, a cocktail or a glass of wine. "A compliment to you, Madame," the waiter would say. "Mister Henri is sorry to disappoint you. He hopes you will return."

In the face of such a pressure I held Mike's table. But he did not come. On Monday morning I sat forward on my seat going to town. I would tell him things.

"Say," I began in the American manner, "I waited and I waited and I waited for you yesterday. Why didn't you come?"

"We went to Lynbrook," said Mike, "but we couldn't find the place."

"But I gave you directions. I told you precisely—"

"Say, you can't mean that big place?" Mike remembered the shabby fellow who slept on the railroad station bench.

"That very place," I said firmly.

"Hoh," said Mike, astounded, "you must be rich."

"Rich is right," said Henri. But that was in 1915.

CHAPTER XXI

Onion Soup for
T. Roosevelt

There are things in this world more subtle than the minds of men can grasp. For all their prying, what convincing words can scientists use to tell each other how an atom of musk during years can throw off a something that in human nostrils becomes that which we call an odor; and yet, itself, be undiminished? Until you can explain that do not laugh when I tell you the simple effective cure I use when I am overcome with a nostalgia for my childhood.

I take down from a shelf in the pyramidal hood of bricks above a fireplace in my restaurant on Long Island a heavy marble mortar and a wooden pestle. I sit quietly holding them on my lap, my hands fondling the shiny surface of the wood which fits my palms and fingers. That is all; but it is enough. I am soothed almost at once as if by the hands that gave these objects their patina.

Before I brought them from the old home of my foster-parents in Contes the mortar and pestle were used to grind salt. According to a legend which I believe, the implements served the Camous family through successive generations for 300 years. Why, I myself saw these tools many times in the hands and lap of Giroumetta, the mother of Papa Camous, and she was 107 years old the day she died and I was seven. She had a big nose and walked always bent from the hips in the animal posture fixed upon her by her years of toiling in the fields. If, walking behind her, I trod upon a living plant she heard and scolded me. Those same keen ears had heard the complaints of the peasants against the Monarchy, the complaints that became the French Revolution. Her ears had heard the tramping feet of Napoleon's soldiers when all Europe shook to that tread. She had seen the Emperor, and while I was small I heard from her lips much that was crammed in her old head, things not to be found in books; and, yet nothing that she could tell me would sound so fantastic in a Frenchman's ears as what I have to tell of recent history.

Eventually I am going to tell you about Henri, the Outlaw. I have been one, surely! My story is one of the underground treasure, of a secret passageway, of subterranean chambers and whispering conspirators. My store of wealth in a form that, certainly, had become contraband, was taken from me. Gunpowder has been exploded under my roof-tree by fleeing agents of government shooting at my son. Oh, yes, I have been an authentic outlaw. But when I revive these occurrences in my mind I find it best to take into my hands the marble mortar and the wooden pestle from the old kitchen in Contes. In this way my soul is soothed as if by some inscrutable means these objects placed me *en rapport* with Sandrina, my Mama Camous, who, thank God, still lives, in France.

What tales I have with which to astound old Giroumetta could I but communicate with her. I could, for example, tell her of Mrs. Mollie Netcher Newbury, one of the first of my patrons and for many years a friend. I have never seen her Boston Store in Chicago but I remember the first significant clue that revealed to me it was a highly successful establishment. My own restaurant at the time was still a little place which was crowded when sixteen persons dined there simultaneously. In those days, long before this lady had surrendered to the reducing madness, she was among the earliest to arrive on a Sunday for dinner. One day as I greeted her and received from her shoulders her coat of marvelous gray softness, she cautioned me:

"Careful of that, Henri! It is worth one hundred thousand dollars."

Blanchette, the *vestiare,* who is as much a part of the premises as myself, rolled her eyes with concern. I rolled mine, too. Surely I decided, I would never dare to descend the stairs into the wine cellar leaving only a woman or two to guard such a treasure. So, I soothed Blanchette, still murmuring, *"quelle responsabilité,"* by receiving back from her the precious garment. Then I placed beside my customer a chair, on the chair a linen tablecloth, then the coat and on top of it another linen tablecloth. "Madame," I said, "I think you had better be the policeman for this coat and then each of us will enjoy your dinner."

I have wished many times since that the hair that grows upon Henri was such a species of chinchilla so that I might reap a fortune from my own skin. Mrs. Newbury does not come so often nowadays; she travels widely, but whether in Hindustan or China or Egypt her post-cards come telling me she misses Henri. What she really misses is Henri's cooking. A true gourmet, that lady. How she can endure to fast for fashion I do not understand.

Ah, the jewels I have seen in my establishment, both the hard bright stones of radiant fire and the lovely ladies adorned by them! But what lady ever came so freighted with jewels as my friend Diamond Jim Brady? He came regularly about noon on every Sunday and two or more times during the week for dinner or luncheon. Invariably he telephoned because he wished to begin eating the moment he arrived. I think no zoo could afford to keep such a magnificent appetite as Mr. Brady nourished. His dinner bill, without wines, which he did not drink, never went below $30.

For dinner he would have two portions of melon, two plates of soup, a whole sea bass, mushrooms, a complete duck, three vegetables and three desserts. He swallowed orange juice a half-pint at a gulp. He consumed oysters until one's arm grew tired with the effort of opening them; forty-two, I swear. I tell you he was as voracious for the last mouthful as for the first. Sometimes I jested as he moved away from the table by asking him, in a tone of sorrow, "Oh, you are leaving when more Crêpes Suzette are being prepared for you?"

"What, Henri," he would exclaim happily, "you mean it? Don't you cry! I'm sitting down again."

There came a time when I could not jest with my friend about his appetite. I think it was in 1915 and all the news I had from France told of the misery of my friends, of men suffering and dying at the front, of their children, their wives and their old ones going without food. It was on a day that I was deep in such sorrow that I sat with Mr. Brady as he devoured a duck. I had carved it in a way he liked, each piece attached to a bit of bone. Mr. Brady held the ultimate piece in his jeweled fingers, his mouth open, when I spoke.

"I would be a rich man if I had a few more customers like you," I said. Something unwonted in my tone held his attention. Ordinarily I played the buffoon for this one who was my friend. Then I went on: "If you could see the miserable people who rise before me as in a vision every time I open a letter from France, I think you would be glad to give that morsel of duck to feed them."

I spoke out of my heart, because I could not control my tongue. I wounded him as only a friend can wound. Mr. Brady's eyes remained fixed on that piece of duck before his mouth until, suddenly, tears spilled from those kind eyes and took their places among the diamonds on his waistcoat. He returned the piece of duck to his plate. Needlessly and without justice I had spoiled his appetite! I have never been more contrite. I apologized. I explained. The more I talked the better Mr. Brady began to grasp an understanding of what miseries of the helpless had shaped my original comments. Nothing I could say restored the appetite of Mr. Brady that day; he left and I was morose, I tell you.

The next day a secretary telephoned for him to inform me of a truly magnificent benefaction Mr. Brady had bestowed upon the orphans of the Allies. I know the amount was about half a million dollars and I know that golden egg came from one of Henri's ducks. The following Sunday to my indescribable relief Mr. Brady telephoned he was coming at one. The place was crowded when he arrived and practically all my customers were, on my premises, as one big family. I had prepared a wreath of flowers and fresh pine branches to represent happy America and of dead grass and withered branches to represent the miseries of France. My idea was further delineated by the flags of the two countries, but the customers did not see the flags; they saw only that ridiculous wreath which they supposed was one of Henri's jokes. They chuckled and laughed with anticipation but when I presented that piece to Mr. Brady he knew I was not joking. I wept and tried to speak what was in my mind, what would have been in the mind of any native of France at such a time; but what happened was that Mr. Brady rose to his feet and embraced me. That was more than a gesture. He outweighed me by more than I should want to lift and I weighed at that time 267 pounds. Nevertheless the two of us cried on each other's shoulders, and became happy. That is why there is something of a *double entendre* in the title of my place: Original Henri Restaurant. Where else in the world would such things happen between a man and his best customer?

On another day of the war Commodore William K. Vanderbilt was having luncheon at my place. I had served him often in Europe and admired him. On this occasion he overheard the compliments of a gentleman who was departing after a luncheon. The man had said he could not get better food in France.

"Henri," said Commodore Vanderbilt with twinkling eyes, "I'll bet if you had known the identity of that one he would have had less pleasure in his meal. It was the German ambassador, Von Bernstorff."

Oh, I was rabid on the subject of the war. I displayed the French flag with the American and irritated some persons to fury but one who agreed with me was the former president, Theodore Roosevelt. Often when he was driving between his home at Oyster Bay and the city he would stop. Invariably, I think, he wanted onion soup. The first time he came he was dubious because he thought mine would not be so good as some he had eaten in France.

The way to make it, Henri style, is to slice, on the bias, three red onions previously peeled. I put these slices in a casserole containing a tablespoon of hot butter. Into this bland substance the onions surrender all their juice. Properly this should be accomplished over a slow fire. This part of the process is complete when the onion slices have turned the color of gold. Three onions, I find, are sufficient to provide the flavor for soup for two persons; four may make sufficient for four or five, but for myself, when I am hungry, I want six onions. Henri likes his onion soup thick, but even I want them well cooked. The breath of a raw onion is completely uncivilized; but a thoroughly cooked onion, remember, leaves you inoffensive, even desirable.

When your onions have turned the proper color then you add to them about a quart of cold chicken or beef consommé. Now permit this to boil thoroughly; between a half and three-quarters of an hour. The final action is to toast a slice or two of bread or a handful of croutons and then in the heat of your oven melt on these grated parmesan or Swiss cheese. Launch these cheese-laden rafts gently on the boiling hot soup, cover the pot and then place it in the oven for ten minutes. This part of the process gives to the soup the flavor of the cheese. It is, therefore, most important. When you serve send along as an escort a saucer of grated parmesan for the use of those whose taste is less delicate than yours and mine.

"Henri," said Mr. Roosevelt many times, "I think I like your onion soup better than that I have eaten in France."

Well, I myself do not say it is better. I am content to know it is as good.

I was grossly fat in the summer of 1917 and one hot afternoon, until I was sore and breathless just above my equator, I was prodded by an emphatic and distinguished forefinger. It belonged to the former president, Theodore Roosevelt. That day he was telling me something and that was his way: to pound on you with his finger, biting off a shrill word with each tap. This would continue until you surrendered, saying, "Sir, you are right."

Not that we disagreed; indeed, no. I think he came sometimes not because he was hungry but because I boldly flew above my house along with the flag of the United States the tricolor of France. Neutral? Me? Hah! That was precisely the way he felt, that Roosevelt.

"They cannot win, those Germans," I said.

"Henri," he said, "you are restoring my appetite."

"When the intelligences trained at West Point arrive on that Western Front, then—"

Well, I had said the wrong thing. He pushed back his chair. He stood up and confronted me so that his face was no more than eighteen inches from mine. My bulging stomach would not permit a closer approach:

"You are like a lot of people in this country," he said. I had been tapped vigorously precisely ten times with his forefinger when he had spoken those ten words. His other hand was thrust deep in the pocket of his morning trousers. "You think this is a West Point war. It is a war calling for all the genius with which this country has been built. West Point?"

At that moment I thought the percussions of his finger were breaking through the walls of my gall bladder.

"If you send a muttonhead to West Point, he will become a muttonhead officer. West Point is a good military school. It is not a place where miracles of creation occur."

Well, finally I succeeded in saying that he was right, that I did agree with him. He looked at me sharply and then resumed his seat, still talking. Consequently I did not ask him what he would like to eat on that hot day. Instead I spoke quickly to a waiter who brought a magnificent *galantine* which I personally sliced thinly, and then placed those slices on a plate garnished with discs of cucumber. *Galantine?* Is there in your neighborhood a *charcuterie?* In France there would be. In America probably you will be compelled to make your own. It is not too difficult; and nothing is so appropriate on a buffet.

You take cooked meats, choice pieces of chicken free of bones, some veal, slices of roast pork, tongue and ham. These are laid in a mold interlaced, flatly. Between the pieces you must introduce whole truffles, pistachio nuts, also a few cherries that have been preserved in sherry. A paste made of ground pork, veal and one or two eggs all seasoned with salt, pepper, sherry, cognac and herbs is required. How much sherry and cognac? Be reasonable; sufficient to flavor the dish and to make your paste easily handled with a spatula. The meat paste must fill all the interstices of the meat slices and then completely enclose it. The whole loaf, one of three or four pounds, should cook about one hour in a slow fire. Served cold it is tempting to gaze upon and delicious to taste.

Next I gave Mr. Roosevelt a salad. Because I knew he would be breathing upon the people with whom he discussed the war, I was very gentle with the garlic and each leaf of lettuce was delicately colored with the purple vinegar of wine and the amber of olive oil; but it was not dripping and in the bottom of the bowl when the salad was lifted to a plate there was nothing. A greasy waste in the bowl represents the reverse of finesse. Because of mine, when Mr. Roosevelt said goodbye to me that afternoon he walked a trifle less briskly. He did not know how to stroll; yet he was relaxed. He had time to see my youngest child, feel its cheek and to see with a sudden alertness the widow's black worn by a woman working for me, a French woman whose small child was the orphan of a French soldier. Ah, he had to hear about that, so on that hot day when finally he departed for Oyster Bay, he who had come for luncheon, it was almost time for dinner.

CHAPTER XXII

LOBSTER HENRI, FOR JOFFRE

Another who came often for onion soup was Alfred Gwynne Vanderbilt, the son of the Commodore. On a day late in April, 1915, he came dressed all in gray, to say *au revoir* and have a farewell luncheon in the company of two of his friends.

"But I would not sail on that boat," I said showing him the lifted palm of my hand. "Those Germans—"

"What's the matter, Henri? Are you losing your courage?"

"No, but I do not endorse suicide for my friends. Let your valet use that steamship ticket! But I know you: you will go anyway. So, then, excuse me a few minutes!"

My errand took me to the cellar, my wine cellar. In that place of darkness with cement floor and concrete walls deeply imbedded in the earth the only draughts were those caused by Henri's bulk in motion, and he walked, I tell you, as softly as a nun. Each corridor of racks was for me an avenue of adventure that was at once soothing and thrilling. I had been the architect of that place. The wines that slept there were of my own choosing and all were good; most were truly great. There below the earth, as naturally and comfortably as the roots of my maples to the uttermost hidden tendrils were alive and growing happily in the blackness of the soil outside the walls, I had rooted my dignity.

Actually I went about my work in the cellar with the finesse of a brain surgeon. The wines must not be disturbed. I do believe I would have slapped into silence anyone, assistant or interloper, who raised his voice down there to a rude tone. There were rack upon rack of bottles of sherry that more than seventy years before had been sleeping in a cellar of a Queen of Spain. There were Burgundies, Bordeaux and Champagnes of all the best years, of eighteen seventy, eighty-six, ninety-three, ninety-eight, nineteen hundred, nineteen four, six, eleven and fourteen. Aye, fourteen was a good year as if nature had sympathized with France in the trials to come. Oh, yes, those were magic fluids in my care. This day my errand into the cellar took me to a place I could find in the darkness, the shelves where I had my bottles of Napoleon brandy. Aye, those were treasures. I brought a bottle into the light it had not seen in several years, and then only briefly, and hastening to the restaurant placed it in the hands of Alfred Gwynne Vanderbilt.

"Bon voyage," I said.

"Henri," he shouted with enthusiasm, "a corkscrew at once!"

"No," I said, "this bottle has a sister which has already been violated; we shall drink from her. But this bottle is to keep you content and, maybe, warm when you are at sea aboard the *Lusitania*."

I have wondered many, many times about that bottle. Remembering his impetuosity I have dared to hope he had begun to enjoy my gift before the terrible hour of the explosion. It is not because of courage I hope this; he had an abundance of that in his blood; but in the bottle he would have found philosophy.

The sinking of the *Lusitania* was only one of many war incidents that steeped me in sadness. Every mail brought me news of some tragedy, a friend killed, a widow in want, children crying for food. I was sending more than I could afford; that was why in Contes a change was made so that the street in which the little Henri had lived near the top of that hillside village now is called Rue Henri Charpentier.

Then on an occasion when the warship *Admiral Aube* had brought Marshal Joffre to the United States, a friend of mine from Paris telephoned me to be prepared on the following day to receive Papa Joffre for luncheon, a party of four with platoons of French sailors marching as his escort. I thought my home village of Lynbrook would want to recognize this visit of such a man by having him greeted by a few people of distinction so I told the Mayor. What a day! My premises were engulfed by humanity. The schools were emptied and there were 20,000 faces watching Marshal Joffre as he mounted the steps to my threshold. What I said to him then about France caused that splendid old man to lift his white moustache in a wide smile; he opened his arms and we embraced. I was a little concerned when I saw my tears were falling on the dark blue tunic of that great soldier; but I was content when I saw his tears falling on my white apron.

Lobster Henri was one of the things I fed that day to the man who had saved France at the Marne. I spoke to that lobster when I placed him, alive, in cold water; "My big fellow," I said, "you are to go to sleep relaxed and peaceful, so your meat will be tender when you blend your being with that of a hero." Parsley, a few grains of white pepper, bay leaves, a carrot, an onion spiny with cloves and some salt joined that lobster. If he had been plunged into boiling hot water he would have died with every muscle taut and tough. Common sense, is it not? Oh, I am sure that lobster, if he understood, was glad to die knowing he would be living again so gloriously within the hour. He remained boiling in that bath for about fifteen minutes and then was placed on a board to dry, after which his flesh was cut in small cylinders the shape of scallops. A small white onion, chopped thin, was cooked in butter until it was golden; then chopped mushrooms were added and cooked until these two had blended, which was after about fifteen minutes. Into this went the lobster. It is not easy to become immortal. Because there was an excess of humidity in the pan a pony of brandy was poured over the mixture. This caught fire and in the blue flame precisely the right amount of moisture was carried off, thereby intensifying the wonderful flavors that remained. Then I added a lump of butter as large as my thumb and when it had melted I poured in a cup of double cream. When this began to bubble from the boiling heat I poured in a glass of sherry which gave its flavor and its bouquet to the sauce before I removed the pan from the fire.

I thought when he ate that lobster Papa Joffre would embrace Henri again. Afterward he had Crêpes Suzette until little scallops began to appear at the edge of his tunic from the stretching between one gold button and another.

Scattered at tables in my park outside the restaurant were the sailors from the *Admiral Aube*, two hundred and fifty at least. I know they consumed a fifty-gallon barrel of wine, and then another and another; red wine that I had imported because of its excellence so I could bottle it myself. But when Henri, who became dizzy with emotion at the sight of one red pompon on a sailor cap, saw his premises overrun with pompons he became delirious. All that shipload were my guests.

There was one, a boy of fourteen, a *petit mousse,* what the British call a cabin boy. His name was Bernard and in his merry eyes and features I seemed to see the reflection of the little Henri who had so nearly starved in London. I took him for my own that day.

"But one so small," I said as I watched him fill his interior with Crêpes Suzette, "what can he do in a war?"

"Small," agreed Bernard, "yes, but Monsieur Henri, I have participated in two battles. I carried water to the bridge and my captain told me I had carried myself, Bernard, like a man."

His father was dead when he talked and he was concerned about his mother and three smaller children. Word of this concern began to spread among my regular customers who were present and enthusiastic. They turned out their pockets and presently the cabin boy stood before me, bewildered, holding in his hands his cap in the manner of a basin. It contained coins and bills of a total of about $250 and he was explaining to me that he was beginning to be afraid something might happen to his ship before he could deliver this treasure to his mother.

"One of my men," I said, "will take you to the post office and then Uncle Sam will be responsible for the delivery of that money to your mama."

Then he jumped so as to encircle my neck with his small arms and asked: "Can I call you papa?" What other country, I ask you, produces boys so free of shyness, so willing to display to another admiration, affection, gratitude? I held him close as if he had been my son. Afterward most of those sailors who feasted that day in my place in Lynbrook were drowned in the North Sea, and among them was Bernard, the *petit mousse.* But on every visit that I made to France in the years to come, until he died, I went to pay my respects to Papa Joffre and invariably he recalled with smackings of his lips the lobster, the Crêpes Suzette and the other surprises of his luncheon at Lynbrook.

CHAPTER XXIII

WINE FOR BERNHARDT

Another who came about 1917 was Madame Sarah Bernhardt. I received her outdoors. One of the gentlemen of her party of ten and myself carried her in a chair into the restaurant. Ah, she was light, for by that time one of her legs had been amputated. She appeared only rarely in public because of this affliction and on the stage between the rising of the curtain and its fall she kept in one position, leaning on a chair, using a hand and her marvelous voice to reduce an audience to tears. All who were in my restaurant rose and saluted her as we carried her chair to the table where she was to dine. How she responded to that applause!

"Madame, you will humor me," I said, "if you will for soup eat *Petite Marmite,* Henri Quatre."

"Certainly," she said.

How I carried on to please her. I behaved with all manner of exaggerations until, after much laughter she said if she were younger she would wean me from the restaurant business and take me into her company for professional training as a comedian. Then it was time for me to speak and in a few words I created in her own memory a vision of the past. I mentioned Havre, the Frascati, Baptiste the waiter, the hot soup and myself, the little assistant waiter who fell and spoiled her dress but managed, heroically, to keep all the burns for his own skin.

"You!" she said, with the tone she might have used upon the stage.

Then from time to time she shook her head from side to side as details of that incident recurred to her. I excused myself. When I returned from my bedroom I carried a sealed envelope which I opened with a flourish and then, bowing low, placed in the hand of Madame Sarah Bernhardt that handkerchief of cambric and point lace which she at once recognized, the one she had soaked with olive oil to soothe my blistered fingers. Oh, that was a great night in both our lives. I think I considered hundreds of the choicest bottles in my cellar each time I selected one for Madame's party. Each time it was a ceremony! But, of course, the bringing of wine was always a ceremony.

You must treat wine as gently as a mother treats her youngest baby. Habitually, Bordeaux and Burgundies, a few bottles at a time, were placed tenderly, each in a straw basket, ten days or so before they would be carried from the cellar. This was done so that the chosen bottle would have rested; not on its side, but almost in the position in which it is opened. In that way the impalpable units of sediment which exist in all wines would have again surrendered themselves to the operations of the law of gravity. I remember going out of the cellar that night with a bottle of Montrachet, Grand Vin, a white Burgundy to be served with the fish. At such times I was protean; in the space between the racks which had become too narrow for my vast bulk I assumed a giraffe-like form so that not one bottle should be disturbed by my passage. Outside the cellar the Burgundy in its basket could hardly have suspected it was in motion so fluidly did I advance to the top of the stairs. Never hold a bottle of wine upright. Such a one as I speak of would go to the table at that same angle at which it has rested in its basket. It would be carried in my left hand so that with my right I could defend it. If I encountered a waiter with an armful of plates he would know that his duty was to drop and smash the plates rather than jostle Henri while he bore wine. The wine coming from the cellar had the right of way!

With the Montrachet I tilted the front of the basket just enough to slip beneath it the edge of a plate. Then I removed the tinfoil, being as careful not to disturb the bottle as if it contained nitroglycerine. You should always remove the cap of tinfoil because if there should be a trace of mold beneath it one little speck would spoil the wine for a connoisseur. Then, using all my power to hold the bottle immobile, the cork was twisted until it left the opening. Would you believe me,

Madame Bernhardt watched Henri open the bottle with as much concentration as audiences always observed her when she moved and spoke upon a stage. No faintest noise told of the emergence of the cork from the bottle. Then with my finger clothed in linen of a napkin I carefully wiped the inside of the bottle neck so that the glass pathway of the wine would be undefiled by a trace of cork. Next I smelled as solemnly as a pig hunting truffles. It was as it should be, so I poured into a glass a finger's-width of wine and held it arm's-length between myself and a light. The faintest of topaz in color! After I tasted it I spoke. "Madame Bernhardt," I said, "ladies and gentlemen, *parfait!*"

When the duck was served I brought from the cellar a chateaubottled Burgundy that Madame knew as well as she knew any one of the characters she acted. It was a Beaune, Clos des Bressandes, full-bodied, ruby-colored, fit to be blood in the veins of an angel. Her eyes met mine as she tasted and then seemed to vanish upward so that I saw for a second only the whites.

With the Crêpes Suzette sending forth fragrance Madame saw me begin to pour an old, old Emperador, a sherry so fine—well no matter what most persons think, the connoisseurs who know that wine will believe me when I say that Madame, when she tasted it, seized my hand and touched it with her lips. And in the entire evening all the wine she drank would not have filled eight tablespoons; but it was enough; she was not quenching a thirst; she was tasting; she was living.

I tell you she embraced me when it was time to depart and she whispered: "How glad I am I once was kind to the little boy who has become Henri, the restaurateur." And there was such a lilt in her voice as I carried her in her chair to her automobile that I do believe spiritually she wore again two legs. Wine can do that, but not to people who guzzle; only those who sip it find the magic.

CHAPTER XXIV

THE MOON ON A PLATE

I have been accustomed all my life to the delights of gratifying my appetite in the open air. So it is to be expected that I may know things about the serving of cold food out of doors. I know, for example, that it is a gastronomic crime to take chicken from the oven and shove it into an ice-box. When you cook chicken or any other meat that is to be served cold, permit it to cool slowly in the atmosphere of the kitchen. In that way it is transformed into something with a rich flavor; but when the hot chicken goes into the frigid ice-box the bird loses none of its humidity; it becomes something very like a cold storage bird.

I have in my restaurant a refrigerator as big as the living room of the average family; nevertheless I have a *garde à manger* in which foods that have been taken from the oven complete the processes of cooling. Slow cooling is highly important in preserving flavor. A shaded place where food is protected from flies or other contaminating influences is sufficient. My own belief is that what is appropriate food for a hot day is good also on a cold one and vice versa. One's internal temperature does not vary with the weather, consequently I am of the fixed opinion that only our need of energy should govern the character of the food we eat, whether the time is winter or summer. Nevertheless on the hot days anyone is entitled to have his appetite pampered as if he were an invalid. A paper-thin slice of ham in Summer, that is something you can digest without raising your temperature. Aye, provided you have tasted it! There is something to make me irritable: when I have expended energy to present thin shavings of meat, of ham, of roast beef, of veal, of chicken, of tongue, to see some clumsy person cram all kinds into his mouth as if he were a fugitive wolf. The manner of eating is important to the reputation of chefs and maîtres d'hôtel.

Where is the finesse then? The one who does not swallow a morsel of food until it no longer imparts taste to his intelligence, that one never suffers from indigestion nor skin disease nor from a whole catalogue of diseases which I dare not list here lest I be prosecuted for practising medicine without a license. I believe it, and the honest doctors agree, that the magic buckler against disease is a simple thing, merely proper habits of eating. I know it is so out of my own experience and, too, Camous told me when I was a small boy.

Finesse? Sometimes it is almost necessary to insult a customer to employ it. I remember one very hot day in August of 1919 when the rich shipping man, Joseph Moran, came to see me. "I have a party of six for dinner," he told me. "Please serve something to keep everybody in a mood to endure the heat in good humor."

Well, Henri is never one who has to consult cookbooks or almanacs or to seek advice from anyone. Immediately I said: "How would you like to have the moon on a plate? That is nice and cool, hey?" Since I jest habitually with my old customers Mr. Moran was ready for me.

"Some new kind of cake?"

"Not a cake," I said. "What time will you come?"

"Seven-thirty."

"Oh, no! That is a crowded hour." Then I call to my chef, Armand, and I say: "We cannot take Mr. Moran before nine-thirty, can we?" Since Armand is always alert for the hidden meanings in what I say he replied: "There is no room for Mr. Moran's party before nine-thirty."

Well, that made Mr. Moran mad. "A fine way to treat an old customer," he complained.

I was pretty near to losing my own temper when I remembered what it is, finesse. "I promise you at nine-thirty such a meal for a hot night as will make the lovely ladies of your party fancy themselves living in an enchanted world."

I think that day the farmers were praying for rain it was so hot but Henri prayed with so much more verve, so much intensity, that there was no rain and my establishment was crowded. Most of the dining room was like a verandah with so many windows open that the table I had saved for Mr. Moran's party was as cool as possible. I followed the principles of Camous and served him first with a hot consommé, in that way replenishing the energy which had gone from those people during the day of discomfort. Since they were feeling better they ate happily, Mushrooms Henri, squab and *Salade Fleurie.*

Then I came in person to offer the dessert.

"Mr. Moran," I began—

"Joe to you, Henri."

"Monsieur Joe," I resumed, "will you be good enough to follow me into the garden with your friends? I want you to enjoy your dessert in a cooler place."

"Come along," said my friend Joe Moran to his guests, "this fellow Henri has to be humored."

In a place in my garden where the trees had not been tolerated so that the flowers and grass might have full intercourse with the sun I had installed a table. The linen had transformed it into a lovely, frosty cube of white. On the top surface were six slender candles and the waiters were already scampering out of sight as we appeared. They had placed on each plate a *Coupe* Monte Carlo, composed of ice and fruit. But in the center of the table was a cut glass bowl of enormous circumference and for its contents crystal clear, placid water; also the appropriate garniture, flowers. Even as we had walked out of doors the full moon swam above the tops of the trees as if it were eager to peer down into the heart of my fragrant garden. Then as the guests were seated I expelled all my breath in a skillfully guided pouf and extinguished the candles. That was how I captured the moon. It was reflected in that bowl of water as fully shaped as if it had been a turkey to be eaten. Then, while the ladies were still squealing with delight, I placed in Mr. Joe Moran's hands a carving knife and fork.

"Sir," I said to him, "serve your people!"

Mr. Moran had tears trickling down his face then and so did Henri. All the people in my restaurant came to see that cool prisoner before he could make his escape. Above their comments I heard him saying: "Henri, call me Joe and make me proud I have such a friend."

Well, that was the way I served the moon on a plate.

I am not the first to do it. Oh, no, I do not make such a claim, for it is an old trick that was known to the ancients, but in this world of bustling and cafeterias it is a thing that is neglected. It is, as I tell you, a piece of finesse.

According to my philosophy no problem is stated when someone asks what to eat on a hot day. If you have nothing to eat then it becomes a problem; but if you have anything, eat it and be grateful. The grateful being is always comfortable.

CHAPTER XXV

BELASCO'S APPETITE

Scenery is as much a problem at the table as it is in the theater. I tell you that on the high authority of the great dramatist David Belasco. His keen intelligence was quick to sense this kinship between our arts. How I miss him now! Our acquaintance began in Martin's but it ripened when he began coming to Lynbrook. Oh, what stimulating conversations we had! On philosophy, cuisine, the theater, music, service, humanity, women. For more than twenty-five years I put things into his stomach which, by the magic of metabolism became ideas that he could put back into my head.

"Henri," he said to me one Sunday afternoon when he had come into my place, "as I see Marcel or Pierre approaching with a casserole to display a pair of chickens browned as only a Frenchman knows how to brown them, I could cheer. No! I could cry! But with satisfaction. It is like that moment in my theater when the house lights go down and the footlights come up. Anticipation! That's it! That's the key to your secret and to mine."

If you think I would let Mr. Belasco stop there you do not know Henri! Right away I plunged into my cellar and, with the careful hurried pace of one carrying nitroglycerine out of a burning building, returned with a bottle of Pommard, 1888. With silent clappings of his soft and gentle hands he applauded my technique as I drew that cork so carefully it did not squeak in grief as it was parted from its bottle.

He smiled, too, at my scheming. He knew that bottle was the ticket with which I proposed to enjoy the play of his conversation.

You remember that priestly collar he affected? In fancy I see him now with his white hair as a saintly wreath above his face and his hand resting as an invalid's just below his throat. Usually he spoke softly, as if he were instructing some actress how Camille should proceed with dying. Yet while he talked softly his velvety black eyes were fixed on mine. It was all a trick! You think I do not know that? It was one of those subtle things that all good restaurateurs must penetrate by instinct. Besides, no one with his belly filled with the food and wine of Henri could be so feeble as he appeared to be. Mr. Belasco spoke softly so that I would listen to him with all my mind. He was a great one, a real teacher. I think I remember every word he said!

"My friend," he told me after his Adam's apple had moved as he swallowed my Pommard, "your art is kindred with mine in that you too must keep your patrons absorbed in what is happening and also keep them excited about what is to come. Is it not so? If an audience were to walk out of my theater at the end of the first act I would be ruined. If your patrons leave after the soup I am sure you would strangle yourself."

"Sir," I told him, "you are right." Then I filled his glass again.

"In 'The Return of Peter Grimm' there was a piano. Remember? There was a clock, a telephone, a hat rack, a Bible and other things. The audience learned about the Grimm family out of that Bible's fly-leaf. Kathrien played that piano. Marta wound that clock. Peter talked over that telephone about his work. Every object on that stage was put there to help me tell my story. I have watched you many times. Some day I think I will make a play about such a one as Henri Charpentier and I will know how."

The significance of what Mr. Belasco was telling me lies in this, that the pieces of scenery he mentioned were really in the category of properties, objects which had a part in the development of the action of the play. Believe me, it is so at the table: the decorations except for flowers should be an active part of the meal. They should be edible. If you are like the ladies who patronize me now you will challenge me by asking me to demonstrate what I say. *Bien.*

One time when I had returned from America to my home village of Contes where it was erroneously believed that I had become an American millionaire, I was invited to Berre de Contest, a neighboring village higher in the Alps, perhaps four miles from what afterward was named the Rue Henri Charpentier. It was an occasion! Two restaurateurs were the guests of honor and I was one. The other was a distinguished native, my friend Louis Barraya, the proprietor of the Café de Paris. We were a party of twelve and the luncheon arrangements had to be improvised in the auberge of Christini, a man too good to stand in awe of old friends like Henri and Louis. Nevertheless he was perspiring that day, I tell you, when I arrived, the first of the party to come.

"My old one," I said to him, "what is the matter? Why are you nervous on such a simple occasion? We are hungry. We are thirsty. We shall all be glad to be together. Why stew yourself like a tough old rooster?"

"Easy for you to talk, Henri," he chided me, "you a restaurateur who have at your back all the resources of America. But regard me up here, like a goat, on this mountain. How am I to prepare a suitable meal? Tell me!"

"Don't shout!" I cautioned him. "What's the matter? Are there no flowers in your garden?"

"We grow eagles' nests on this high rock," he told me. "What little soil we have is dedicated to our vegetable gardens." When people speak in the self-righteous tone that fellow used you may know they are going to be difficult. Contrary was my friend, and not inventive. But he was a talented cook and he had something very rare in this world, gratitude.

"Um, um, um, my poor dear friend Christini," I said with false sympathy. "I have often felt sorry for you when in America. I have thought of you by turns baking and freezing high on this barren mountain."

"So?" The long moustaches of Christini moved forward like the horns of a goat preparing to charge. He had exhaled a powerful blast of garlic-scented indignation. "So, in that barbarous America you feel sorry for me. Christini, dwelling in this paradise. You, come!" He leveled a forefinger at my chest as if he were half a mind to thrust it through my gizzard. Then he stamped out of doors, into his garden. I tell you, he had not exaggerated. It was a paradise in which he lived, a rugged paradise perhaps, but you should have seen youthful Madame Christini and that garden! The tomatoes were scarlet to such a degree as to make an artistic soul like Henri writhe with sheer delight. Don't ask me why mountain tomatoes should be so vivid. Possibly it is the unobstructed kissing of their skins by ultraviolet rays of the sun. Certainly the big peppers of that hillside garden were varnished with such a green pigment as I do believe is not to be seen in our lower and heavier atmosphere. The lettuce heads were as firm as the calves of the Christini legs, and of the color of the sea close to shore.

We chose the best as if for a competition in a country fair, taking young onions, cucumbers, beets and carrots until we had filled a wicker basket.

"Now Christini," I said when we were back in the auberge, "we have no time to waste because when the others come they will be thirsty and hungry. We must be ready to sit down when they appear."

"As if I did not know!" he burst forth with fresh despair.

"Give me your biggest platter, infant," I commanded him and when he brought it I was filled with envy for it was a very old thing more than a yard long and half as wide at the middle. It was a piece of ancient porcelain treasured up in that Alpine village for who can say how many generations. The tracery of brown cracks in the glaze over its gray-whiteness created such a longing of possession in me as was never to subside. But I went to work.

Diagonally I arranged a row of tomato slices so that it became a stripe of scarlet on the platter; then in turn I arranged other stripes of cucumber slices, of raw carrot thinner than paper. Madame hastened, in response to my shoutings, to deliver to me some beets that she had boiled that morning. Sliced they gave me the magenta stripe my palette needed. The white was made of slices of cold boiled potato. But for every stripe of vegetable on that platter I provided as a companion a wide band of anchovy fillets. And all these stripes moved in echelon in a corridor formed of salami. In those mountain villages salami is highly esteemed.

Since I was a small boy I have been an admirer of those little gray animals, the donkeys of Southern France and Italy. There is a strong appeal for me in their floppy ears, their tiny flint-like hoofs, their patient dispositions and their astonishing ability to stagger home with enormous loads piled on their backs. Perhaps it is because they envy us humans who ride upon them that they have in their flesh such a delicious flavor when they are minced into a sausage skin. After all, I do believe that their flavor is simply the subtle means by which the donkeys take a short cut into more intimate life with mankind. By inducing us to eat them they became emancipated, transmogrified! But wait, not all salami is made of donkey. I hasten to tell you this lest you be prejudiced.

I did not cut thin circles of that sausage, but thick ones and then, with the heavy carving knife I whacked out domino-shaped pieces and then cut them in half. With quick chops of the knife I reduced the remaining pieces of irregular shape into a double handful of pungently flavored meat crumbs. Similarly I reduced the flesh of a double handful of black ripe olives and made thin circles of green from the flesh of brine-cured olives. In the geography of that interesting platter these things became mountains. There was also a hill of chopped lettuce. Do you not see what I had devised? An assortment of hors d'œuvres. This stood in a commanding place on the table, resting on top of a bowl that was large enough to be the porridge dish of the papa bear. But that was not its function, as you shall see, nor were the hors d'œuvres what they seemed to be.

There was excellent sherry in the rock cavern cellar of my friend Christini. When all of us were gathered we who had been boys together toasted one another. Then we sat down to soup and as we ate noisily and swallowed white wine we all feasted our eyes on the rich colors of the platter. Each hungry man ate a dozen times, in fancy, the contents of that noble platter. But when the soup plates were cleared away I took that platter which I so greatly admired and with one thrust of a carving knife along its surface swept its burden into the big bowl. You see, the hors d'œuvres became the salad!

I myself made the French dressing in a marble dish as ancient as the platter. It had been rubbed with garlic and the vinegar was a wine that had soured, keeping its purple color. Finally I adjusted to the completed dish finely chopped tarragon, chives and chervil.

The rest of our meal that bright noon was a mountain cheese brought to the table in a wicker netting in which it had been hanging in the cellar. Oh, yes, and the figs! But the two of us who were restaurateurs were thrilled by the richness of the color in the food we had eaten. Our meal had been dramatized for us. We had eaten it in anticipation until digestion was half accomplished before we swallowed.

I told Mr. Belasco about that Alpine luncheon one time and he nodded in complete agreement with me.

"It is possible to starve with the eyes," he said. "In color we know there is sustenance for the soul; but there is also, I suspect, sustenance for the body. I think the brown skin of your chicken as it comes from the oven is, after all, my favorite color. But what about that platter, Henri?"

"Ah, Mr. Belasco, my friend Christini presented it to me for a souvenir. It hangs on the wall of my villa."

"Hah!" he complained, "you Frenchmen!"

Table decoration is a phase of the art of the restaurateur which too many ladies accept as a formal, a conventionalized thing of fixed rituals; the linen must be so, the flowers so. Ah, they are far too solemn. Life is something to be enjoyed and to be expanded by the imagination.

I tell you it makes me warm inside now to realize that the high art of the restaurateur is no more than a development of the thing which in the kitchen of the home is recognized for what it is, the love of the mother for her family.

So, when my chef exercises his imagination, when he contrives something rich in color, distinguished as to shape and likewise enchanting to the palate I do not want it devoured swinishly. No! I want it to be appreciated. Please, I would say to any husband or any son, when the mama or her adjutant, the cook, produces something from the kitchen that reveals the pains of creation, be appreciative. Do not be a hog. If you voice admiration for a meat pie before you profane it with a fork then when you ask for more, you are giving a shrewd compliment. Next time the food will be even better.

I will tell you how my friend Charles Scotto, who is chef at Pierre's in New York, invented a dessert one time by accident. It was before the war when the big English liner that is now called the *Berengaria* was a German liner, the *Imperator*. It was a great occasion. The general manager of the line, Herr Albert Ballin, was attending, with two hundred other guests, a dinner aboard the ship at her pier. The Prince of Bavaria was to be the guest of honor. It was a great occasion in the life of any chef as you may suppose.

Scotto had caused a great many pineapples to be converted into pleasing dishes. The tropical fruits had been hollowed skillfully. The spiny leaves and top of each pineapple had been contrived into a cover. These hollow pineapples were to be packed with a mixture of pineapple ice and fresh strawberries all flavored with orange cordial, curaçao. There was also a sauce of whipped cream with purée of raspberries. The guests were filing into the great dining salon of the ship when the director of the line visited Chef Scotto and asked what the dessert would be.

"It is called *Rêve de Bébé,* dream of a baby," said Scotto proudly, and gave the details of its preparation.

"Ach," exclaimed the director, "Herr Ballin is forbidden to eat ice dessert. Sherbet for him is impossible."

"Well," said Scotto darkly, "he may have strawberries with sugar and cream."

"A special dish for Herr Ballin at a dinner to the Prince of Bavaria? Nein! Can't you change it?"

"For two hundred people with the meal now being served, you ask me to change the dessert, is that it?"

"Yes," said his German boss.

"All right," said Scotto, "I will do what is impossible: I will change the dessert. Throw the pineapples into the sea!"

Even as he spoke he invented a new thing. He clapped his hands and began to set his subordinates at the task. They brought gallons of milk, crates of eggs, and other material in proportion. But if he were preparing for four persons he would proceed with but a pint of milk. While that was boiling he would mix two ounces of butter with four of sugar and a little grated lemon peel. To this he would add six ounces of flour, and then pour into this the boiling milk, beating it until it became a smooth substance. Then it would be boiled again while the yolks of six eggs were added, after which it would be removed from the fire. As it became lukewarm he would fold into it the white of six eggs, whipped stiff. Then he would pour this into a buttered *soufflé* mold that had been spread with powdered sugar, and then he would cook it for fifteen minutes. It may be served with almost any fruit.

"But did you really throw those wonderful pineapples into the sea?" I asked Scotto.

"But certainly not," he replied. "I myself presented them to the crew, deck hands and stokers. And they applauded me."

CHAPTER XXVI

A Kitchen Phidias

Aye, that is another kindred thing binding the Belascos of the theater with those of us who govern life at the eating table: we want applause for our efforts and if we fail to get it we may have tantrums. And that is true of all who cook. I say this because I know that Mama Camous in her peasant kitchen lovingly modeling a lump of dough into a bread doll baby was, sympathetically and actually, close to those temperamental fellows of the great hotels who are sculptors in ice. I knew one who was a Phidias if you will believe me. But listen:

This fellow was a subordinate of Scotto. In the kitchen of Pierre's this sculptor worked all day at his water-marble. Believe me, I am aware of what constitutes greatness in my own domain and this fellow had it. Camous was a dreamy fellow, too, and he showed me how to carve ice. Salier was one of the greatest of kitchen sculptors. And him I knew very well, too; first at the Métropole in Monte Carlo; then at the Café de Paris and next at the Métropole in Cannes. He could model a castle of ice to be placed on the table of a king and any architect who saw it would gasp with astonishment. Poor old Salier; his fingers relaxed finally a year ago. He was eighty, an artist all of whose dreams had melted into tears. But Scotto's man I do believe was the greatest of all.

Ice is a wonderful medium for an amateur sculptor, a fascinating substance, truly. A carpenter's chisel and a wooden mallet are the first tools. With these you may give a rough form to your vision. Then with a hot flat blade or a soldering iron, proceed to give what you wish to create the fine line of perfection. This fellow who worked for Scotto was skillful as a god. He was the keeper of the *garde à manger;* that is he prepared the cold dishes and the garniture. You see it is only in cold dishes and desserts that the tradition of elaborate decoration persists among those of us devoted to first-class cuisine. This man worked all day long in an atmosphere of a refrigerator, shaping his dreams. No mallet for him; he used the heel of his palm to animate his chisel. For a party of three hundred this fellow would provide thirty or thirty-five separate pieces of sculpture. A swan took time but he could contrive the shape of a fish in ice almost as quickly as you could create the vision in your mind: a can of caviar on the back of such a fish becomes an appropriate thing, eh? or a goose so lifelike as to appear bewitched into crystal would be fashioned by him so that it could be borne into the dining room as the dish of an actual goose's liver in jelly. He would take a three hundred–pound block of ice, divide it in half-a-dozen pieces and then shape each one according to your wish or his fancy. Pierrot and Pierrette? *Oui!* And it was done. A crescent moon as a couch for a maiden, pure at least in her substance, playing a mandolin? He repeated that theme many times. His Indian heads were exceptional for one who perhaps had never seen an Indian. But his portraiture was astonishing. In his blocks of ice he could shape anyone you might show him. The features would remain sharp, photographic, so long as the figure was kept in the ice box; but in the atmosphere of the dining room his portraits soon became blurred, even became caricatures. It was breaking his heart. He did not see he was neglecting the higher art of cooking to pursue his specialty. No! So last year he threw off his white apron, told despairing Scotto farewell and sailed away for Tahiti! Gauguin did that, too; so I will not tell you this fellow's name lest he be embarrassed when he returns from exile, a master of color as well as form. Nowadays he paints, but I suspect that he gets the money for his pigments by carving ice in a South Sea Island hotel kitchen.

Did you know that a revolution in cuisine had released chefs and their assistants from the slavery of a foolish extreme in decoration? The leader of this revolution was the great Escoffier. What Escoffier did was to bring to an end the custom of decorating hot dishes. We still decorate cold dishes, which can be prepared well in advance of a meal, but for hot dishes garniture is all that is required. If that garniture be supplied by intelligence then it will be better than decoration.

Oh, I have spent a large slice of my own life decorating hot dishes. I have worked in a frenzy of inspiration carving designs in a border of noodle paste trying to please my foster-brother, and master, Camous. I have carved carrots, beets, potatoes, parsnips and other root vegetables into shapes like flowers. Now what was the trouble with all that? The patrons were made too much aware that the food had been handled. After all, the food is to be eaten. But there was a further difficulty and that was in the time element. The process of decorating hot dishes was dreadfully time-consuming. That did not matter when all the first-class hotels were conducted on a table d'hôte basis. There is much to be said for that scheme of service. Yet Escoffier was the first man to see that a change had to be made. The world had become—and I regret it—less leisurely. Because of the invention of automobiles, high-speed elevators, airplanes and all the other familiar utensils of transportation, ladies and gentlemen were not having more time, but less. They came, even to the supper table, in a mood of impatience. "Hurry, hurry, hurry," they cried. Well, Escoffier accepted that challenge. Do not forget that he was a great inventor himself but he invented not alone numerous recipes, he also invented new tools. One, a silver serving dish called the Escoffier dish, has compartments and a fitted cover. It is a metallic guarantee that what the chef prepares carefully will not be mishandled by the careless waiter. He was too great a chef to tolerate anything less than excellence; he simply altered circumstances to fit his destiny. With that dish with its compartments noodle paste borders were no longer required as reservoirs to keep the blonde sauce of your fish from forming on the waiter's tray a mésalliance with the brown sauce on somebody else's meat.

Before Escoffier made his changes at the Carlton in London no steak ever arrived at a table in a first-class restaurant unaccompanied by a beet or carrot carved in the likeness of a rose. The vegetable flower would be nestled, perhaps, in watercress. No sober diner ever ate such a flower. It represented waste. It was a piece of nonsense. Today the garniture of watercress remains. It should be selected watercress, crisp, brightly varnished and stems not too coarse. Such a garniture requires nothing else. It is appropriate and complete.

Now, you see? I am not a fanatic about decoration. I want to see imagination employed in the preparation and in the serving of food. But, please, never let me see any garniture that is not designed to be eaten; indeed, never let me see any that does not of itself set the appetite on fire! That is the function of garniture. Truffles and tarragon leaves, white of boiled egg, these are all tempting things in the right place and much more sensible than all that foolishness which Escoffier banished from the first-class kitchens. But these remarks relate to hot dishes. With cold ones the fancy of the chef is permitted to indulge itself. The cold dish is, as I say, prepared in advance. If it is brought to the table lavishly decorated that decoration does not represent any waste of the time of the person who is to eat it. Consequently with cold dishes you may, as did Escoffier, invent as though you were Mr. Edison.

You may create edible flowers with Spanish pimento, with leek stems and tarragon leaves. You may send a cold fish to the table resting on a mosaic pattern achieved with rectangles of corn cut from the cob four grains wide, with slices of carrot, of cucumber, lima beans, green peas and tomato slices. If you have no flowers and wish for something to brighten your table use the green husks from the corn cobs. How? Fix them inside a belt of green, and therefore invisible, thread encircling the dish in which the corn is brought to the table.

I am really grateful to have seen the end of that old-fashioned custom of embroidering good hot food with all manner of noodle paste trimming. For me, Henri, there is beauty in a natural tomato, but something obscene in any effort to disguise its shape. Today if I were asked to serve a saddle of lamb for the King of England (I have done as much for his son and I did as much for his father) the royal decorations would be confined to garniture, truly. On one side, that saddle of lamb would be supported by artichokes and asparagus tips. On the other side there would be a squad of brown, roasted potatoes, some lettuce, more artichokes and a fresh scarlet tomato. "Your Majesty," I would say, "even though you are a king eat this and be grateful. You live in a castle therefore do not expect me to waste time and food building one for you out of mashed potato!"

CHAPTER XXVII

THE LIQUID JEWELS
OF LYNBROOK

When the war was over and the Allies victorious, I was struggling to live after an attack of that influenza which had sent to the cemeteries of Long Island so many long boxes they were piled one on top of another in grisly rows. I had an overpowering desire to see Papa and Mama Camous; but before I returned to Europe there was a debt I wished to pay. Long years before I had while in great trouble borrowed $3,000 from one of my oldest customers, Mr. William Castle. He had sent back the note I had given as security. I had offered to repay the loan earlier but he had asked me to put him at the bottom of my list of creditors and now only one name remained there, that of this man who had known me when I was a waiter in Martin's and who had rejoiced to see me succeed. By that time I had two cellars, the second under the house in which I lived and each was stored with fluid treasures. My emeralds were bottles of old green Chartreuse, my—but, I must remember not to behave as if I were the victim of a fixed idea. Yet I must tell you I had thousands upon thousands of bottles of the best the world afforded of wines and liqueurs. That was the physical form in which I had chosen to keep my wealth. It was a way I understood and loved. Henri was no miser of gold!

I arranged a dinner to which I invited all of the customers who had a place in my heart as well as in my books. One who was there was Mr. Frank O. Burridge, who came to Lynbrook every Saturday and Sunday for twenty years. In the Franco-Prussian War of 1870 his father, an American doctor, had been attached to an ambulance serving the French army and young Burridge had, consequently, lived in Paris during the siege, and gone hungry too.

That night I served ducks, and appropriately they were Long Island ducks. Few people understand how to prepare them, no matter where they come from. Although it is excellent material to grease a swimming duck's feathers, a duck's fat is not fit to be eaten in my opinion. So, put your cleaned, picked duck in a pan over a hot fire and permit him to exude the last drop of his fat, watching to make sure he does not burn. That requires about twenty minutes. Throw away that fat and try again to render out more of it. When this process is complete you are ready to roast your duck; not before under any circumstances. Not all chefs understand this.

Put butter in the pan with the duck when you begin to roast him. Baste constantly and turn the carcass frequently. Then (it will be an hour and a quarter later) remove the duck from the pan. The stock consisting of the butter and the juice of the duck should become the base of a sauce. Take a glass of any good, strong wine, sherry, port or Malaga and pour it into the pan along with thin slices of orange. Cut a piece of orange skin, as thin as a piece of silk. Slice this in strips and add to the sauce. Now, reduce it over a hot fire until it is almost like marmalade in appearance. Next place your duck on a big silver platter, and arrange around his feet and along his sides long spirals of orange peel. Down the median line of his breast and abdomen place at intervals pieces of orange cut round in the shape of buttons and precisely in the center of each of these put a maraschino cherry. Arrange half slices of orange with the peel in a series of scallops around the edge of the platter. Then varnish your duck with the sauce. A Long Island duck is a handsome bird in that condition and should be worth seven dollars.

Well, when Mr. Burridge gazed upon his duck on the night of the party he said: "How different this is from the roasted rats I had during the siege of Paris. And, Henri, I did not have a whole rat ever; only half a one."

"Sir," I said, "I am glad you do not complain about the portions served here."

The one disturbing subject of our conversation that night was the impending change in civilization as it was understood in the United States. All alcohol was to be abolished. People who drank it were to be pariahs. Those who sold it were to be burglars, safe blowers, the lowest of scoundrels. What I thought of it all was well known to every one. A short while before, in July, 1919, when prohibition was assured I had put the flag above the entrance to my premises at half mast. That was no gesture of mockery. It was an action of sincere sadness. To one born a Frenchman, the method by which the nation was undertaking to achieve temperance seemed like madness. I genuinely believed the greatest republic on the earth had begun to kill liberty. Pardon me if you do not agree, but please consider that in one day I was losing not alone a career and a prosperous business but my diet as well.

I had sold the contents of one cellar to about two hundred of my customers. For each a locker was built and we proposed to exist as nearly as possible as we had before this affliction. We were, we thought, to become a club. One of those gentlemen paid me $4,000 for a collection of wines and liqueurs which he hoped would last his lifetime. For myself, in despair I moved, oh, so tenderly, a huge stock into the cellar beneath my house. A third cellar beneath the house occupied by some forty employees of the restaurant was equipped with racks and stocked with more wine. All of us were behaving somewhat, I fancy, in the manner of Noah just before his ark went afloat.

Nevertheless on that October night in 1919 my guests and I toasted each other in Veuve Cliquot until, despite the menace of prohibition, happiness was effervescing in my veins like the wine bubbling in the glasses. Finally, in a silver loving cup I returned to Mr. Castle my check for his generous loan. I told things about myself and my struggle that some of those people did not know. Presently all of them were seeing what was coming from my point of view and yet, the important thing, that night, was that I had so many friends. The occasion was the mountain peak of my career.

The next morning I would not permit my employees to scrub the restaurant. The echoes of the warm testimonials, the toasts of affection and admiration, and yes, the tears, must be left until some tangible bouquet of memory was fixed forever into the atmosphere and physical elements of my restaurant. Of course, I am a sentimental fellow.

I was in a splendid frame of mind the day I went to the French consulate in New York to get my passport viséd. And why not? The poor immigrant of 1906 had become, according to the standards of Contes, magnificently rich. Philomene and I by that time had all four of our children, the two sons and the two daughters. Now, as a prosperous restaurateur, as a father of a family and as a citizen of fabulous America, I was all eagerness to appear once more in the streets of Contes, to embrace Papa and Mama Camus, to hear the welcoming shouts of my friends who had survived the war and to let them hear from my own lips the details of the happy outcome of my adventurings. Oh yes, it was precisely in the spirit with which I had prepared to go home from the Cap Martin when I was a boy of ten that I prepared to leave America in 1919. I did think it was a curious twist of fate, that I, born in France, passionately devoted to France, should have to seek, as an alien, permission to return to those who called me their son. But it was so.

As long ago as 1912 I had stood before a judge in New York and uttered words that had tasted bitter in my mouth, and I think, taste bitter in the mouths of many who adopt citizenship. I had said that I absolutely and entirely renounced and abjured all allegiance and fidelity to France. Could I say such words without reservations? Could I renounce the two who had reared me? Could I abjure Mama Camous? She was and is a part of France. That was a terrible moment for a new citizen of the United States but when the judge of the Federal court understood why tears streamed from my eyes he left his bench, all robed in solemn black as he was, and shook my hand with both of his.

When I walked into the consulate I was thinking about those things, about the momentous obligations I had imposed on myself and my children by the step I had taken. I do not enter into such things lightly. So, then, when the employee of the consulate to whom I handed my American passport questioned its authenticity there was an exchange of words in which I delved deeply into all six of my vocabularies. Finally he flung the passport to the floor.

Then I really did inflate myself with wrath. With fingers tensed and ready I ordered him to pick up that document or himself be flung end over end through the window. He picked it up; but he did not visé that paper. In consequence I landed in Genoa, October of 1919, and then, in the town of Bordighera, Italy, Henri the exile prepared a great feast.

There was wine and food, not so good as I could have produced from my own cellar and kitchen in Lynbrook, but nevertheless excellent. There was an orchestra. There were flowers in profusion and then into this scene of splendor there came in their peasant clothes my Papa and Mama Camous. The Sunday suit the old man wore was one he had owned since 1899! How often I rubbed my fingers over the fabric; how sweet it was to hold the calloused fingers of my foster-mother, my *maman nourrice!*

I was possessed then by a great yearning to overwhelm those old people with a proof of my gratitude for my happy childhood. In that town of Bordighera the Queen Mother of Italy had a villa and so when I found there was for sale in the same street another villa I knew what to do. I bought it. A place fit for a queen would be suitable for Sandrina Camous. There was a palmerie, many acres of small palms destined to grow up in pots in hotel and restaurant lobbies. There were other acres planted with mimosa trees and myriads of orange trees. These produce not fruit but flowers to be crushed for their perfume. And in that fragrant atmosphere I brought my Mama Camous to live.

There is on that estate a tower with windows of colored glass and from it one can see all of that blue water of the Mediterranean that lies between Bordighera and Mentone. The two capes are the horns of the crescent which embraces that lovely bay and they seem likewise to embrace the full scope of my career.

Every winter but one after 1919 I soothed myself on the Riviera. I love it as it was loved by those two gourmets, Edward and Leopold. The steep rocks which are neither too high nor too insignificant, speak to me. The flowers have a special smile of recognition for me, the native. The birds sing more sweetly when I walk beneath their trees and mine. At night the moon is swollen with pride and the stars invite me to catch their twinkles in my eyes. The land is tingling with charm and romance.

CHAPTER XXVIII

HENRI, THE OUTLAW

In January, 1920, after an exchange of cablegrams between my son and myself, all my customers came and emptied their lockers of the fine wines which had been stored in them. It had been a silly idea, that one. They could still eat a few things at the Restaurant Henri but the law was unmistakable: it would be a crime for them to drink there. And most of the dishes we were accustomed to serve would be felonies during the process of cooking.

Then in April, 1920, I returned to the United States. The big hotel men of my acquaintance were shrugging their shoulders and watching their business go to ruin. The Hotel Knickerbocker became an office building. So did the Hotel Manhattan. Prohibition, they said, was a *fait accompli*. Why struggle? I did not feel so but I violated the law only in technical ways and not deliberately during many months. Yet I say again it was utterly impossible for me to obey it completely without destroying myself. I went abroad again; this time to France as the passport difficulties had been cleared up with an apology to me.

In June, 1922, when prohibition had been the law for two and a half years, I returned from France and found that more than a score of employees had vanished. The Restaurant Henri had only two waiters and they were half idle. I was on the way to becoming a poor man again. Everyone told me I was the only fool in America. Everyone seemed to be right. The highways were crowded with the traffic of bootleggers.

Everywhere I went I saw people poisoning themselves with concoctions which seemed to transform them into maniacs. What I then did seemed to me then, and seems now, to have been something I need not blush to tell to my dead mother. I began again to conduct a restaurant and, in a few weeks, my waiters returned to work.

I had never been in the business of making drunkards. On the contrary I had always dealt with ladies and gentlemen which is a complete statement of the case.

There was one hideous aspect to the new arrangement in my life. It began when two men walked into the restaurant and displayed badges. They were, it seemed, interested in the publication of a book. What was the book about? Did it matter? Would I not be willing to contribute a few hundred dollars toward the publication of a book telling of the heroism of agents of the United States Government? Well, I paid. I paid month after month and year after year. And the payments put scars on my soul. The finest people on earth were served in my establishment in those years; gentlemen of royal blood; men who will be kings, great generals, judges, financiers; the most distinguished men in the eastern part of the United States, their wives; and now at this minute I realize that all of them were criminals and so I must not name them even though I am convinced they would be proud to name themselves as outlaws along with Henri.

Below the surface of my park there had been built a lengthy hidden passageway which led to a big and unsuspected subterranean chamber. Sometime, I thought, it would be wise to move the best of my store of wines and liqueurs into that secret cavern; especially the numerous bottles of 1805 brandy. My replenishments came to me a few bottles at a time by way of Canada and never, I assure you, from a bloodthirsty bootlegger but always from a kindly citizen who had been prior to 1920 a quite law-abiding liquor dealer. I had always hated to disturb my wines and so I delayed from month to month.

Ten years after prohibition began my oldest son, Camille, spoke to me. He learned his English in America, on Long Island. "Pop," he said, "will you be a sucker all your life? These chiselers do not represent anything. They are just grafters. Quit handing out money."

"My boy," I said, "we are in a situation—"

"Pop," he insisted, "will you listen to reason? Everybody—"

The Original Restaurant Henri was inhabited by a gay throng on a

Friday night in June, 1930. In the chauffeurs' dining room a piano sounded faintly; but there was no other music. Then there was a sudden rush of new customers. A party of six, another party of four and another of two. Tables were found for them.

The three women and the men of these parties of strangers were all in evening clothes and, therefore, not conspicuous among the other guests; except for their thirsts. They wanted old-fashioned cocktails at the table of six. The party of four wished for champagne. But my waiters would not serve these strangers. Then the women began to cajole and implore. Eventually one of them named as her close friends two dear friends of mine. The waiters consulted. The champagne and the cocktails were brought. These parties continued to eat; onion soup, Chicken Beaulieu and Crêpes Suzette. They had four bottles of champagne and then, when their bill for $122 was presented, it began.

In an adjoining room of the restaurant I was talking to some of my friends when my ears were filled with the sound of a revolver shot. Then Camille, my son, appeared in the room, pale and clutching in his hands the dinner checks of that night's business. After him came his pursuers. Other men jumped into the restaurant from the out-of-doors.

"What is it?" I demanded this of Camille.

"Pop," he said, "these fellows are revenue cops."

Then I took charge.

"You don't need to shoot around here," I said. Two of the men had been displaying revolvers and one of these was pressed against the back of my son. My customers, of whom there were about a hundred and twenty-five that night, settled back into their chairs for a little while. Then they paid their checks and departed from one table after another.

All of my employees, my son and myself were herded into the small room which serves me as an office and held there as prisoners.

"Tell me where you keep your wines and give me the keys," he said. "If you don't we'll ransack the place, break all the glasses and everything."

What I said to him is not, I suppose, important but in conclusion I said: "The porter has the keys to everything and will hand them over to you. I direct him to do so."

All night long I heard my wines being carried out of the cellar. My waiters were forced into this labor. I heard a truck depart, with noisy back-firing of its engine; then more trampling feet, the occasional breakage of a bottle, the shrill laughter of women and the departure of another truck load. This continued throughout the night. I had counted the departure of a truck seven times. Then my cellars were emptied but my heart was full of grief.

We all rode to Jamaica in the patrol wagon of Lynbrook. After the formalities of bail I found those kind-hearted policemen of the patrol wagon, Lynbrook neighbors, waiting to ride us home. When we reached there again, at dawn, I found the women, my wife, my little daughter, two women employees, in tears.

I was never punished. That is, the outlaw, Henri Charpentier, was never found guilty of any crime. A Federal judge repeatedly refused to padlock my restaurant. He declined to believe it was a nuisance. Perhaps I am prejudiced but I do agree with him.

CHAPTER XXIX

A New Restaurant

After the sack of my establishment by the prohibition raiders I found myself in a deplorable state of mind. My customers, since they were gentle people, were reluctant to spend an evening in a place from which the soul was gone. So they gave me neither the consolation of their presence nor the means to deal with pressing worries. I had my beautiful trees and I could give them water. I had a garden and the conviction that somehow I would be able to feed my wife and our children; but there were the waiters and the others who worked for the restaurant in Lynbrook. Some had been with me for twenty years. For each one I had such a feeling as made me accept the responsibility for his family. How can I explain that since it is a sense of obligation that seems to come to me out of the past of my ancestors? For that matter how may I hope to explain to anyone other than myself that complete sense of outrage, the whole crashing down of the structure of my life that resulted from the looting of my cellars? Four-fifths of my life, I told myself, were gone. What could be done with the remaining years except to suffer in regret? There was no money to meet a pay-roll any longer. I had the feeling which was intolerable, that somehow I had been an enormous failure. So I went back to France to put myself in contact with things that would give me a perspective. In Lynbrook I was "boss" or "Pop" or "Mister" but in Contes and nowhere else there was one who could think of me only as *"petit."*

It was a sure instinct that took me back to Sandrina Camous, my *maman nourrice.*

There in Contes I began to feel anew the stirring of that which had made me stubbornly hold to my pride when I was a starving child in London, when I was abused in the army and in other periods of stress. Unhappily this spirit, after the affair at Lynbrook, had taken its shape too much from the modeling fingers of anger; it wanted softer touches. I knew that. Reflecting on it now I realize that my need was chiefly for humility. After all, I was not the only one in the world who suffered.

One day I determined to go to Nice and from there to Mentone, to the Hotel Cap Martin. I strode through its doors and stood in the lobby feeling the soft pile of the rugs beneath my shoes. I had an un-lighted cigarette in my mouth. A small page boy, a very small page boy, stood nearby. He looked with unseeing eyes.

"Jean," I spoke softly and he did not respond.

"Petit." This time I spoke more loudly and he turned. His eyes were wide now and in them I seemed to see myself.

"You want to be a hotel man, eh?" I spoke in the patois of Nice and he understood me better than if I had used French words.

"Yes sir!" He spoke with emphasis.

"Then the first thing you must cultivate is an ear wonderfully sensitive. When someone calls you 'Jean' you for the moment be 'Jean.' But what is your name, *petit?*"

"André," he said.

"All right, André," I went on. "Never keep more than one eye on the front door. Reserve one eye for the lobby. Be alert. When I was a page boy here—"

"Oh, sir," he exclaimed with incredulity. "What are you saying? When you were page boy here!"

"A fact," I boasted, "and if you will go with me to the cellar I will show you a stain from ink which I threw there in carelessness and for which offense I was cuffed. They do not paint the underside of cellar steps. It must be there still—"

"It is, it is," said little André with excitement and led the way. And so down in the cellar of that hotel on the Cap Martin I handed to little André a piece of gold as big as if I were Mr. Cyril de Cordova who tips like nobody else I have ever known. And then I sat down on the cellar steps and wept because I was no longer a page boy. I tell you there are a lot of curious processes involved in the making of one Henri.

I believe now that in those moments of weeping my spirit had a new birth. I know it was then that I realized that fears and worries were too big a cargo for the soul of any man. Courage! That, I determined, should be the sole ingredient of myself for the balance of my years, whether many or few. I came home as quickly as I could and tried again to make of Lynbrook what it had been. But how could I accomplish anything when at brief intervals surly government agents appeared and demanded opportunities to make chemically sure that my wine vinegar was not wine, that my children's dentrifice was not alcoholic, that the water in the bowl for the use of the house cat was not in disguise a dish of cocktails? Then the chance came to become manager of the new playground of the rich of Long Island, the Atlantic Beach Club. I took the position never suspecting that it was simply the place where Destiny proposed to reveal to Henri that once more the world could be transformed into the shape of his oyster. How simply it began! Just the voice of a friend coming over a telephone line.

"Henri?"

"Oui."

"Jack Grubman. Listen—"

"My friend! A guitar would not sound so sweetly! How is Madame? How is—"

"Listen, Henri. *La Maison Française,* the French government and Mr. John D. Rockefeller, Jr., are seeking a restaurateur of high quality, of French birth and experience. If you had not quit Lynbrook to be a club manager I would never have suggested that you transplant yourself—"

"My dear friend!"

"Come in to see me quickly. This is a good chance."

Well, after my talk with Mr. Grubman so great was my hurry, so hot was the fire of my ambition that I could not wait for the sailing to Europe of a French boat; instead I went aboard a German boat, the *Bremen,* and when I arrived in Paris, when I had told my part of my story, of my experience, to the gentlemen representing the Maison Française, the Rockefeller Corporation and the French Government, all agreed with me and with Mr. Jack Grubman, that I was the complete recipe for what was needed at Rockefeller Center. I signed the first contract at the American consulate in Paris. At that moment Henri was on the road back.

When I came back to Long Island, Philomene and I, we discussed these things. What about Lynbrook? If prohibition was to be canceled then once again it could be a place of delight for the gourmets. I knew I loved that place but Philomene is a creature of great sagacity. She said: "I will be the proprietor of the Original Henri Restaurant to make sure that our Camille responds to all our teachings. Therefore you proceed to create in New York a restaurant that will in its gay and gentle atmosphere demonstrate what a colossal mistake was prohibition."

So we decided. But a fine restaurant, the finest restaurant is not made without money. Money was becoming very, very scarce in the late Autumn of 1933. I had a little, but I had something worth more than money: I had and I hope I shall have always, a genius for friendship. Never, keeping that talisman, shall I have to worry about Henri. I had to post $14,000 for a guarantee on one of my contracts; there was another big sum demanded of me as a payment on furniture and kitchen fittings. I dare not think now how little real cash I had when there came to me at Lynbrook one of the former employees, Marco Perino, the father of six children. This was just before Christmas.

"Boss," said Marco, "you have been kind to thousands. Year after year I have watched you feed out the back door the money you were taking in at the front. You look to me very much depressed. What is it?"

"Money," I said to him.

"So I think," said Marco, and then he placed in my hand four savings bank books in which for years he had been making small deposits on behalf of his children.

"Boss," he said, "no guarantee of any kind from you. I lend it to you as if you were my father."

Perhaps you did not know that tears had varying flavors. On that day mine were very sweet.

Another day in that period when I was striving to make a fabric of the raveled ends of my affairs there came to Lynbrook an old customer, Mr. Robert Hague, Vice-President of the Standard Oil Company of New Jersey.

"Henri," he said, "maybe you will be needing some cash in this new enterprise."

"Mr. Hague," I said, "the Lobster Henri must have given you pre-science."

"Anyway," he replied, as he pressed a paper into my hand, "here is some and I am wishing it was a thousand times more."

Scotto, taking off for half a day his cap and apron and his great authority as chef at Pierre's, came for a visit during an afternoon at Lynbrook.

"Henri," he said, "you do not smile enough nowadays. This envelope contains something designed not to help you but to help me by making you smile." That envelope contained the wages of Scotto for some months.

Another day a friend of mine who is poor as the devil most of the time came in to see me. He had worked for me in other days.

"Boss," he said, "I am in a great hurry because if I do not hurry I won't have this two hundred dollars which I want to put behind you now. Banks? Pouf! You are my bank."

Those sorts of loans, evidences of pure friendship, are the precious bricks with which I have enclosed my restaurant in Rockefeller Center.

On the very day before the restaurant was opened Mr. Jack Grubman came into it. That gentleman is a direct descendant from King Solomon.

"Henri," he said, "your place is fine but I think the walls are too bare. For so great an expanse of nakedness even a Venus would require a chemise and for your purpose I have at home precisely the garments required."

Early the next morning there arrived a Gobelin tapestry and another equally fine, miracles of weaving, each one a museum piece, and the insurance on them was paid so that I do not have to lie awake at night with worry for their safety. Often I look up at one of them, at a knight fixed in its pattern as by enchantment, and I think to myself that I have such ancestors blended in my own being which is a nice sensation; and then I find myself feeling sorry for those embroidered likenesses of heroic men. After centuries the fumes of my Crêpes Suzette, I think, will be making those poor fellows regret that they do not have stomachs.

CHAPTER XXX

The Goose
Is Not Quite Cooked

Only one thing puzzles me: Why should I continue to work, to engage with problems of great proportions when, always, the past beckons me to enter into a dreamy world of delight, peopled by ladies of Maxim's, by princes and princesses, by Edward and Leopold, by the fabulous talents of Camous, Escoffier, Antoine the carver, Baptiste the waiter and all the others? But I know the answer even while I am puzzling. It is because for me there is the excitement of adventure in preparing such a thing as an order of Crêpes Suzette and then watching after a lovely lady has had her first taste, to see her smile and know that actually what I compounded was not Crêpes Suzette but a later stage in its transmogrification, a happy human being. The seed Camous planted in me has grown until now the restaurateur dominates my being. Sometimes it pleases me to think that I have become another joint in the great arm of Camous and that if he could observe me now he would be gratified. Indeed, sometimes if you should see me lost in thought then you will know that again the great Camous and the *petit* Henri are in conference. Many of my thoughts when voiced are but echoes of him.

"Hey," he would say to a cook or a waiter, "why don't you take a knife and cut off the ends of your fingers so that no nails will grow upon you? Then you could not have nails in mourning. But if you won't cut off your fingers then please me by cutting the nails until they are shorter than the fingers."

Again I see him in one of those kitchens where we worked together and he was angry. He would push his stiff white chef's hat a little to one side so that it slanted like a donkey's ear when it is annoyed. Then he would put his beard in his mouth and bite it and talk to himself words that no one else could understand. At such a time you would know that the chef, Camous, was very, very angry; that he might kill a lion with one stab of a knife. One day possibly three hundred people had come to the Frascati from Paris for dinner; all the orders were à la carte; nothing was wanted by that army of customers that had been prepared in advance. Just before those people came you might have heard in the kitchen the drip from the ice-box but within a few minutes the big, steamy, hot chamber was roaring with sound. When you understand one of those battles of mealtime then only will you be able to interpret the commands, the responses and the other outcries. I heard: *"Faites marches,"* and knew that some other splendid thing had been placed on the fire. These were not ham-and-egg orders. For each patron there was a need in a succession according to whim, of a soup, fish, an entrée, a *timbale* of something, a roast, vegetable, salad, dessert, coffee and liqueurs. From the caviar on to the waiter's tip there was never a mistake. Now how could that be in a place that sounded as if a battle were being fought? The subordinate cooks were all shouting, *"bon," "bon," "bon"* and each *"bon"* was a signal that an order was understood. Sometimes I would hear *"aller retour"* which meant that a cook was telling a waiter to go to the dining room and return by which time the order of food he desired would be ready. Whenever Camous heard that phrase *"aller retour"* he would become alert; if he heard it twice from the same cook he would begin to bite his beard.

As a *commis* it was my job to listen for a cook to express a want, such as "three grouse." Instantly I would start running for the *garde à manger* and quickly as clapping your hands I would be back with the birds. Now a grouse is never put to the fire until the waiter is actually there ready to receive it because it must be cooked just to a point, with the juice running. It was such an order that fired Camous to a rage. He knew that a waiter who had come for grouse had been told *"aller retour."* He came plunging along the alleyway between the ranges and the tables heedless of all who were in his path. He seized that dilatory cook and shook him until I heard the man's teeth rattle. He put him down in the manner that a soldier would stab his rifle with bayonet at an object on the ground. Then Camous snatched up the grouse that I had brought and had them cooking before I could complete a wink of astonishment. When the waiter had received the grouse and scampered off toward the swinging doors to the dining room Camous looked up to focus his rage once more upon the recreant cook but all that was left of that fellow was his cap and apron; they were limp on the floor where he had thrown them in lieu of his resignation.

When I began to hunt for a chef for my new restaurant I wished with a great longing for Camous but that foster-brother, that preceptor of mine, has been dead now for a long time. I searched my mind for an available one who had worked and learned his craft in those playgrounds of Europe where Camous became great. Having found one do you think that Henri tells that fellow how to cook? Oh, no indeed, for chefs are like poets and each one must be permitted to express himself; for that matter, so are restaurateurs. When I step into a kitchen of my restaurant in the Maison Française be sure I step lightly even though it is my own and every lady who has a cook will know why that is. I am content to look upon him, note his black hair, his trimmed black moustache, his brown eyes and to remember that he is a native of Mentone, born so close to the Hotel Cap Martin that probably his mother inhaled the odors from its kitchen. But after all a chef is by no means all of a restaurant.

Afar off in Egypt there sing today a species of quail no bigger than sparrows. Their flesh is something to tempt the ancient kings to walk forth from their silent tombs. These tender little birds are caught, drawn and plucked by brown men subject to superstitions with which I am not in accord; but they are a part of my restaurant. Those Egyptian quail are an exquisite delicacy I could not have but for those brown men. We serve very few and lose maybe ten dollars doing it but if a gourmet enters and demands Egyptian quail it is better that I should not be embarrassed by offering him something else even when my own palate tells me that American quail are better.

Truffles are another matter. Those muzzled pigs and dogs of France that hunt with delicate noses until they come upon their hiding places a foot or a foot and half in the earth, those creatures, too, are a part of my restaurant. In old Martin's we would use of truffles about four pounds in a night and when at the Restaurant Charpentier we serve as much then I shall know in truth that prohibition has become no more than a bad dream of history. With duty, one pays 225 francs for two pounds of truffles. For what reason? In a truffle, I would tell you though the words were my last, there is a flavor so delicate, so splendid, that it cannot be described. It is a piece of Heaven attained on earth.

Once more I find myself buying from France *morilles* which are special mushrooms. The people who hunt for those in Provence, they too, are a part of my restaurant. These mushrooms are dark gray and vaguely, because of the holes in their texture, resemble pumice stone. The odor is as fine if not better than that which you may snuff from a cooked truffle. A few pieces of *morille* on roast pork or chicken or veal lifts those things from the barnyard to the topmost Heaven. When I am tired, down and, in spite of the Salvation Army, out, I take some for myself with roast pork and red wine. For me the combination is a magic carpet. I close my eyes as soon as I have shut my lips upon a morsel. It becomes a part of me as I taste. That is the sense, my taste, that wafts me over the gigantic buildings of New York, across the sea and lowers me tenderly amid scenes that I love. I see in the South of France, anywhere from Marseilles to the Riviera, or, possibly, in Spain, some old woman or a young one, bare-legged, hunting among the olive trees for those wild things which never can be cultivated and which appear so infrequently as if to mark and bless the spot where some sacred foot had touched the ground. For the poor peasant it is easy to believe that this is the case because in one rare day, if he or she is very lucky, very well favored, a fortune may be revealed in some sudden sprouting of *morille*. Think what eight or ten pounds of these things would be worth to a peasant when the price in a French market often is as much as the equivalent of a dollar and a half a pound. Heigh ho; one little piece in my mouth and in fancy I can see an olive orchard and in the shaded grasses what appears to be a stone and Henri knows that stone is a *morille* mushroom.

I never could, I think, be made to see any fascination in an addiction to narcotic drugs when in a bewildering catalogue of foods as yet untasted there are so many unrealized exquisite sensations for the palate. It may be true of the cobbler that his shoes are the shabbiest; but of the restaurateur believe that he eats with the most complete appreciation the best of his viands except when you are his friend whom he loves and then, and then only, you may eat better. If you have been cultivating your palate as one cultivates an ability to appreciate music; oh, my friends, do as I: some day, close your lips upon a sip of red wine of vintage quality and then take a morsel of roast pork and *morille*.

The memories of our later days become fogged when youthful ones remain clear but one that is carved into my mind like the pattern on a buffet table ham is of my experience on the opening day of the Restaurant Charpentier in Rockefeller Center. What happened? Almost the worst!

In the beginning it had been decided that there would have to be a dumb-waiter to facilitate the service between the kitchen and the dining room. Now, at the very moment when my place was most crowded with old Lynbrook patrons, with the finest people I know, that dumb-waiter became stuck in its shaft. I think one of the boys accidentally put into its shelving a casserole with a handle projecting; certainly the mechanism would go neither up nor down. My place was like a man with a fish bone in his throat. In the dining room were hungry stomachs, delicate perceptions, numerous true gourmets and close observers of life. Should I fail at such a time?

To the *commis* who brought me word of the sudden cessation of service I was gentle in a ferocious kind of way; I thrust him from my path so he would not be hurt by my hurry. Through the doors and down the too-small flight of steps I hurried putting myself at the bottom of a bottle neck through which nothing could pass. Down there were most of the frantic waiters, each one like a mother when the house is on fire, only here the children were such things as sea bass just from the "salamander," *Petite Marmite* with the croutons just gone afloat in the tureen, grapefruit cocktails, oysters, lobster specialties, Chicken Beaulieu and a hundred other things. Each waiter thought honestly that the particular thing he was bringing was the one most likely to suffer by delay. That was the situation into which I stepped. Why are your boys sent to Annapolis, to West Point? Why are crown princes carefully educated? For emergencies! Now, in this situation, I knew I was a restaurateur in all my fibers. I took command.

"Stop!" To some I spoke in English; to others in French; to some in Spanish. When I had everyone's attention I outlined the plan for a bucket brigade to pass the used dishes and silver down the narrow steps while the entrées, the wines and everything else were proceeding up into the dining room. Things began to move; but in my heart I was aching with disappointment not to be upstairs where I could be shaking hands and clinking glasses (mine, except for a few drops, empty, of course) with old, old friends. Oh, how I hated to miss that reception! But I was glad to be confident that my maîtres d'hôtel, Louis, Jean and Jules, would be carrying on with aplomb, with exquisite courtesy, with finesse. To myself I was saying: "This battle is nearly won." I saw that the desserts were passing from hand to hand up the flight of steps. Along came a masterpiece of the chef, a Cake St. Honoré. It is made with small puffs stuffed with cream and candied oranges; the inside is cream Monte; the whites of eggs beaten stiff with a cup of cream and thickened in a double boiler. That cream can be decorated with any kind of fruit and on this day of days, please believe me, our Cake St. Honoré was a thing for architects to study. Whose hand slipped I do not know. I do not wish to know until the District Attorney is my best customer and finds me so indispensable to his happiness he will permit me to murder. That soft stiffness of cream and white of egg fell and shattered itself on the head of a pantryman. Do not wonder if my voice for one agonized instant was heard by my patrons in the dining room.

But of forty-six who served with me on that feverish day only two were cowards and quit; they were not of the stuff that is required to make good waiters. My own excitement did not subside by one degree for eleven days when I confronted a figure which revealed that two thousand were the number of customers who had been turned away without service. My French blood can not tolerate that kind of success. It is waste.

———

Well, this Henri Charpentier is pretty nearly cooked to a point; but in his little oven he is pretending to be not quite brown enough, since for many many years to come he wishes to delude Destiny into the belief that a particular goose is not quite done, and should be left for a time in its bubbling juices, to improve further its flavor.

Recipes
by
Henri Charpentier

Quantities Given Are for Four Persons

MEATS

STEAK D'AGNEAU MASCOTE

3 lbs. of lamb steak—center cut (4 slices)
Butter (approximately 3 tablespoons)
2 tablespoons white wine or sherry

Place meat in saucepan with small quantity of butter and cook under a high flame until browned on each side (about 12 minutes). Remove meat and add to the remaining juice the white wine or sherry and 2 tablespoons of sweet butter.

TO SERVE: Pour sauce over meat, garnishing with truffles, sliced artichokes and small potatoes which have been fried in butter.

NOISETTE D'AGNEAU ARLESIENNE

2 racks of lamb (5 lbs.)
1 eggplant
4 fresh tomatoes, peeled and seeded
1 lb. potatoes
½ cup Sauternes
8 tablespoons butter
1 tablespoon olive oil
1 teaspoon chopped onion
Salt and ground pepper
1 teaspoon of chopped parsley

Cut racks of lamb into 8 pieces and remove the bones. Heat in a saucepan on top of the stove some butter mixed with olive oil. When it is very hot place the meat, seasoned with salt and pepper, in the pan. Cook for about 12 minutes (6 minutes on each side). Peel and slice the eggplant. Fry in oil or butter (8 minutes). Place the tomatoes, quartered, in very hot butter to which has been added the chopped onion. Cook this for 10 minutes under a high flame, add salt, pepper and parsley, then cook for an additional 2 minutes.

Fry in hot butter the potatoes cut in small squares.

Take meat from pan and add to the meat juice, while very hot, the Sauternes. Boil over moderate flame until the wine turns brown (2 or 3 minutes). Remove from fire and add a small quantity of sweet butter.

TO SERVE: Place on the meat the eggplant and on the eggplant the tomatoes. Pour over this the sauce. Arrange potatoes on the side.

EMINCE DE BOEUF PALOISE

2 lbs. of beef
½ lb. sliced fresh mushrooms
6 tablespoons butter
1 tablespoon oil
1 glass of dry white wine
1 tablespoon of chopped parsley
1 tablespoon of chopped chives
Salt and ground pepper

Remove all fat from the meat and slice beef, not too thick. Heat 3 tablespoons of butter and 1 tablespoon of oil. When very hot add beef seasoned with salt and pepper. Cook five minutes, turning constantly. Remove meat from pan, placing it on hot plate at the side of the stove. Pour out the oil and butter, and without washing the pan, add the wine. Cook for two minutes; add mushrooms and chives (which have previously been browned in butter), cook for an additional 2 minutes and pour over the meat. Garnish with chopped parsley. Heat 2 tablespoons of butter and pour on top.

BEEF À LA MODE (BOEUF BRAISÉ À LA MODE)

4 lbs. of roast beef
Butter
2 cloves of garlic
2 onions
2 bay leaves
1 pint of purée of tomatoes
2 fresh tomatoes
1 pint of red wine
2 carrots
1 piece of celery

Roast the meat for about 10 minutes until it is browned.

In a separate pan place a small piece of butter. Heat the butter and add garlic, carrots and celery. When browned, combine with the meat, add wine, purée of tomatoes and fresh tomatoes. Cover and cook slowly on top of the stove for two hours. When a fork plunged into the meat comes out clean the meat is thoroughly cooked. Remove meat, skim all fat from the sauce and strain.

Serve with garniture of cooked carrots, onions, mushrooms and green peas.

TRIPE MENTONNAISE

10 lbs. of belly tripe, cut in strips about ½ inch wide and 2 inches long.
4 pieces of celery
10 medium-size onions, minced fine
6 leeks, minced
2 bay leaves
Salt and ground pepper
2 cloves of garlic
2 small bunches of parsley
12 fresh tomatoes, peeled and seeded
2 cloves
¾ qt. of white wine
½ pt. olive oil
1 teaspoon of thyme

Pour the oil in a large pan and when hot add the onions, leeks and celery. Cook until light brown using moderate fire. Then add garlic, bay leaves, parsley, thyme, tomatoes, cloves, pinch of salt and ground pepper and the tripe. Pour the wine over this and cover tightly. Place under medium flame or in oven of moderate temperature for twenty-four hours. Season to taste before serving.

PAUPIETTE MENAGÈRE

3 lb. hip of beef
½ lb. country sausage—skinned
1 clove of garlic
1 tablespoon chopped onions
1 tablespoon chopped parsley
8 tablespoons butter
1 cocktail glass of sherry
1 pint of Burgundy
2 tablespoons of parmesan cheese
Salt and ground pepper
1 tablespoon of dried mushrooms
½ lb. noodles
1 sliced carrot
1 sliced onion
Parsley root, chopped
Celery
1 bay leaf
½ teaspoon of powdered thyme
1 teaspoon of flour
3 tomatoes, peeled and seeded
Olive oil

(Cut meat in 8 slices and pound with handle of large knife. Place dried mushrooms in hot water for half an hour.)

Heat 4 tablespoons of butter, add onions and brown. Combine with this the garlic chopped fine and the mushrooms. Cook for 2 minutes and let cool. Then mix the onions, garlic and mushrooms with sausage meat, seasoning, chopped parsley and sherry. Divide the filling into 8 portions and spread over meat slices. Roll each piece of meat and tie as you would a package. Heat the remaining butter with some olive oil. When it is very hot add the meat. Let it brown thoroughly (10 minutes). Then add carrot, sliced onion, celery, bay leaf and thyme. Cook an additional 5 minutes. Spread flour on the meat, add Burgundy and about 2 pints of boiling water (just enough to cover the meat) and the tomatoes. Cover and cook for 45 minutes or more. Strain the sauce.

Serve with boiled noodles, buttered and spread with parmesan cheese.

FRICANDEAU DE VEAUX AUX EPINARDS

1 lb. leg of veal (one piece)
small veal bones
½ lb. pork lard, unrendered,—2 slices
1 carrot, quartered
1 onion
3 pieces of celery
½ of a bay leaf
2 cloves of garlic
4 tomatoes
3 pieces of parsley root
1 glass of white wine
1 cup of salt
Pepper
4 lbs. of spinach
Butter

Put ¼ of a bay leaf on each lard slice. Place the meat between the lard slices so that the bay leaves are against the veal. Tie with string.

Heat butter in a deep pan; add veal, veal bones and garlic. Brown on top of the stove for about 20 minutes, turning meat several times. Cover the pan and place in oven of medium temperature for half an hour. Then add the onion, carrot, celery and parsley roots. When vegetables are browned (ten minutes), add wine. Five minutes later add the tomatoes. Cook for additional 15 minutes. Remove meat and permit sauce to cook for ten minutes before straining.

Meat should be basted every ten minutes while in oven. Wash spinach thoroughly, place in boiling water with 1 cup of salt to retain fresh green color. Boil for 12 minutes. Strain carefully, squeezing out any surplus water. Heat 2 tablespoons of butter; add spinach, salt and pepper. Cook for a few minutes.

TO SERVE: Pour sauce over meat. Serve spinach separately.

GRENOUILLE PROVENÇALE

2 lbs. of frogs' legs, medium size
½ lb. butter
1 tablespoon of olive oil
1 tablespoon chopped parsley
2 cloves of garlic, powdered
½ cup of milk
½ cup of flour
Salt and ground pepper
Juice of half a lemon
1 teaspoon chopped chives

Dip frogs' legs in milk seasoned with salt and pepper and pass through flour. Heat 2 tablespoons of butter and 1 tablespoon of oil. Add frogs' legs. Cook until browned (about 12 minutes). Remove to plate placed on corner of stove. Pour over lemon juice, add parsley, chives and pepper. Brown remaining butter, until hazel nut color, moving pan constantly. Add garlic and quickly pour over frogs' legs.

Garnish with lemon slices.

BRAISED SWEETBREADS, SAUCE MADEIRA

2 pair of fresh sweetbreads
¼ lb. butter
1 glass of white wine
1 cup of Maderia
1 sliced carrot
1 sliced onion
4 chopped tomatoes
3 pieces of celery
½ of a bay leaf
1 pinch of thyme, powdered
1 cup of beef broth
4 veal bones, chopped in small pieces

Place the sweetbreads and bones in 1 gallon of cold water. Boil ten minutes, remove from stove and run cold water over them until thoroughly cooled. Separate the sweetbreads and remove veins.

Cook in melted butter, for five minutes, the carrot, onion, celery, bay leaf and thyme. Add sweetbreads and bones, cover and cook for additional ten minutes until liquid has evaporated and vegetables are browned. Pour in the white wine, tomatoes and beef broth. Cover with buttered waxed paper and pot cover, place in oven and cook for fifteen or twenty minutes, basting frequently. Remove covers and roast for five minutes, basting twice. Then remove the sweetbreads but boil the sauce for ten minutes more *on top of the stove*. Strain the sauce, replace on fire and add Madeira permitting wine to cook two minutes. Add 1 tablespoon of butter when sauce has been taken from the fire. Serve with buttered peas.

MINUTE STEAK

4 sirloin steaks (2 lbs.) without bone, ¼ inch thick
Olive oil
1 teaspoon shallot
1 teaspoon parlsey
1 teaspoon chives

Have a pan with a little olive oil very hot. Add the steak and brown on one side for two minutes. Turn and brown the other side for a little under two minutes. Serve on a hot plate with a handful of chopped shallots, finely cut parsley and chives on top.

STEAK SAUCE PAYSANNÉ BOURGUIGNONNE

4 lbs. thick steak
¼ lb. butter
2 tomatoes, peeled
½ lb. mushrooms
1 teaspoon shallot
1 tablespoon olive oil
1 clove garlic
Salt and ground pepper
1 glass Burgundy wine

Set the tomatoes to cook in butter in a small covered pan. In a larger pan, put a tablespoon of butter and heat. When it is not quite boiling, add the shallot, chopped fine. When the shallot is a golden yellow, add the mushrooms, four or five whole, and the rest chopped. Reduce the heat under the pan about two-thirds, and begin to add Burgundy, a very little at a time. When the mushrooms are nearly cooked, you can add a full glass of wine, one-fifth at a time, over a hot fire. With the final fifth of wine, add the puréed tomatoes. Then turn down the flame to keep the sauce hot until the steak is broiled. To a tablespoon of olive oil, add the oil of one-tenth of a piece of garlic, salt and pepper. When the steak is ready, transfer it to a hot platter, place the whole mushrooms along the top, add the seasoned olive oil to the sauce, drench the steak in sauce and serve.

SOUPS

GERMINY

½ lb. sorrel (sour grass)
8 egg yolks
4 tablespoons of rice
Butter
1 quart chicken consommé

Cut the sorrel very fine and place in a pan with a small quantity of butter. Cook about ten minutes. *Cool thoroughly,* then add egg yolks, and very slowly, one quart of boiling consommé. When serving add a tablespoon of boiled rice to each plate.

PETITE MARMITE HENRI IV

2 lbs. beef with marrow-fat
1 chicken
4 lbs. beef and veal bones
3 onions
3 long turnips
4 carrots
2 celery tops
1 cabbage
Salt and ground pepper
¼ teaspoon chervil
1 teaspoon chives
¼ teaspoon parsley
1 bunch of leeks

Salt and pepper the beef and brown in a casserole over a hot fire for about ten minutes. In another casserole similarly brown the chicken, moving it so that it does not burn. Remove the marrow from one bone and set it aside. Then combine bones, browned beef and chicken in a pot containing six quarts of cold water. Roast the onions with skins on until brown and fragrant and add to the soup pot. Then add turnips, peeled carrots, leeks and celery tops. Put the cabbage in a separate pot, cover with cold salted water and boil. When it is cooked, rinse in cold water, and continue cooking in some broth taken from the large soup pot. Skim the soup whenever froth forms. After an hour of boiling, remove the meat, chicken and vegetables and continue boiling the consommé for another four hours, skimming when necessary. Replace small pieces of chicken and carrot just before serving. Slice the raw marrow crosswise and lay the slices in cold water. Toast croûtons covered with grated parmesan cheese in the oven. When ready to serve, add two slices of marrow-fat to each portion, placing on each slice minute quantities of chervil, chives and parsley. Add croûtons, and serve.

PURÉE MONGOLE

¼ lb. string beans
¼ lb. lima beans
¼ lb. peas
1 medium onion
½ stalk celery
¼ lb. white navy beans
1 pt. milk
1 qt. beef or chicken consommé
5 tomatoes
½ cup heavy cream
1 tablespoon sweet butter
Salt and pepper

Cover the string beans, lima beans, peas, celery and navy beans with water, add one onion, and cook to a purée. Pass this through a sieve. Combine the milk and consommé, boil, and add to the purée. Peel the tomatoes, add onion, salt and pepper, and boil to a purée. Combine in one pot a mixture of two parts bean purée to one part tomato purée, and boil for twenty minutes. Place the cream and butter in the bottom of a tureen and pour the boiling soup over them. Stir thoroughly before serving.

JELLY CONSOMMÉ

1 veal bone (2 lbs.)
3 lbs. brisket beef
1 carrot
1 onion
1 clove garlic
1 stalk celery
Salt and pepper
A few drops Worcestershire sauce

Cover the bone and beef with water, add the carrot, onion, garlic and celery, salt, freshly ground pepper and Worcestershire sauce, and boil for about two hours. Strain into a glass dish and cool. It will be thick when cold. *If* you insist on stiff jelly, add gelatine before cooling.

ONION SOUP

6 red onions
2 quarts chicken or beef consommé
2 tablespoons butter
8 slices bread
Parmesan cheese

Peel the onions and slice them on the bias. Heat the butter in a casserole. When it is hot, add the onions and cook them thoroughly, over a slow fire, until they are golden in color. Then add the cold consommé and boil it thoroughly, from thirty to forty-five minutes. Toast the bread, cover it with grated cheese and melt in the oven. Place the cheese-covered slices gently on top of the boiling soup, remove the soup from the fire and set it, covered, in the oven for ten minutes before serving.

FISH

FILET DE SOLE QUEEN VICTORIA STYLE

1 sole
Onion
Carrot
Parsley root
1 spoonful fish stock
1 truffle
2 tablespoons double cream
Milk
Butter
Puff paste
Parmesan cheese
Chablis wine
1 spoonful brandy

After cutting fillets, boil fish bones and scraps with the onion, carrot (chopped in strips), and parsley root (sliced). Add salt and pepper. Boil thirty-five minutes, add Chablis and brandy, then fish stock. Stir in a teaspoonful of butter and two tablespoons of double cream. Chop the truffle fine, add most of it to the sauce, and pour the sauce into a double boiler to keep hot. Dip the fillets in cold milk. Melt 3 tablespoonsful of butter in a saucepan and brown the fillets to a golden tan. Place each fillet on a piece of puff paste, cover with sauce, and sprinkle with crumbs of grated parmesan cheese and powdered truffle. Place the platter under the broiler just long enough to form a very thin skin on the outside of the sauce.

LOBSTER HENRI

3 large live lobsters
1 large onion
1 carrot
2 pieces root parsley
1 bay leaf
1 whole clove
2 tablespoons salt and whole grains of white pepper
3 tablespoons butter
½ lb. mushrooms
1 small white onion
1 pony brandy
1 glass sherry
1 cup double cream

Place the lobster in cold water, with parsley, bay leaf, the carrot, the large onion stuck all over with cloves, salt and a few grains of white pepper. Bring to a boil and boil fifteen minutes. Remove, dry on a board, and cut the flesh into small cylinders. Chop the small white onion thin, and cook in butter until golden, add chopped mushrooms and cook about fifteen minutes. Then add the lobster, pour on a pony of brandy, and when the flame disappears add a tablespoon of butter. When the butter has melted add the cream. When that bubbles add the sherry. Remove from the fire and serve.

ÉCREVISSE WITH SAUCE PROVENÇALE

4 lbs. live crawfish
1 lb. sweet butter
1 clove garlic
1 tablespoon parsley
1 stalk celery
1 peppercorn
1 bay leaf
2 small onions

Place the crawfish in a pot of cold water, with the onion, celery, peppercorn, bay leaf and a little parsley, bring to a boil and boil for five minutes. While they are boiling, mash the garlic on a plate and throw away the solids. To the oil on the plate add salt and pepper and a few sprigs of parsley cut fine with scissors. Work this substance thoroughly into the butter. Cover the boiled crawfish with this butter paste and place in a hot oven for ten minutes.

OYSTERS

Cover oysters on the half shell with butter paste made as for écrevisse, and place in a hot oven for 12 minutes. Sprinkle with finely chopped shallot and serve. Sherry and cream may be used instead of the butter paste, or Chablis and cream, omitting the shallot.

BOUILLABAISSE MARSEILLAISE

3 onions, sliced
3 celery stalk tops, chopped
4 cloves of garlic
2 bay leaves
2 pinches of thyme
Parsley roots
Chopped leek
1 teaspoon saffron
1 tomato, peeled and seeded
1 glass of white wine
4 lbs. of fish in equal amounts as follows:
  Lobster
  Halibut
  Catfish
  Sea Bass
  Pike
  Mussels
Olive oil

Heat olive oil and add onions, celery tops, garlic, bay leaves, parsley roots, leeks and thyme. (Tie thyme in small piece of cloth to avoid discoloration.) Cook until browned (about 10 minutes). Cut fish in large size pieces and place in the pan with the onions, etc., the lobster, pike, catfish and mussels, tomato, saffron (which has been placed in hot water to remove the color) and wine. Pour over this one quart of boiling water. Cover tightly and boil rapidly for ten minutes. Add sea bass and halibut. Boil for additional five minutes. Remove fish and strain gravy.

Serve with French bread slices which have been toasted and spread with oil flavored with garlic (to flavor place garlic cloves in cruet of oil).

SEA BASS NIÇOISE

4 sea bass—¾ lb. each
2 tablespoons chopped onion
6 tomatoes, peeled, seeded and quartered
1 clove of garlic
Butter
1 bay leaf
Salt and ground pepper

Brown the onions in butter, add garlic, bay leaf and tomatoes. Cook about 12 minutes.

Dip the fish in milk, seasoned with salt and pepper, and pass them through flour. Combine with the tomatoes and cook for 12 minutes.

TO SERVE: Cover fish with sauce and garnish with chopped parsley and lemon, one slice of which is placed in the center of the platter. On this put a rolled anchovy filet. Remove the pepper from an olive, replace with capers and place on the anchovy.

FILET DE FLOUNDER
HENRI CHARPENTIER

3 lbs. of flounder (8 small filets)
5 tablespoons of butter (sweet)
2 tablespoons of chopped shallots
10 sliced fresh mushrooms
½ lb. noodles
½ cup of white wine
1 cup of chicken broth
1 cup of heavy cream (40%)
Salt and ground pepper

Heat 2 tablespoons of butter in a saucepan, add filets, shallots, mushrooms, chicken broth and wine. Butter one side of a sheet of waxed paper and use as a cover, fitting it inside of the pan. Cook for 10 minutes over a medium flame. Remove filets, add cream to sauce, increase flame and boil until sauce has thickened to mayonnaise consistency. Remove from fire and add 3 tablespoons of butter and lemon juice.

Place in salted boiling water half a pound of noodles. Cook 15 minutes; strain. Heat butter in a pan, add noodles seasoned with salt and pepper. Cook for a few minutes.

Serve filets using noodles as a base; cover with sauce.

COLD SALMON OR HOT SALMON

3 lbs. fresh salmon
Parsley root
1 onion, sliced
1 bay leaf
½ teaspoon grain pepper
3 tablespoons of salt
½ gallon of water
Juice of 1 lemon
1 carrot

Place all listed ingredients in half a gallon of cold water. Boil for three minutes, not too rapidly, remove scum, lower flame and permit to cook slowly for 15 minutes.

Let fish cool in the water it was cooked in, then place in ice-box.

Serve with mayonnaise.

Serve with Hollandaise sauce and boiled potatoes garnished with parsley, if eaten hot.

POULTRY

DUCKLING À LA PRESSE

2 ducklings (about 12 lbs.)
1 glass sherry
1 liqueur glass brandy
1 tablespoon butter
Salt and ground pepper
Cayenne pepper
1 glass port

Roast the duckling (strangled, not beheaded) four minutes on each side, and two minutes or less on the breast. Remove the skin and cut the meat into small thin slices. Keep these warm on a silver platter while preparing the sauce. Mash the liver in a pan with the sherry and half the brandy. Squeeze the carcass of the duck in a press to extract the last drop of blood. Heat the butter in a pan over a moderate flame. When it bubbles add quickly a dash of cayenne and the port and brandy, which will catch fire. When the flame disappears pour in the duck blood, stirring steadily. Then work in the liver, add a pinch of salt and a sprinkle of black pepper and cook for two minutes. Pour the sauce, still boiling, over the slices of duck, and serve.

SUPRÉME DE VOLAILLE

4 breasts of chicken
½ lb. butter
Salt and ground pepper

Melt the butter in a small uncovered copper casserole. Season the chicken with salt and pepper, and put it in the hot butter, over a full flame. The butter should cover the chicken completely. Cook in the boiling butter for four minutes, and serve.

ROAST DUCK

2 ducks (about 12 lbs.)
1 glass sherry, port or malaga
4 oranges
Maraschino cherries
½ lb. butter

Put the cleaned duck in a pan over a hot fire, watching to see that it does not burn, until most of the fat has been extracted. Throw the fat away and repeat the process. When all possible fat has been discarded, put 3 tablespoons of butter in the pan and place it in a very hot oven. Baste constantly and turn frequently, for an hour and a quarter. Remove the duck from the pan, and add to the butter and juice remaining the glass of wine, thin slices of orange, and a very thin piece of the outer rind of an orange, cut in fine strips. Reduce this mixture over a hot fire, almost to the consistency of marmalade. Place the duck on a large platter and surround it with long spirals of orange peel. Down the center of the breast place round pieces of orange like buttons and a maraschino cherry on top of each of these. Arrange half-slices of orange with the peel in scallops around the edge of the platter. Then varnish the duck with the sauce.

CHICKEN BEAULIEU

2 chickens (about 3 lbs. each)
½ lb. sweet butter
1 lb. small white onions
2 lbs. small potatoes
6 hazel nuts
1 artichoke heart
1 dozen ripe olives
1 small tomato
4 slices truffle
1 glass of sherry
Salt and ground pepper
1 clove garlic

Heat butter in a casserole with salt and pepper until it bubbles. Then add the chicken and cover. Cook about forty minutes, or until tender. Meanwhile, in another casserole, heat ¼ lb. of butter, and add the vegetables in the following order: first onions, then potatoes, then hazel nuts, artichoke heart, and olives (with the stones left in), then the tomato, peeled. Cook the truffles in the sherry, arrange the chicken in a nest of vegetables, and garnish with truffles.

POULET CHAMPEAU

2 roasting chickens (2½ lbs. each)
½ lb. butter
2 lbs. small white onions
2 lbs. potatoes
1 cup Sauternes
1 cup chicken stock
1 tablespoon powdered sugar
Salt and ground pepper
½ bay leaf
2 carrots
1 small piece of celery

Heat in a casserole ¼ lb. of butter. Season the chickens, inside and outside and place in casserole. Roast in oven, basting every five minutes. In 18 minutes add 1 raw onion, quartered, bay leaf, carrots and celery. Roast for an additional 7 minutes, remove chickens, strain the butter sauce and add to it the Sauternes. Place onions in cold water and boil for 10 minutes, then strain. Heat some butter in a saucepan, add onions and chicken stock, cover the pan and place in an oven of medium temperature. When the onions have absorbed the broth (approximately 18 minutes) add powdered sugar and fresh butter. In five or six minutes the onions will brown. Watch carefully to avoid burning. Serve chickens with sauce, onions and small squares of fried potatoes.

GARNISHES

FRIED PARSLEY

Fry 2 bunches parsley in deep pork fat, boiling hot, for four or five seconds. Serve as a garnish with fish.

MALAGA GRAPES

2 lbs. Malaga grapes
1 glass Malaga wine
¼ lb. butter
1 tablespoon grated truffle

Cover the grapes with water and cook slowly for half an hour or until they are swollen. Have ready in another saucepan the butter and wine, very hot. Transfer the grapes to this mixture and cook furiously for five minutes. Use as a garnish with poultry.

VEGETABLES

ARTICHOKE HEARTS PROVENÇALE

4 big or 8 medium artichokes
1 clove garlic
1 teaspoon salt and pepper

Boil the artichokes for twenty-five minutes. Strip off the leaves and clean the beards from the hearts. With a spatula, turn the hearts in salt, pepper, and a very lightly pressed clove of garlic, until each is delicately seasoned. Brown the hearts in a frying pan (five minutes). Just before serving, add the garlic again, turn it two or three times among the artichoke hearts and take it out.

POTATOES FRIED IN BUTTER

Cut potatoes in the shape of fingers, wash and dry thoroughly. Put in a saucepan with plenty of butter, cover and cook over a hot flame, for twenty minutes, turning every two minutes to brown thoroughly.

MUSHROOMS HENRI

3 lbs. mushrooms
½ lb. butter
1 teaspoon shallot
1 glass sherry
1 pony brandy
1 cup heavy cream

Heat the butter in a saucepan. When it begins to bubble add the chopped shallot and cover. When the shallot is brown and soft add the mushrooms, whole, and cook uncovered for seven minutes. Then add the sherry, little by little, and the brandy. When the brandy stops burning, stir in the cream, and cook until thick—twenty or twenty-five minutes.

ZUCCHINI AND EGGPLANT PROVENÇALE

    2 medium-size zucchini, peeled and sliced
    ½ medium-size eggplant, peeled and sliced
    4 tomatoes, peeled, seeded and quartered
    1 teaspoonful of chopped parsley
    1 clove of garlic, chopped fine
    2 teaspoonfuls of chopped onion
    1 cup olive oil
    Salt and ground pepper
    2 green peppers, cut
    2 tablespoons of parmesan cheese

Heat the olive oil in a very large pan, add zucchini, eggplant, salt and pepper. When brown place in strainer for about 12 minutes. Be sure that all the oil has drained off.

Brown onion in hot butter, add garlic, parsley, tomatoes and green pepper. Cook about ten minutes.

Place on the bottom of a casserole the zucchini and eggplant, add the other vegetables, spread with parmesan cheese and cover with 2 tablespoons of olive oil. Bake in oven for 10 or 12 minutes. Serve in casserole.

COLD DISHES

POACHED EGGS WITH VEGETABLES

Boiled carrots, peas, potatoes or other decorative vegetables
Hot jelly consommé (see page 199)
6 eggs

Arrange the vegetables on a big platter with spaces in the design to accommodate six poached eggs. When the eggs are in place cover them
with the hot consommé and put a border of the consommé around the
platter. Avoid putting jelly on the vegetables. Cool and serve.

GALANTINE

Assorted cooked meats:
   1 chicken, about 3 lbs. boned
   ½ lb. veal
   ½ lb. roast pork
   ¼ lb. tongue
   ¼ lb. ham
2 eggs
1 glass sherry
1 liqueur glass cognac
1 teaspoon herbs
1 truffle (whole)
1 tablespoon pistachio nuts
12 cherries preserved in sherry
Salt and pepper

Interlace flatly slices of cold meat in a mold. Introduce between the pieces truffles, pistachio nuts and preserved cherries. Make a paste of ground pork, veal and eggs, season with salt, pepper and herbs and enough sherry and cognac to make the paste easily handled with a spatula. Fill in all openings between the meat slices with this paste and cover with more paste. Cook in a slow oven—about an hour for a three or four pound loaf. Serve cold, sliced thinly and garnished with cucumber slices.

SALADS

SALADE FLEURIE

4 leaves romaine
2 endives
4 leaves lettuce
4 leaves escarole
½ bunch watercress
1 bunch dandelion
1 bunch barbe de capuchin
1 cucumber
1 diced hard-boiled egg
1 teaspoon tarragon
1 teaspoon parsley
1 teaspoon chives
1½ tablespoons purple wine vinegar
4 tablespoons olive oil
Salt and ground pepper
1 pinch English mustard

Arrange the salad stalks in a deep dish in concentric circles using different varieties to simulate petals, and inserting lengthwise slices of peeled cucumbers with flattened ends to help them stand upright. Place a small head or heart of lettuce in the center, leaving a depression. Fill this depression with a center of crumbled egg yolk, surrounded by a ring of chopped tarragon, another of parsley, a ring of chives and finally a ring of chopped white of egg. When ready to serve the salad, mix a dressing of vinegar and olive oil, salt, pepper and mustard, beating it into an emulsion. Tilt the salad and scrape the heart of the flower—egg, tarragon, parsley and chives—into the dressing, and serve at once.

SLICED CUCUMBERS

3 cucumbers
4 tablespoons olive oil
1 tablespoon wine vinegar
Salt and ground pepper

Slice cucumbers crosswise. Mix separately a dressing of oil and vinegar, salt and pepper, beat lightly, and pour over the cucumbers just before serving.

EGG DISHES

SHIRRED EGGS

2 eggs (per person)
2 tablespoonsful butter
Salt
Pepper

Use a small dish or ramekin for each egg. Put on a hot range, with one tablespoonful of butter in each dish, and when it is bubbling slide the egg in gently and cook for two minutes. Add a pinch of salt to each, and grind a sprinkling of pepper over the top.

SCRAMBLED EGGS

12 eggs (3 per person)
¼ lb. butter
1 lb. bacon, or jelly

Break and examine the eggs separately. Combine them and beat to a smooth creamy consistency. Have a double boiler hot and containing most of the butter, melted. Pour the eggs in and continue to beat slowly, alternating direction. Add more butter before they begin to stick to the pan. When they appear granulated, add quickly small pieces of crisp bacon or pieces of jelly, and serve. A dash of whipped cream may be added to the center of the dish.

DESSERTS

ŒUFS FRITS A LA FRANÇAISE

2 cups of olive oil
8 eggs
8 slices bacon
Pint tomato sauce
½ bunch parsley, washed and dried thoroughly

When oil is very hot slide in one egg at a time. With a wooden spoon quickly fold white of egg over yolk, turning egg three or four times. It will take about 30 seconds to brown.

Heat tomato sauce in a little butter. Place in deep plate, put the eggs on top, then broiled or fried bacon strips and garnish with parsley which has been dipped in the boiling olive oil.

SABAILLON

4 egg yolks
3 tablespoons vanilla sugar
1 pony sherry
¾ glass white wine

While water in a saucepan is heating, stir the egg yolks together in a small, deep casserole, slowly adding the vanilla sugar. Beat until the sugar is dissolved, and then mix in the sherry and white wine. Place the casserole in the pan of boiling water and beat with an egg beater until thick. Scrape out the mixture and serve in glasses.

CRÊPES SUZETTE

4 eggs
3 tablespoons flour
3 tablespoons milk
A pinch of salt
1 tablespoon water

Stir the ingredients smoothly to the consistency of thick olive oil, or until it will pour back silently and smoothly from a foot or more above the mixing bowl. Heat in a round-bottomed frying pan 2 tablespoons of sweet butter. When it bubbles pour in enough paste to cover the bottom of the pan. Move the pan to spread the paste thinly, and keep it moving. After one minute, turn the pancake upside down, then turn it again and again, until it is nicely browned. Fold the circle in half, and again to form a triangle.

THE SAUCE

Small piece of orange skin
Small piece of lemon skin
2 tablespoons vanilla sugar
5 ponies of blended maraschino, curaçao and kirschwasser
¼ lb. sweet butter

To make vanilla sugar add a vanilla bean to a mason jar of sugar, cover and set aside for a few days, after which it can be kept on hand, and used as needed. At least a day or two before making Crêpes Suzette, slice a thin piece from the outer rind of an orange, large enough to cover the ball of your thumb, and a smaller piece of lemon rind. Cut both into thin strips, add to 2 tablespoonsful of vanilla sugar, cover and put away until the sugar absorbs the flavoring oils. To make the sauce, melt the butter in a thin silver pan. When it begins to bubble pour in three ponies of the blended cordials. This will catch fire. When the fire goes out add the sugar and lemon and orange peel. Then plunge the folded pancakes into the boiling sauce. Turn them, and add two more ponies of blended cordials. When the fire dies down again they are ready to serve.

MACÉDOINE OF FRUIT

1 apple
2 slices fresh pineapple
4 figs
2 peaches
2 oranges
2 bananas
6 tablespoons sugar
Small pieces orange and lemon rind
1 tablespoon kirsch
1 tablespoon maraschino
1 tablespoon curaçao
1 pear

Peel and slice the fruits separately, catching the juices in separate dishes. Crush two peach stone kernels in a salad bowl, and add the sugar. Slice a piece large enough to cover the ball of the thumb from the outer rind of a lemon, shred it and add to the sugar. Do the same with an equal piece of orange rind. Distribute this flavored sugar in equal portions over the various fruits in the refrigerator. Then mix the juices and add the kirsch, maraschino and curaçao. At the last minute combine the fruits and pour the liquid over them. Cherries and dried seedless grapes may be included if preferred.

SOUFFLÉ CITRON

1 pint milk
2 tablespoons butter
4 tablespoons sugar
6 tablespoons flour
6 eggs
Grated lemon peel

Boil the milk. Mix the butter and sugar and a little grated lemon peel. Mix in the flour, and then add the boiling milk, beating the mixture till smooth. Return the mixture to the stove, and when it is boiling add the yolks of the eggs. Remove from the fire. When it is lukewarm fold in the whites, whipped stiff. Pour into a buttered soufflé mold spread with powdered sugar, and cook in a moderate oven for fifteen minutes.

SOUFFLÉ ROCKEFELLER

2 tablespoons of sweet butter
3 tablespoons of flour
1 pint of milk
1 vanilla bean
8 egg yolks
6 egg whites

Melt in a pan the sweet butter to which is added the flour. Mix with a hand whipper. Add, very slowly, boiling milk in which there has been placed a vanilla bean. Remove from fire and add egg yolks, two at a time. Beat whites of eggs stiffly and add. Place the mixture in a deep receptacle which has been greased with butter and sprinkled with powdered sugar. Allow to remain in oven 15 minutes. Avoid frequent opening of oven door.

ORANGE SURPRISE ORIENTALE

4 oranges
2 pints of orange ice
6 egg whites
Small quantity maraschino

Remove top from orange and thin slice of skin from bottom. Hollow out and refill two-sixths of the shell with orange cubes mixed with maraschino. Add orange ice until five-sixths of the shell is filled. Cover generously with stiffly beaten egg whites. Place under grill for two minutes. Serve immediately.

If decoration is desired use pastry tube to apply egg whites.

COUPE AUX MARRONS

2 pts. vanilla ice cream
½ pt. sweet cream, whipped
4 tablespoons marrons glace in syrup. Cut.

Place in bottom of sherbet glass one tablespoon of marrons glace, add one scoop of ice cream, surround with whipped cream and decorate with one whole marron.

TARTE BOURDALOU

TARTE

8 tablespoons flour
2 tablespoons sugar
8 tablespoons sweet butter
2 eggs

Mix sugar and flour, add butter which has been softened, and eggs. Knead well and place in ice-box for half an hour. Roll and place in buttered pie mold. Place wax paper weighed down by beans over the flat surface of the dough to keep it even before placing in oven (15 minutes).

FILLING

1 pint of milk
1 vanilla bean
½ tablespoon sugar
1 tablespoon flour
3 egg yolks
4 macaroons, chopped
8 pears or peaches
1 teaspoon of almond flavor

Boil milk to which a vanilla bean has been added. In a separate vessel mix sugar, flour and egg yolks thoroughly. Add boiling milk slowly. Place on fire and stir constantly until boiling point is reached. Do not boil the mixture. Strain and when cold add macaroons and almond flavor. Pour half the mixture into the pastry shell, add a layer of cooked, halved pears or peaches and cover with remaining filling. Place under grill for a few minutes.

ŒUFS A LA NEIGE

1 pint milk
1 cup of cream (heavy)
1 vanilla bean
6 egg whites
1 pound of sugar
Small piece of lemon peel
8 egg yolks

Boil milk, vanilla bean, ½ cup of sugar and lemon peel.

Beat egg whites very stiff and with a tablespoon drop gently into the slowly boiling milk. After 2 minutes of cooking turn the egg puffs and cook for an additional 2 minutes. Remove with spoon strainer and place on dry cloth.

Mix the egg yolks with the remaining sugar. Add cream to the boiled milk and re-boil, then take the pot from the fire and gradually add to egg yolks, stirring constantly. Place the mixture over a medium fire and cook until thickened, mixing rapidly. Do not boil. Strain 2 or 3 times and when cool place in ice-box.

TO SERVE: Place sauce in center of plate, egg puffs on the side. Use sauce dish for remaining sauce.

RIZ AUX APRICOTS

½ lb. of rice
2 pints of milk
1 cup of heavy cream
1 pint of whipped cream
1 tablespoon of sweet butter
1 can of apricots
½ lb. of sugar
3 slices of candied pineapple
Maraschino cherries
1 vanilla bean

Cook rice in boiling water for five minutes, strain and place with vanilla bean in boiling milk. Cook under a low flame for 15 minutes, stirring every 2 or 3 minutes. Rice should be creamy. If necessary add another cup of hot milk. Remove from fire and pour into deep bowl. Add cream, sugar and butter. Cool and place on ice. When cold, fold in the whipped cream. Pour ⅓ into serving dish, cover with layer of apricots; ⅓ of creamed rice, another layer of apricots and remainder of rice. Decorate with candied pineapple (cut), and maraschino cherries.

SAUCE

HOLLANDAISE SAUCE

6 yolks of eggs
1½ lbs. sweet butter, melted
6 drops of lemon juice
Salt and cayenne pepper
¼ glass of cold water

Place egg yolks and water in deep pot. Put the pot in a pan of boiling water over a moderate flame. Stir constantly and rapidly with hand whipper for about 5 minutes until mayonnaise consistency is reached. Remove from fire and slowly add melted butter, a tablespoon at a time, salt, cayenne pepper and lemon juice, stirring constantly. Put through a fine strainer.

MISCELLANEOUS

CANAPÉ MAISON

4 slices of white bread
4 medium-size tomatoes, sliced
2 chopped hard-boiled eggs
1 teaspoon chopped chives
16 anchovy filets
Olive oil
Salt

Toast bread and spread with olive oil. Place on each slice tomatoes, salt, then spread with chopped egg, 4 anchovy filets, chopped chives and a little olive oil on top.

TARTINE ALSACIENNE

4 slices of white bread
4 slices of boiled ham
1 pound of grated Swiss cheese

Toast bread on one side, place ham on untoasted side; spread generously with cheese. Place under grill until melted (7 or 8 minutes). Serve very hot.

ADVICE FOR A LADY
WITH A
MARKET BASKET

APPLES

Split the stem. If it is soft and sappy it is a fresh apple, probably tree-ripened.

PEACHES

Take those which are fragrant. Peaches with beautiful skins and no odor are usually tasteless.

GRAPEFRUIT

Those with unblemished thin skins are most desirable. If there are black spots where the fruit was attached to the stem, beware.

ORANGES

Test for fragrance by scratching skin with fingernail. As a general rule unblemished, brilliant skins are indications of ripeness and consequently of flavor.

MELONS

Open and taste. There is no other way to be sure of the quality of this variable fruit. Fragrance is a fairly sound test, however.

STRING BEANS

Fresh string beans have solid stems. Avoid those of anemic pallor.

OYSTER PLANT

Should snap crisply. If it bends before breaking the plant is fibrous.

CARROTS

Should be firm and the tender green portion near the leaves cover only a narrow margin. If the green has spread the vegetable is overgrown and probably tough.

CABBAGE

Young and tender cabbage has closely packed leaves and only slight odor. Watch out for splits. They indicate worms at the center.

SWEET POTATOES

Select those with smooth skins. If there are little rootlets attached the sweet potato will be fibrous and unpalatable.

BROCCOLI

Take that which has short, crisp stems.

TURNIPS

Test with fingernail. If incision does not fill with liquid the turnip will be stringy.

CHESTNUTS

Fresh, raw chestnuts suitable for cooking wear tight skins. If the skins can be rubbed off easily the chestnuts are probably stale.

SPINACH

Select straight leaves of deep green hue. Curved leaves mean overgrowth.

RADISHES

The center leaves should be small and the flesh crisp.

COFFEE

The crack in the bean should be almost invisible. If widely spread the flavor and aroma will be diminished.

CHICKEN

A young and tender chicken is soft to the touch at breast bone and second leg joint. Contrariwise, if those places feel tough the chicken is old.

PORK

Meat should be very white, with plenty of fat.

BEEF

Beef should be streaked with fat.

LAMB

Look for meat of a delicate pinkness. Lamb that is red in color is of poor quality.

LETTUCE

Should be firm and crisp. If it has been plunged in water to revive it the inside will be soft.

PARSLEY

If fresh it will be fragrant.

MUSHROOMS

Raise the skin. The flesh should be white. If it is dark the mushroom is spoiled.

WATERCRESS

Leaves should be brittle and so brilliantly green they appear varnished.

PEAS

Press fingernail into pod. If sap does not appear in the wound the peas are not fresh.

EGGPLANT

The stem and attached green segments should adhere firmly to the skin; the pulp and seeds should be white. If the segments have begun to detach themselves the plant has started to spoil and the inside will be spotted with black.

TOMATOES

If vine ripened the tempting odor can be detected at arm's length.

CAULIFLOWER

Flesh should be tightly packed and white. When it has spread, another and unsavory growth has begun.

ASPARAGUS

Stem should be smooth near the cut and pink-white in color. The top should be tightly folded. If leaves have already formed the asparagus has lost much of its savor.

ARTICHOKES

Slice off the blackened end of the stem. If the cut shows white and moist they are fresh.

FISH

Eyes should be brilliant and tongue moist. The fish should be very slippery, not sticky.

OYSTERS
CLAMS
Rap the shells together. If they sound like stones the inhabitants are alive and edible.

CRABS
A live crab is a good crab.

MUSSELS
Select the heavy ones.

ABOUT THE AUTHOR

Born in France, HENRI CHARPENTIER immigrated to the
United States in the early 1900s and opened the origi-
nal Henri Restaurant in 1906. Queen Victoria, Marilyn
Monroe, King Edward VII, Sarah Bernhardt, and J. P.
Morgan were among his friends and patrons. He died in
1961.

A NOTE ON THE TYPE

The principal text of this Modern Library edition
was set in a digitized version of Janson,
a typeface that dates from about 1690 and was cut by Nicholas Kis,
a Hungarian working in Amsterdam. The original matrices have
survived and are held by the Stempel foundry in Germany.
Hermann Zapf redesigned some of the weights and sizes for Stempel,
basing his revisions on the original design.